NOVELL'S®

Guide to BorderManager™

NOVELL'S®

Guide to BorderManager™

SANDY STEVENS AND J.D. MARYMEE

Novell Press, San Jose

Novell's Guide to BorderManager™

Published by
Novell Press
2180 Fortune Drive
San Jose, CA 95131

Library of Congress Catalog Card No.: 97-77817

ISBN: 0-7645-4540-X

Printed in the United States of America

10 9 8 7 6 5 4 3 2 1

1B/SW/QR/ZY/FC

Distributed in the United States by IDG Books Worldwide, Inc.

Distributed by Macmillan Canada for Canada; by Contemporanea de Ediciones for Venezuela; by Distribuidora Cuspide for Argentina; by CITEC for Brazil; by Ediciones ZETA S.C.R. Ltda. for Peru; by Editorial Limusa SA for Mexico; by Transworld Publishers Limited in the United Kingdom and Europe; by Academic Bookshop for Egypt; by Levant Distributors S.A.R.L. for Lebanon; by Al Jassim for Saudi Arabia; by Simron Pty. Ltd. for South Africa; by Pustak Mahal for India; by The Computer Bookshop for India; by Toppan Company Ltd. for Japan; by Addison Wesley Publishing Company for Korea; by Longman Singapore Publishers Ltd. for Singapore, Malaysia, Thailand, and Indonesia; by Unalis Corporation for Taiwan; by WS Computer Publishing Company, Inc. for the Philippines; by WoodsLane Pty. Ltd. for Australia; by WoodsLane Enterprises Ltd. for New Zealand. Authorized Sales Agent: Anthony Rudkin Associates for the Middle East and North Africa.

For general information on IDG Books Worldwide's books in the U.S., contact our Consumer Customer Service department at 800-762-2974. For reseller information, including discounts and premium sales, contact our Reseller Customer Service department at 800-434-3422.

For information on where to purchase IDG Books Worldwide's books outside the U.S., contact our International Sales department at 650-655-3078 or fax 650-655-3281.

For information on foreign language translations, contact our Foreign & Subsidiary Rights department at 650-655-3018 or fax 650-655-3281.

For sales inquiries and special prices for bulk quantities, contact our Sales department at 650-655-3200 or write to the address above.

For information on using IDG Books Worldwide's books in the classroom or for ordering examination copies, contact our Educational Sales department at 800-434-2086 or fax 817-251-8174.

For authorization to photocopy items for corporate, personal, or educational use, contact the Copyright Clearance Center, 222 Rosewood Drive, Danvers, MA 01923, or fax 978-750-4470.

For general information on Novell Press books in the U.S., including information on discounts and premiums, contact IDG Books at 800-434-3422 or 650-655-3200. For information on where to purchase Novell Press books outside the U.S., contact IDG Books International at 650-655-3021 or fax 650-655-3295.

John Kilcullen, *President & CEO, IDG Books Worldwide, Inc.*
Brenda McLaughlin, *Senior Vice President & Group Publisher, IDG Books Worldwide, Inc.*
The IDG Books Worldwide logo is a trademark under exclusive license to IDG Books Worldwide, Inc., from International Data Group, Inc.

Rosalie Kearsley, *Publisher, Novell Press, Inc.*
Novell Press and the Novell Press logo are trademarks of Novell, Inc.

Welcome to Novell Press

Novell Press, the world's leading provider of networking books, is the premier source for the most timely and useful information in the networking industry. Novell Press books cover fundamental networking issues as they emerge — from today's Novell and third-party products to the concepts and strategies that will guide the industry's future. The result is a broad spectrum of titles for the benefit of those involved in networking at any level: end-user, department administrator, developer, systems manager, or network architect.

Novell Press books are written by experts with the full participation of Novell's technical, managerial, and marketing staff. The books are exhaustively reviewed by Novell's own technicians and are published only on the basis of final released software, never on prereleased versions. Novell Press at IDG Books Worldwide is an exciting partnership between two companies at the forefront of the knowledge and communications revolution. The Press is implementing an ambitious publishing program to develop new networking titles centered on the current IntranetWare version of NetWare and on Novell's GroupWise and other popular groupware products.

Novell Press books are translated into 12 languages and are available at bookstores around the world.

KC Sue, *Publisher, Novell, Inc.*

Novell Press

Publisher
KC Sue

Events and Publicity Manager
Marci Shanti

Web Specialist/Publisher Support Liaison
Robin Wheatley

Acquisitions Editor
Jim Sumser

Development Editors
Mandy Erickson
Katharine Dvorak

Technical Editor
Paul Reiner

Copy Editor
Nicole Fountain

Production Coordinator
Susan Parini

Graphics & Production Specialists
Vincent F. Burns
Linda Marousek
Maureen Moore
Dina F Quan

Quality Control Specialist
Mark Schumann

Proofreader
Arielle Carole Mennelle

Indexer
Ty Koontz

About the Authors

JD Marymee began his computer life with TRS-80s back in the good old days of 16K RAM and cassette program loading. He soon found that the computer industry was in need of knowledgeable people and that college instructors knew less about microcomputers than he did. He began working full time at a computer distributor circa 1983. After several bouts as a technical support engineer and salesperson, he started teaching Novell classes in 1985 and joined Novell's Educational division in 1988 in Provo, Utah. He continued this (along with some consulting) until 1990 when he was asked to head up a new part of the Educational division. After completing that task, he jumped into Systems Engineering with the infamous Corporate Integration Manager group. There he was routinely beat up (and enlightened) by customers of all shapes and sizes. Severely scarred, he moved to the marketing organization, which was even worse: it mandates instant lobotomies. His responsibilities now include O/S integration efforts (such as Windows NT), platform products (including NetWare), and distributed services (such as BorderManager).

Like JD, **Sandy Stevens** has been involved in computers since the early days, venturing into PC networking while it was in its infancy. Taking the abundance of practical knowledge she gained from the School of Hard Knocks and the small amount of knowledge she gained in college, Sandy became a certified Novell instructor and certified Novell engineer in 1989 and began a career of teaching and consulting in the San Francisco Bay Area. She later joined Novell, was beamed to Utah, and became an instructor for the prestigious Novell Technology Institute. The desire to be more involved with Novell's products prompted a move to the NetWare product team. There she was a technical marketing manager and later a product manager for NetWare 3, NetWare 4, NDS, and other distributed services. Today, Sandy prefers an entrepreneurial lifestyle to corporate chaos: she works as a freelance writer and consultant.

Foreword

Novell BorderManager began shipping in August 1997 to solid market demand and virtually no competition. No other product on the market provides an integrated set of network services as does BorderManager.

This is a new business in the industry; to be more exact, a new business in a new space — the network services space. Novell is leading the way in this business and this space with this product, which leverages the capabilities of the Internet for customers.

BorderManager is a technology that will blur the distinction between the Internet and intranet. It's a product likely to spawn the ubiquitous deployment of virtual private networks. As this book demonstrates, it is possible for customers, suppliers, and distributors to safely share information over the public network at enormous cost savings.

BorderManager reduces cost of network ownership and enables the extension of a customer's network to the Internet. It is the industry's first integrated family of directory-based network services that manages, secures, and accelerates user access to information at every point where any two networks meet. It enables the enterprise to expand from a strict yes/no firewall system to a secure point-to-point encrypted network where security is less of a technology issue and more of a business issue. BorderManager transforms an intranet into something that enterprises can embrace to advance their business externally. The boundaries of a corporation or institution now can be defined by its security policy.

Novell created the Border Services product family in the spirit of providing the most of the public network. *Novell's Guide to BorderManager* provides customers a comprehensive look at product installation and benefits, using real-life customer scenarios. The book provides a revealing look at the development of the Internet and places BorderManager — and the need for such a customer solution — squarely in the middle of the networking computer revolution.

Novell is delighted with the way the marketplace has received BorderManager and is looking forward to broadening its Border Services portfolio with additional innovative solutions.

Dr. Eric Schmidt
Chairman & CEO, Novell, Inc.

Foreword

In business, a strategic inflection point is a moment in a company's history when new opportunities present themselves; opportunities that offer staggering growth potential. Strategic inflection points define new market structures—new rules that obsolete the old way of doing things; new rules that catalyze a company's ascension to new heights.

Technology is a powerful catalyst for strategic inflection in contemporary business. For Novell—as for many enterprises—the intranet/Internet phenomenon is a strategic inflection point. As a major innovator of networking software, Novell was essential to the growth of networking proficiency in the business enterprise. Novell technology is the prominent choice among high-performance, scalable business networking solutions. As a network technology vendor and a business enterprise, Novell is in the exciting position of catalyst and beneficiary of the Internet era.

The driving force behind Internet growth rises from the competitive advantages it gives those businesses that are capable of exploiting it—competitive advantages, such as timely contact among employees, customers, and vendors; direct access to vast amounts of information; and an economical backbone for enterprise computing.

As a nascent business technology, however, today's Internet has many well-known limitations and problems—and tremendous unrealized potential. Internet clients experience relatively slow and increasingly inconsistent performance. And whereas corporate networks may implement effective access control policies, today's Internet is an open, public network within the grasp of millions of users and is susceptible to a variety of external attacks. Similarly, directory-based networks implement effective administrative domains, while the Internet is a cooperative architecture with little uniformity among its administrative policies.

There is a crucial impedance mismatch within the emerging enterprise fabric—a mismatch of performance, stability, access control, and administration. This impedance is the driving force shaping a new technology space—the managed border. The intranet/Internet seam is a well-known border. A border, however, is any intersection among networks with distinct performance, access control, or administrative character. For example, an individual company's intranet may be partitioned along departmental borders for access control purposes (Legal, Accounting, Finance, Sales, Manufacturing, and so on). Technologically, the strategic inflection occurs at the border—the best place to implement services and infrastructure facilitating consumers' access to global resources.

Novell is uniquely positioned for border management, given our high-performance platform and installed base. BorderManager's established administrative points enable access control, improve performance, and most importantly provide convenient administration. Because IntranetWare supports open Internet standards, this management is effective throughout heterogeneous, multivendor enterprises.

Beyond managing intranet/Internet boundaries, however, BorderManager enables administrators to craft multiple intranet boundaries within their private enterprises. For example, managers may easily create access-control boundaries constraining who may browse documents hosted by their Legal or Human Resource departments. Hospitals may readily construct intranet boundaries constraining medical personnel to browsing patient information and accounting personnel to browsing financial records. This is our vision for applying BorderManager throughout the enterprise.

Novell's Guide to BorderManager is a comprehensive, practical presentation of the suite of technologies encompassed by Novell's BorderManager. The authors draw from deep experience with protocols, security, management, performance, and services required to safely integrate business networks with the outside world. I am confident that their advice will help you craft innovative solutions that will enable your enterprise to take advantage of this new inflection point—the Internet!

Drew Major
Chief Scientist, Novell, Inc.

Preface

Organizations across all industries are extending their private business networks to the Internet to improve communication with customers, employees, and business partners and to have real-time access to a wealth of information. As private networks are extended to the Internet, issues of performance, security, and manageability arise. Novell BorderManager is the industry's first directory-enabled solution that addresses all of these issues in a single product.

What You'll Find in This Book

This book is designed to be a comprehensive guide to BorderManager. It is unique in that it is the work of not only the authors, but also many key BorderManager experts within Novell. This combined effort brings you the most thorough and technically accurate BorderManager reference available.

The book begins with a look at how the Internet is being used as a business tool, and the problems encountered when connecting private networks to the Internet. It then presents detailed information on how Novell's BorderManager solves these problems. In addition, real-world scenarios are included that present problems and solutions for a broad range of organization types. An installation guide provides step-by-step instructions for installing and configuring each BorderManager component. Finally, detailed information is provided on establishing network security policies and managing BorderManager.

How This Book Is Organized

Listed below is a brief summary of what you'll find in each chapter.

Chapter 1: The Internet

This chapter provides you with an overview of Internet technologies, their evolution, and how they are used today. It gives you the foundation necessary to understand how BorderManager works and how to implement it.

Chapter 2: Controlling the Borders

This chapter covers some of the problems companies face when connecting their private networks to the Internet. The majority of this chapter focuses on securing the borders between your intranet and the Internet. The chapter discusses several areas that are typically vulnerable in an intranet and then covers how today's firewall technologies provide a solution to these weaknesses.

Chapter 3: Novell's BorderManager

This chapter provides detailed information on the various BorderManager components. It describes how BorderManager enables organizations to directly address the security, management, and performance issues encountered when connecting to the Internet; and it describes each of the BorderManager technologies in depth.

Chapter 4: BorderManager Solutions Scenarios

This chapter provides practical case scenarios to help you determine how best to implement BorderManager in your organization. These scenarios are based on real-world businesses and provide you with examples of how the BorderManager technologies can be implemented.

Chapter 5: Installing BorderManager

This chapter discusses how to install the many components of BorderManager. It provides step-by-step instructions for installing the IntranetWare platform, base BorderManager product, and each BorderManager component.

Chapter 6: Configuring BorderManager Components

This chapter covers how to configure BorderManager components that were installed in Chapter 5.

Chapter 7: Defining and Setting a System Security Policy

This chapter describes the process of establishing a security policy for your network and then describes the specific technologies that enable you to carry out the terms of the policy. It describes the role of a security policy and presents practical guidelines for creating your own security policy. The guidelines presented are then used to create a security policy for a fictional company.

Chapter 8: Administering BorderManager

This chapter provides a basic reference of where to go to administer each of the BorderManager components, along with a walk through configuring several typical uses of the BorderManager. The purpose of this chapter is not to reproduce the information provided in the BorderManager documentation, but to provide a concise explanation of what administration options are available in each of the tools.

Appendix A: Request for Comments 1631 The IP Network Address Translator (NAT)

RFC 1631 describes the IP Network Address Translator (NAT), which is a significant component of Novell BorderManager.

Appendix B: Request for Comments 1918 Address Allocation for Private Internets

RFC 1918 describes address allocations for private intranets, another important component of BorderManager.

Appendix C: Web Server Acceleration with Novell BorderManager — A case study of www.novell.com

This Novell Research AppNote provides a case study of Novell's use of BorderManager to redesign its Web configuration and increase security and reliability while boosting performance by an order of magnitude.

Acknowledgments

This book is the product of many hard hours of the hard work of many people. We would like to acknowledge these individuals, as without their help, we never could have written this book.

First we would like to acknowledge Carrie Prewitt, Eric Burkholder, and Jim Thatcher who took time out of their very busy lives to contribute to this book. Carrie, your efforts went beyond the call of duty (and even the call of friendship!): thank you. Eric, your willingness to give what little time you have (while traveling 200,000 miles on an airplane) to help us with this project is an example of your never-ending passion for technology and undying friendship: thank you. And last but not least, Jim, thank you for the unbelievable marathon weekend. Never have we seen an individual produce so much in such a short time frame. Thanks for being there for us in a pinch: you're a great friend.

Next we'd like to acknowledge our editor, Mandy Erickson. Mandy, thank you for keeping this book focused from start to finish. Your attention to detail and ability to stay calm when the pressure is on is remarkable. Thank you for helping us make this book the best that it can be.

We would like to acknowledge Paul Reiner, who provided the technical edit for this book. Paul, your knowledge and experience is unsurpassed. You are truly a walking technology encyclopedia! Thank you for ensuring the technical accuracy of this book, as well as always being there for sanity checks. We value your opinion as well as your friendship.

We'd also like to acknowledge Jim Sumser at IDG Books Worldwide who has been with us from the beginning of our very first book. Jim, it's nice to know we can always count on you to help us through whatever challenges we encounter. Thank you for your support, patience, and understanding. We know you wonder at times, but we'll always come through for you!

We'd like to acknowledge our copy editor, Nicole Fountain, who waited ever so patiently to receive the manuscript and then worked double time to complete the edit. Thanks for making the finished product perfect.

We would especially like to acknowledge Eric Schmidt and Drew Major for taking time out of their busy schedules to provide their thoughts on BorderManager and this book. We'd like to thank Steven Jay for his assistance with Eric's foreword, as well as Dayle Woolston and Carrie Prewitt for their assistance with Drew's foreword.

We would also like to acknowledge Katharine Dvorak and all of the others at IDG Books Worldwide who contributed their time and efforts to this book—our thanks to all of you.

We would like to acknowledge KC Sue, Lois Dudley, and all those at Novell Press who made this book possible. Thanks for your commitment to producing quality books.

And finally, we would like to acknowledge all of those who either directly or indirectly helped make this book possible. Though your name is not mentioned, your efforts are appreciated: thank you.

J.D. & Sandy

Contents at a Glance

Contents

CHAPTER 1

The Internet

So, you want to learn about BorderManager. BorderManager can make managing an intranet easier. It can also protect it from the untamed wilderness and vast, unexplored savannas stretching off into the sunset. . . sorry — it's just so easy to get excited about network technologies. To understand BorderManager, you need to know how the Internet works, as intranets are simply private Internets. This means learning a few things about Internet protocols and everyday applications.

This chapter provides you with an overview of Internet technologies, their evolution, and how they are used today. It gives you the foundation necessary to understand how BorderManager works and how to implement it.

Some Light History

The Internet stemmed from one concept — the sharing of information. It was originally funded by the U.S. government, in the 70s. The Advanced Research Projects Agency (ARPA) recognized the widespread use of computers, and the benefit of enabling researchers to share information being generated and stored on computers. In 1983, this meant sharing files, but first, a method of moving data electronically (and reliably) had to be invented.

Today, we assume that computers communicate with one another. Almost all computers that ship to businesses or homes have some form of connectivity built right into them. For business, we buy computers with Network Interface Cards (NICs) — many come built into the motherboard and are not even optional. At home, we use modems — and most of us use those modems to connect to the Internet. Many of us also use those modems to connect to our corporate intranets; we don't even consider how data moves over the network.

The Internet architects didn't have this luxury. They had to create a reliable method of moving data from one computer to another (and it had to be independent of the type of computer). What they came up with was the Internet protocol (IP). The IP initially developed was one of the first efforts to create a generalized network protocol. As problems arose, the original protocol was modified, and more protocols were developed to remedy each problem. As a result, the IP has become a suite of protocols and applications.

SHARING INFORMATION THE HARD WAY

In 1978, researchers shared information by moving files from computer to computer. To view the contents of a research file, you had to move the file to your computer, and then fire up your favorite editor or word processor to read it.

There were two main problems with this method; the first was one of accuracy. Suppose we created a document about skydiving safety and you wanted to read it. In the pre-World Wide Web (WWW) days of the Internet, you would open an application and copy the file to your computer. You could then read it using your favorite editor or word processor. If we updated the document, however, we had no way to inform you. The file you stored on your computer would gradually become more and more inaccurate as we created more and more updates. Accurate, timely information is crucial when skydiving. If your altimeter was showing the wrong information because you didn't have the latest information to set it correctly, you wouldn't know you were about to become a human lawn dart.

The second problem isn't life-threatening, just infuriating. Suppose we created the document in a word processor and saved it in a form that your favorite word processor couldn't read? To answer this question and address the previous problem, architects of the WWW contemplated ways for everyone to read the copy in a standard format.

SHARING INFORMATION THE EASY WAY

One of these architects was Tim Berners-Lee, a researcher working at CERN (the European Laboratory for Particle Physics) in 1989. He was creating a method of sharing data among teams of researchers who were working around the globe. CERN was already using Internet protocols and applications, such as FTP and Telnet (discussed later in this chapter) to share information, but these methods were awkward. Berners-Lee recognized that providing information to a group of people on a network meant creating a common format that could easily be followed, and accessed, using a common protocol.

Berners-Lee chose to start with the U.S. government's Standard Government Markup Language (SGML) as a common format. SGML is an internationally recognized language for describing documents. SGML is like a programming language for documents. Hypertext Markup Language (HTML) is a special implementation of SGML that supports dynamic links between documents. With

HTML we can create a reference in one document that points to an entirely separate document. Dynamic links almost single handedly created the World Wide Web.

Berners-Lee needed a way to move a document from the computer it was stored on to the computer that would view the document. To do this, he developed the Hypertext Transfer Protocol (HTTP), which ran over the IP to fetch data for display. Following this development, he needed a place to store documents for retrieval, and a program to display them. Berners-Lee then developed the Web server — the place where we go to get documents, and the Web browser — the program we run on our computers to display documents.

Web servers and lots of linked documents didn't make the WWW into the universal town hall it is today. Almost all credit for this can be given to one program, the National Center for Supercomputing Applications (NCSA) Mosaic Web browser. Mosaic enables you to move through WWW documents, intuitively, by following links. Text that indicates a link is usually colored; by clicking the text, you open the next document.

By 1994, most computers were capable of using Mosaic to browse the WWW — more than 100,000 copies a month were being downloaded. As more and more people could access WWW documents, more companies and organizations put up Web servers and Web pages. By March of 1996, there were over 300,000 registered Web site names; and in March of 1997, there were more than 1 million.

Today, anyone can put up a Web server with documents that anyone else can read. Web servers are electronic billboards that have created a new, international culture with highly varied opinions and content. All of this was made possible by a browser. Mosaic has since been usurped by companies, such as Netscape and Microsoft, that have created more advanced browsers (but Mosaic's place in history is secured).

Today's Use of the Internet

The WWW provides an incredible new opportunity for manufacturers, service providers, stores, and consumers to come together in one place. The Internet has the potential to make the Mall of America, in Minneapolis, look like a corner grocery. You can browse electronic book catalogues (offering more titles than could ever be assembled in a physical store), retrieve information about cars, purchase airline tickets, read sports updates, and check stock prices. The list is growing by the minute, but the Internet faces significant hurdles before it becomes Mall of the World. Not to worry — there are solutions. That is the purpose of this book, but first let's explore the ways in which businesses use the Internet.

CORPORATE INTRANETS

Publishing a document that many people can read anonymously is quite useful. For instance, one copy of an employee handbook can be created, and individual employees can access it. This is infinitely better than maintaining paper copies of the handbook. When updates are made on a paper handbook, the author must copy it and mail the copies to each employee. Employees must constantly update the information to ensure its accuracy.

Many companies publish employee handbooks, job listings, company events, phone books, contact lists, help desk information, and even departmental home pages on corporate intranets. Authors of this material aren't sure who will want the information, but they know someone will. Intranets provide a simple way to create a company bulletin board.

REACHING CUSTOMERS

The WWW provides another solution to a common business problem — establishing and maintaining relationships with customers. The business world quickly recognized the value of the Internet. The *.com* domain, which represents commercial enterprises (as in `www.novell.com`), is the fastest growing domain. Nearly all major companies have a Web site. Organizations such as hospitals, Internet service providers (ISPs), and design, advertising, and architecture firms have all leapt onto the Web. Almost every big budget movie has its own Web site — even before the movie is released! Delivering goods and services to consumers on the Internet presents many problems, however.

Who Owns the Data?

First, the issue of data ownership arises. One good example of this is the `www.altavista.com` Web site. AltaVista is a Web search engine produced by Digital Equipment Corporation. The Web address of the Digital site is `www.altavista.digital.com`. So what is `www.altavista.com`? Well, it's really `www.`

`altavista.digital.com`, repackaged by AltaVista Technology, Inc. of California. AltaVista puts the data from `www.altavista.digital.com` into a Web page and sells advertising space around the data. Digital makes no money from this even though it owns the data. Because everything published on the Web is essentially in the public domain, it is permissible for anyone to reference any data. Permissible, except for the intellectual property laws of the United States — and there are quite a few. Currently, many lawsuits are brewing.

The Issue of Trust

Another issue involves trust. In the traditional security model of the Internet, access to information is anonymous. Merchants are not interested in who you are until they want to charge you for a service, or for the goods you want to purchase.

Your ISP, for example, charges you a fee to access the Internet. Because your ISP doesn't want just anyone getting its service for free, and it must bill you for your service, it provides you with a username and password. You must log on using your username and password, and you are responsible for keeping them private. Someone else using your username and password can be likened to someone stealing your credit card and then going shopping.

When cruising the electronic highways and byways, you run across all kinds of sites offering additional services for sale. If you sign up with a stock-trading service, you provide credit and account information and the service gives you another username and password to provide you with access. You must remember and protect this username and password as you do the ones given to you by your ISP. In fact, for every service site you want to use on the Internet, you will get a new username and password. This can become a record-keeping nightmare.

Why can't we just have one username and password? Good question! It boils down to trust. Currently, there is no way anyone can trust anyone else on the Internet. Your stock-trading company doesn't trust your ISP, so it won't accept and use the username and password given.

Cleartext

A third problem facing companies that do business on the Internet is that all protocols and access to data are "in the clear." This means that the data moving through the Internet is not encrypted — it's *cleartext* (as cryptographers call it). As most of the Internet's original information was free and public information, this was not a problem; however, now we have information or services to sell.

Suppose you want to purchase a new set of speakers for your computer at the local electronics shop. First, you go to the store and pick out the speakers you want. In this case, the speakers cost more than the amount of cash you have at the moment, so you use a credit card. The clerk takes your card and gets validation from the credit card company that you have the credit available to make the purchase. The clerk gives you a receipt to sign and compares your signature on the card with your signature on the receipt. At this point, he/she may even ask you for photo identification. This is a sophisticated procedure that includes several validations of who you are and the credit you have available.

On the Internet, this is a problem because there is no way to prove your identity. Today, several sites on the Internet enable us to make purchases using credit cards — they are similar to mail order phone purchases. We choose a product, and then we must supply information: name, address, phone number, and of course, the credit card number. The problem is that anyone could intercept the credit card number and pretend to be the card's owner. It isn't difficult to find information about a given user on the Internet.

Furthermore, weaknesses in the IP and Internet infrastructure make it possible for others to intercept part (or all) of your conversations on the Internet. This isn't as easy to do as the press would have you believe, but it is a real concern. When you sign on to the Internet, you have no way of knowing which route your data will travel, and almost anyone can intercept it.

To Each His Own

A final problem is that the content of the WWW is highly, shall we say, varied. It contains information that may be appropriate for some and very inappropriate — even offensive — to others. How do we keep our employees (or even our kids) from accessing certain information when the WWW and the Internet are basically accessible by everyone? How do we protect proprietary data from people outside our companies? How do we publish information within our companies that is not intended for all employees?

The solutions to all these problems are firewalls, screening routers, application gateways, and proxy servers — all of which make up BorderManager. This book addresses all of these solutions, but you need to understand how the Internet works to use them effectively.

Internet Protocols

Why does the IP suite exist, and what does it do? To answer this question, you must understand how data is moved around the network. At some time, you have probably seen the seven-layer OSI model of the network. All of its nuances will not be discussed here, though it does offer a few clues to the previous question.

HOW DOES DATA GET DELIVERED?

Data is delivered as electrical signals on a wire. Generally, this is done in one of two ways. To illustrate the first way, picture a classroom full of students (see Figure 1.1). A student yells out a name with a message. If your name was yelled, you accept the message and everyone else ignores it — this is how Ethernet works. A message that includes an address is broadcast to everyone. The workstation whose address matches the broadcast keeps the message, and everyone else throws it away.

FIGURE 1.1

In an Ethernet network, a message is broadcast to all workstations. Only the workstation whose address matches the broadcast accepts the message — all others discard it.

Mary, your mother is waiting for you.

OK!

To illustrate the second method of delivering data, picture the same classroom full of students. All of the students are arranged in a circle and a blackboard eraser is passed around (see Figure 1.2). If there is a message attached to the eraser, each student looks at the name on the message. If the student's name is on the message, he/she copies the message, attaches a message, then passes the eraser to a neighbor. If the message is not addressed to a particular student, that student passes the whole thing to a neighbor. You can't talk unless you have the eraser — this is how the Token Ring works.

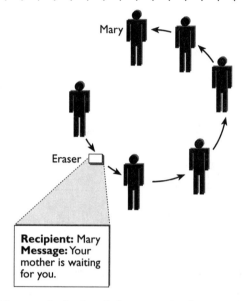

FIGURE 1.2

In a Token Ring network, the token is passed in a circle from workstation to workstation. A workstation can send data only if it has the token.

Mary

Eraser

Recipient: Mary
Message: Your mother is waiting for you.

The problem with both of these methods is scalability. As described in the previous Ethernet example, Ethernet communication can be likened to everyone yelling names and messages when they have something to say. If a lot of people in a room are yelling names and messages, it gets very confusing. In Token Ring, it takes awhile for the token to get to everyone if the ring gets really big. To make this work, you have to limit the number of people in a group. When too many workstations are put together in one group, or segment, things slow down. Even if there aren't many computers on the segment, they may just have a lot of information to send and it will slow things down.

This is where IP comes in; it enables us to define and name multiple rooms. Now, if I want to send a message to you and you are in a different room, I must include your room name in addition to your name. Because we can't all be in the same room, we just make lots of rooms — or networks. A router must determine how best to deliver messages among the networks.

IP Addressing

The designers of the IP recognized the merits of naming the network, and the computers on the network. They defined an addressing scheme that is 4 bytes (or 32 bits) long. The addressing is usually represented in one of the following forms:

- dotted decimal (137.65.4.227)

- dotted hexadecimal (89.41.4.E3)

- binary (10001001 01000001 00000100 11100011)

The binary representation of address is included because it is important to remember that all IP addresses are binary numbers. Part of the address is used to identify which network (or room) you are in, and the other part identifies you. The part that identifies your network is called the *Network ID*, while the part that identifies the computer is called the *Host ID*.

Network Classes A, B, and C

When the IP protocol was being designed, there weren't many computers and PCs were not prevalent. Because there weren't many computers, it was generally assumed there wouldn't be many big networks. Those big networks did develop, however, with a pile of computers attached to them. These large networks came to be known as Class A networks.

Provisions were also made to include small-, and medium-sized networks. The IP designers expected that there would be more medium-sized networks that wouldn't have as many computers attached to them. These types of networks are known as Class B networks. Small networks, called Class C networks, were expected to be the most prevalent type of network. Table 1.1 illustrates the number of networks and computers available in each network class.

TABLE 1.1	CLASS	NUMBER OF NETWORKS	NUMBER OF COMPUTERS
IP Network Classes	A	126	16,777,214
	B	16,384	65,534
	C	2,097,152	254

Class A networks are large, and they have many computers attached to them (not many exist). Class B networks are more common and have a fair number of computers attached to them. Class C networks are small, and very abundant.

LIMITATIONS OF THE IP

The IP suite is useful because it is so common (everything supports IP). It does, however, have several problems that need to be dealt with operationally. BorderManager offers solutions to these problems.

Running Out of Addresses

The most obvious, and most often-discussed, problem with the current version of IP is that there just aren't enough addresses to go around. Theoretically, we should be able to name 2^{32} computers or network devices, which works out to 4,294,967,296 addresses. Four billion addresses should be enough; however, the current implementation of IP calls for a four-byte address that is broken up into Network ID and Host ID (as shown in the preceding table). Each class has a set number of addresses with which it names networks and computers. For example, imagine owning a small business with five computers. I give you a class C (the smallest address range possible) that can handle 254 computers. Because you have only five computers, the rest of the 250 addresses are lost. For large corporations receiving class A assignments with 16 million addresses — but need only 500 thousand — millions of addresses are lost. Addresses are also lost because each class has a certain number reserved for various administrative functions.

The people at INTERNIC.NET have sent out e-mail messages requesting unused addresses back. Most network administrators are simply amused by such requests. Addresses are so limited that some companies even sell their unused addresses.

Administration

Even when the right class of network address is assigned for the size of our networks, IP-address administration is a manually intensive task. If forced to use network addresses that don't fit our network, we tend to start looking for bulk-purchasing deals on headache remedies.

Security

Spectacular hacks into IP networks have caused loss of service, and millions of dollars in repair. These problems stem from the fact that addresses are virtual. Anyone can address a workstation with any address — even yours. This is known as *spoofing*. Advances in operational procedures and technologies (including proxies and firewalls) have made hacks less prevalent, but they are still a daily occurrence.

IP administrators often number routers by starting at the top of the address space and working backwards. An example for a class C network is 151.157. 239.254; the next router might be 151.157.239.253, and so on. This makes it easy to remember where the routers are located. Of course, this also makes it easier for a hacker to find your routers, and use the information to divine the logical structure of your network and break in. There are solutions to both of these problems, which will be covered in Chapters 2 and 3 when we discuss Network Address Translators (NAT), IPX to IP gateways, and IP to IP gateways.

OTHER APPLICATIONS

There is more to transferring data than just the highway carrying it on your intranet and the Internet. Application-layer services, such as Web browsers and Web servers have their own protocols that use the IP highway.

TCP and UDP

Two primary protocols run over the Internet Protocol: the Transmission Control Protocol (TCP), and the User Datagram Protocol (UDP). TCP was designed to guarantee delivery of a packet from one computer to another, and it has robust error-checking features. TCP supports three application-layer services (and their protocols) that are crucial to the WWW today: FTP, Telnet, and HTTP.

The User Datagram Protocol performs the same job as TCP, getting a packet from one computer to another, but it uses a different method. TCP creates a connection between computers that can be used to track the data being sent and received. This provides a high degree of reliability to any program that uses TCP — but not for free; a lot of overhead is required to set up and maintain connections. UDP forgoes the overhead to maintain connections between computers and, as a result, does not guarantee delivery of the data.

FTP and Telnet: The Original Internet Applications

Think of IP as the highway, and TCP and UDP as two different kinds of trucks carrying data on that highway. Users aren't concerned with the highway, only the data being transported. The first really useful applications for transporting data on the IP highway were the File Transfer Protocol (FTP) and Telnet.

FTP is both a protocol specification and a file-transfer program; it is highly reliable because it runs over the TCP. You can run a local FTP program on your computer and open a connection to an FTP server. FTP servers are all over the Internet, and most of them support *anonymous FTP*. This means that when the FTP server requests a username, you type in the word anonymous (in many cases, *guest* is also used). Most of the time, however, the FTP server doesn't even request a username. The site `ftp://ftp.nic.ddn.mil` is a great example of an anonymous FTP site. You can use FTP to retrieve any Request for Comment (RFC), on any Internet protocol, as shown in Figure 1.3. (Internet standards are still called RFCs even after they move out of draft stage and are accepted as standards.)

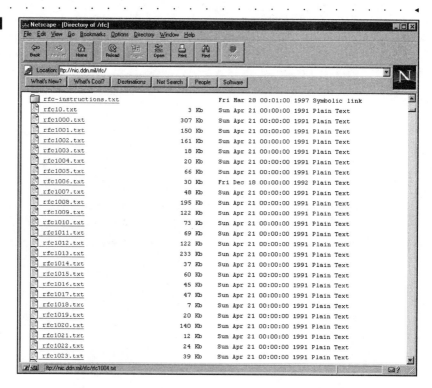

F I G U R E   1.3

HYPERLINK
ftp://ftp.nic.ddn.mil *is an example of an anonymous FTP site, in which FTP can be used to retrieve any RFCs on any Internet protocols.*

Most of the computers that comprised the Internet in the early days were UNIX computers. Because the UNIX operating system (OS) requires terminal emulation to access programs and applications running on the UNIX host, the Telnet application was created to access the UNIX host over the network using terminal emulation.

GOPHER, VERONICA, and WAIS   Today, information on the WWW is accessed by browsing. Users access a Web page and browse through the links on that page to get to other pages. The Gopher browser permitted us to do the same thing. With Gopher, the browser presented a directory structure, and directories and files were displayed as hyperlinks. The user moved up or down the structure by clicking a directory, and could retrieve a file (via FTP) just by clicking the name. Gopher was a precursor to today's Web browsers but it only permitted the user to retrieve a file, not retrieve and view the file in one step like Netscape or Mosaic.

The name Gopher seems to have several histories depending on who you ask. One is that the Gopher programs were originally developed at the University of Minnesota, where the team mascot was a Golden Gopher. Another is that when you use a Gopher browser, you spend a lot of time "burrowing" in the information hierarchy, much like the rodent burrows in the ground. Others claim that gopher is a pun on the slang, "go fer" (as in "go fer this" or "go fer that"). Whatever the origin of the name, it has had quite a legacy.

VERONICA, is an acronym for Very Easy, Rodent-Oriented, Net-Wide Index to Computerized Archives. Two of the first VERONICA servers were named Archie and Jughead. Perhaps, they had a thing for Archie comics? In any case, we've definitely gone over the edge when our acronyms are big enough to be words.

One annoying thing about Gopher was that in order to find anything, you had to know where to look. VERONICA, a search tool for Gopher servers, enabled users to put in a query to search 5,500 Gopher servers and more than 10 million Gopher "items" for files and directories whose titles contained the keyword. This made life a little simpler, but it pummeled the living daylights out of the network. In addition, it only looked for your keyword in the filename or directory name — not in the contents of the file.

WAIS was a joint project among four companies — Dow Jones & Co., Apple Computer, Thinking Machines Corporation, and KPMG Peat Marwick — to produce an information-retrieval system that supported personal, corporate, and wide-area information. The major goals of the system were to provide the capability of searching a file's contents, and to view text from different source applications. Therefore, if you wanted to look at a document that was generated in WordPerfect, you wouldn't need WordPerfect to view it.

The WAIS protocol was developed to enable a client to query a server. With the client program, you could type an English-language request that was then entered into the WAIS protocol and sent to a WAIS server. The server would execute the query, assemble the answers, and send them back to you. Sounds a lot like using one of the current Web search engines, does it not?

WAIS servers were being installed in the Internet as early as 1991, and the protocol and servers are still around today. In fact, there are several WAIS gateway products and an Internet specification on how to convert between WAIS and the current HTTP-request types.

HTTP

HTTP is the protocol spoken between Web browsers and Web servers. It is a simple request/response client/server protocol, but it has some interesting advanced features. It enables the browser program, in the request header, to provide the server with information about the browser. It can relate what kind of data it will accept (like HTML), what kind of data it can decode (like x-zip), and even which document pointed to the requested document.

The Modern Internet

The modern Internet has come a long way. The evolution of the early Internet technologies has lead us to the current WWW, yet many of these original protocols are still around today. There are thousands of Gopher and WAIS servers on the Internet, and they're almost like the COBOL programming language. Old code never dies — it just gets harder to support! BorderManager recognizes these protocols and is capable of accelerating and managing them.

Now it's time to discuss current protocols and how they work. Figure 1.4 shows the World Wide Web.

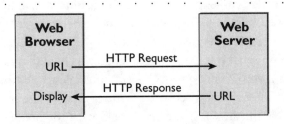

FIGURE 1.4

Modern Internet protocols and the World Wide Web

The basic cycle is very simple. With a Web browser, you can request a site, by name, or a document, by location. The browser converts the request into an HTTP request, which is then sent to the appropriate server. The server receiving the HTTP request examines the request and tries to fulfill it. Many times we will ask for a site, such as `mars.novell.com`, rather than a specific page or document. Web servers are programmed to have a default page, or document, that will be served if the user hasn't asked for one. By convention, the page is usually named default.htm or defaul.html.

If a specific document is requested, the server will look at the Uniform Resource Locator (URL) in the request and retrieve it. If the server finds the document, it formats an HTTP response and sends it back to the requesting workstation with the document data attached (usually in many packets). The browser program unpacks the requested data and displays the document as the HTML document has been formatted.

The benefits for people using the program are obvious: they need not know anything about HTML, HTTP, or even Web servers — all they need to know is the name of the desired page, or where to click in a document. This enables administrators to centralize information. They can create new links on a Web page to make new information available, and people will discover the new information the next time they access the document. Administrators and Web managers can also write programs that search databases and generate an HTML document on the fly (stock quotation sites are a good example of this technology).

Many people view the Web browser as an advanced terminal — IBM 3270 — and the Web server as a host-IBM 4381 Mainframe. My, doesn't the wheel of technology go round, and round, and round!

THE URL AND THE URN

Although the HTML code and the HTTP requests are hidden, there is one feature in the diagram that is visible: the URL. The URL is a path to a document — a location, if you will. It includes the server on which the document resides and the path to the document on that server. We've all received the "Error 404, document not found" message from our browsers, and it clearly highlights a problem with the URL — that is, it's a hard-coded location. If a document moves to a new location, all other documents referencing it must be updated with the new document name. The Internet Engineering Task Force (IETF) URL Working Group is currently trying to enhance the capabilities of URLs. Part of that effort includes the concept of a Uniform Resource Name (URN).

A URN is much like a Novell Directory Services (NDS) name, in that, we don't know where the desired data is physically stored, but we can get to it anyway. If you want to access a fax number for Bubba Barnstormer, for example, all you need to know is his name. NDS will figure out where a copy of Mr. Barnstormer's fax number is and return it to you. The idea behind the URN is that the data's location is managed by software technology — not the Web administrator. The theory is that we could request a Web name, and if the document wasn't where we expected, the WWW server will still be capable of finding it; no more "Error 404, document not found." It may, however, be a while before this concept is realized.

MIME

Multipurpose Internet Mail Extensions (MIME) provides the means for a Web server and a Web client to communicate the types of data they understand. Everytime a browser requests a document, it sends the server a list of the MIME types it can support (the server maps file types and file extensions to standard MIME data types). In this manner, Web browsers and servers can negotiate the file type that is transmitted between them. There are standardized MIME descriptions for all of the popular image types, documents, and even dynamic data (such as audio and video). If you look in the options page of your Web browser, you can see the listings of MIME types that your browser understands.

THE DOCUMENT LANGUAGE HTML

HTML, as previously discussed, is a special implementation of the Standard Government Markup Language (SGML). It is nothing more than a programming language that describes how a WWW document should be presented on a computer screen. It's standardized so that everyone is on the same page (pun intended).

HTML is a text language; therefore, if you know the right syntax, you can create advanced Web pages using your text editor. Because most of us are not programming gurus, products like Corel WordPerfect, Microsoft Word, and even Excel can save information in HTML format. There are also specialized editors (word processors) that use HTML as their native file type.

HTML documents have several sections, including a header and a body. Here is a sample of HTML code:

```
<HTML>

<HEAD>

<TITLE>Purveyors Administrator's Guide — HyperText Transfer
Protocol</TITLE>

</HEAD>

<BODY>

<H1>HyperText Transfer Protocol </H1>

<H2><A ID="I575" NAME="I575"<A ID="I576" NAME="I576">

<A ID="I579" NAME="I579"<A ID="I580" NAME="I580">

<A ID="I581" NAME="I581"<A ID="I582" NAME="I582">

<A ID="I583" NAME="I583"<A ID="I584" NAME="I584">

<A ID="I585" NAME="I585"<A ID="I586" NAME="I586">

<A ID="I587" NAME="I587"><B>Introducing

HTTP</B></A></A></A></A></A></A></A></A></A></A></A></A></A>
</H2>

<P>Web browsers and servers communicate with each other
using the HyperText Transfer Protocol (HTTP). The World Wide
```

```
Web has used HTTP since 1990.</P>

<P>Practical information systems require more functionality
than simple retrieval, including search, front-end update,
and annotation. HTTP provides an open-ended set of methods
that indicate the purpose of a request. It builds on the
reference provided by the Uniform Resource Identifier (URI),
as a location (URL), or name (URN), for indicating the
resource on which a method is to be applied.</P>

<P>This generic, object-oriented protocol accommodates
distributed, collaborative hypermedia information systems. A
feature of HTTP is the typing and negotiation of data
representation that enables the creation of systems that are
independent of the data being transferred.</P>
```

HTML has several fonts, sizes, and even image types that can be described. The first versions of HTML supported only text and images, but as new and more dynamic content is added to Web pages, more types of data are directly supported by HTML.

Today audio, video, programs (Java), and even virtual-reality content are being distributed via HTML pages. New commands have been included in HTML to support Java Applets, Java Script, and Virtual Reality Markup Language (VRML), to name just a few. Following is an HTML sample from www.novell.com that launches a Java applet on your WWW browser:

```
<applet code="newsbreakerp.class" width="170" height="88">

<param name="FRAME" value="3">

<PARAM NAME="DOUBLE" VALUE="y">

<param name="HHEIGHT" value="12">

<param name="NONSTOP" value="y">

<param name="SIZE" value="10">

<param name="TEXT" value="news0">

<param name="TARGET" value="_self">

</applet>
```

SSL AND SHTTP

To protect digital information, we turn to cryptography. Cryptography is exactly what the Secure Socket Layer (SSL) and Secure Hypertext Transfer Protocol (SHTTP) are about.

Both SSL and SHTTP enable a user (with the right browser program) to create a secure, encrypted link with a Web server. This can happen on the fly: if you are browsing an online catalog and decide to make a purchase with a credit card, you can switch to an encrypted mode to complete the transaction. SSL, from Netscape Communications, was designed to be a more generalized protocol than SHTTP, which was created by members of the CommerceNet Consortium. CommerceNet was formed to promote and build electronic commerce solutions on the Internet; it hosts a number of working groups and public forums. Figure 1.5 illustrates the SSL and SHTTP architecture.

FIGURE 1.5

SSL and SHTTP enable a user to create a secure, encryped link with the Web server to protect credit-card purchases over the Internet.

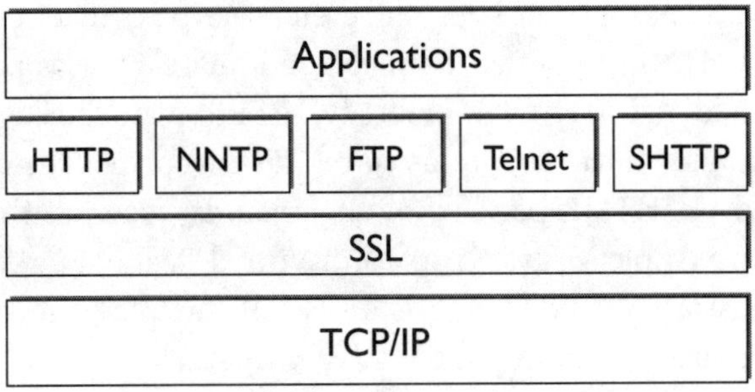

SSL

SSL is a relatively low-level protocol — that is, it provides its features to any Internet protocol. It supports authentication and creates a secure, encrypted pipe from the Web browser to the Web server. Both the Web browser and Web server must support SSL, and the server must be certified by a reputable certificate authority that is also accepted by the browser.

Certificates   Certificates are electronic documents that can be used to verify identity and authority. When buying something from an online catalog, we must be sure that the server is legally connected to the company from which we are purchasing a product. If not, we could open ourselves up to a big financial liability.

Certificates are issued by companies that assume legal liability for their use much like credit card companies assume liability for their use. When you report your credit card as stolen, you are no longer liable for its use or abuse. When a company conducting sales on the Internet gets a certificate for its server, it must go to a Certificate Authority (CA) and pay a fee to register. VeriSign is one certificate authority. When an online catalog company registers with them, VeriSign provides the company with a certificate to install on its servers for use with SSL. VeriSign will guarantee that the certificate is unique to the catalog store and assume legal liability for the use (or misuse) of the certificate.

Figure 1.6 illustrates the SSL certificate exchange process.

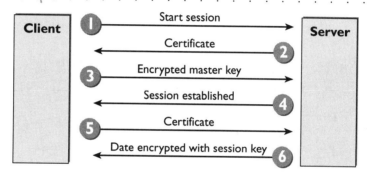

FIGURE 1.6

SSL creates a secure, encrypted pipe from the Web browser to the Web server; when both the Web browser and the Web server support SSL, a certificate exchange takes place.

When we make a purchase from an online vendor, the vendor's server sends us to an SSL-encrypted Web page. Upon first contact with this page, the server sends the VeriSign certificate to our browser with a key to be used for the encrypted link. Your browser looks at the certificate, and its issuing authority, and decides whether or not to accept it. If the browser recognizes the authority — VeriSign, in our example — it enables the encrypted link to be created. If the browser doesn't know what the issuing authority is (Bob's Bait Shop and Certificate Authority, for example), it declines the certificate and protects us from unscrupulous Web vendors. The names of the acceptable certificate authorities can be viewed in the advanced options page of your Web browser.

SHTTP

SHTTP deals only with securing HTTP content. It can be controlled by the author of a document and does not use the same certificate negotiation as in SSL. SHTTP is a bit more flexible than SSL, in that it is not tied to any one certification process. It is connection oriented, like SSL, but encryption is normally handled on a message-by-message basis rather than encrypting all data at all times. There are two major reasons SHTTP is not as prevalent as SSL: first, as shown in the diagram, SSL can be used with any higher-level protocol. It is often referred to as the encrypt-everything-and-don't-sweat-it approach. Second, the prevalence of the SSL-supporting Netscape browser has done wonders for its widespread use. Although SHTTP may provide several technical advantages and efficiency with HTML content, it still has some market acceptance hurdles to overcome.

WEB BROWSERS

The browser's role is to decode and display HTML documents, and images, and to show them on a computer. The browser understands the dynamic nature of HTML, and displays links to other sites and Web pages as highlighted text. By clicking the highlighted text, the browser interprets the commands instructing it to load and display a particular site, or document.

Extending the Browser

Web browsers typically display HTML documents, as well as images. The problem is that the Internet is a free-form construct; nothing can prevent a user from creating new data types that your browser doesn't know how to decode and display. If you can't view the data, what's the point? Fortunately, most browsers have extensibility features that permit the addition of new programs to the browser. Both of today's major commercial browsers (produced by Netscape and Microsoft), can be extended — however, they accomplish these extensions using different methods.

Netscape's product supports plug-ins. By downloading the appropriate plug-in and installing it on your workstation, your browser can display new content. Basically, the plug-in registers as the program to be invoked for a given type of data. When that data is encountered, the browser looks at the MIME type and invokes the appropriate plug-in.

Microsoft extends its browser using a similar methodology, which they call ActiveX controls. This is really a new twist on object linking and embedding (OLE) controls. This solution has cross-platform limitations, however, as ActiveX controls can only be run by Microsoft IIS servers and the I/E browser.

Both products require that the extension be installed on the workstation. Microsoft's product will automatically download the control if the server with which you are communicating supports it. The Netscape browser usually gives you a message about downloading the control, and then takes you to a Web site to retrieve it.

Java

The big problem with today's browsers is that they subscribe to the PC faith. Originally, the PC operating system was designed to be a stand-alone, self-supporting computer without a large staff of operators keeping things running behind the scenes. The operating system programmer assumed that the code had to be compatible with everything that could be plugged into a PC. Before the emergence of the network, this task was relatively easy: there were only so many devices and types of data a PC would contact.

When we connect a PC to a network, particularly the Internet, the number of choices becomes infinite. With a new image, or audio type, we must have code on our computers that can display, or play, the new type. In order to display various sites on the Internet, current browser extensions require that we preinstall all of the new extensions for our browser. Even if we could go out and get them all, within a week someone would create some new type of data for which we'd have no browser extension.

Java solves this problem. When a new image type is brought down to a workstation for viewing, the program needed to display that image is sent along with it. From the viewer's perspective, any piece of data accessed will be displayed (regardless of whether the computer has a program that understands it). This is the basic idea behind *object brokering*. A piece of data that comes with a program to understand it is called an *object*. What's more important is the kind of computer the program is written for: Microsoft ActiveX controls run only in Microsoft browsers on Microsoft operating systems, while Netscape extensions can only be used with Netscape browsers.

Today, all browsers support Java. This means that we have a new opportunity to make life easier. If extensions are written properly in Java, any browser can access any piece of data on the Internet, at any time; people never trip over data they can't use. It will be some time before this idea is a reality, but almost every software company is working toward this goal. There are major hurdles to overcome — marketing issues, mostly — but Java will continue to be a major force in the Internet for quite some time.

Origin Servers

We've discussed the architectures of the Internet, and the protocols used. What about content, you ask? What provides the data that we consume using the Internet Protocols? The answers lie in a class of servers that can best be described as *origin servers*.

Most origin servers are Web servers, although many new types of servers, and services, are becoming prevalent. Most server advancements deal with the new types of content being developed for the Internet (including audio, video, and Java). The content of the Internet has changed greatly over the years. When Tim Berners-Lee was pioneering the WWW, most of the information being shared was text — drawings and technical diagrams were novelties.

Research information, as the primary content of the Internet, is now being pushed aside by commercial enterprise. Graphical content is crucially important to these organizations.

GRAPHIC CONTENT ON THE INTERNET

Today, most of the bytes downloaded for any given Web page are images and, like all types of data, images come in several flavors. The standard image format that all browsers understand is the JPEG format. JPEG stands for Joint Photographic Experts Group, the creator of the format. Other formats include: Graphic Interchange Format (GIF), Tag Image File Format (TIFF), Bitmap (BMP), and PCX. Each of these formats can be used in Web documents, but the browser must have a plug-in extension that helps it understand the data format. Web authors, therefore, shouldn't make too many assumptions about the browser, or the people who will read their documents. As all browsers can understand and display JPEG images, most images on the Web are in this format.

New, affordable hardware technologies have increased image complexity and, hence, image size. As a result, more complex images are appearing on Web pages — much to the dismay of dial-up Internet users everywhere. As we go from simple line drawings to black-and-white, grayscale, and color images, the amount of data required for each image increases (as does the size of the file required to store it).

The pictures that you see are composed of pixels, also called pels. A pixel is simply a spot on the screen where a dot can be placed. The type of dot determines the type of picture that can be displayed. Magnifying a photograph in a newspaper reveals a small conglomeration of dots, and a newspaper has only two kinds of dots — black and white.

To display the different shades of gray, we place some of the dots closer together. This trick, which fools the human eye, is called dithering. It can create an entire black-and-white photograph using only two colors of dots. Dithered black-and-white images are easy to store, as they produce image files that are very small compared to the actual size of the photograph.

Early computers generally came with monochrome monitors, but by the time browsers entered the scene, almost every computer monitor was color. For some unfathomable reason, people with color monitors like to view color images. This is how image-file sizes start getting bigger — and they can get quite unwieldy. To store dithered black-and-white images, we need only one bit per pixel. A 16-color image needs four bits per pixel to describe all 16 colors (four times the data required by black-and-white images). To display 256 color images, we need eight bits per pixel. The really amazing quality images today have up to 16 million different colors. This is almost indistinguishable from a photograph, but we need three bytes per pixel to store the image.

The smaller the dots, the better the picture looks on the screen. A 4-by-6-inch photograph (such as a family vacation photo) stored as a 300-dots-per-inch, 24-bit (three-byte) color image looks photographic on our monitors — but it requires 6.4 megabytes to store. Ouch! The good news is that there are more efficient ways to store these images.

Most modern image-file types store their data in compressed form. Compression technology is permeating networking because it really helps increase efficiency and performance on the Internet. The JPEG format is one image format that takes advantage of compression for efficiency.

AUDIO AND VIDEO

As previously discussed, low-cost imaging hardware is driving the content of the Internet. Scanners and digital cameras are just the beginning. Low-cost digital video cameras and video-capture hardware and sound boards are making it trivially easy for anyone to include multimedia information on the Web. The complexity and size of video and audio information has given rise to a whole specialized breed of origin servers.

Audio

Audio content is simpler and more widely used than video, but it has its own idiosyncrasies. The most popular audio formats are WAV and RealAudio. Both formats record and store audio in a file, but RealAudio also has several specialized features for real-time audio. Files recorded in the WAV format can be very large — a computer playing even a short clip has to read the file quickly to prevent the sound from being distorted. This is where things come up short on the Internet. If the file is stored on your computer, access to it is fast. However, most of us dial into an ISP using a modem, so we can be sure it won't be as fast.

The human ear is an amazingly sensitive organ that easily detects gaps in audio playback. Consider your CD player; if you bump it while it's playing, it will probably skip and drop some music — unless it has special circuits to compensate. Reading large WAV files over the modem doesn't make for good audio playback because the program producing the sounds gets ahead of the file transfer to your computer. The result is similar to your CD getting jostled — skips, and drops. This problem has lead to a new way of distributing sound in real time over the Internet.

The RealAudio format for encoding audio employs advanced compression technology to make it efficient (even over lower speed links). It has its own transport protocol that can reduce the quality of the sound being sent over the Internet, so as not to skip whole sections of sound. This technology is used to broadcast radio, television audio, NASA space-mission audio, and more — right onto our computer desktops!

RealAudio is proprietary, but it is so efficient it's gaining wide market acceptance. It requires special client software and, if you're using real-time sound from the Internet, a specialized origin server called a *RealAudio server*.

Video

Video is a relatively new technology for the Internet. Even a short movie in low resolution, without any sound contains a large amount of information. Video is generally limited to corporations, as link speeds of 1Mbps (or more) are typically required to see a video of marginally good quality.

There is a growing market for small, inexpensive digital-video cameras for personal computers. This market is currently driving some innovative software solutions for network video. Two technologies are achieving success in markedly different areas: VDO Live is addressing the problems of broadcasting video, while

CUSeeMe is attacking videoconferencing. Both of these technologies have dedicated servers, and protocols, for maximum performance and image quality. They also have specialized client software that is registered with your Web browser to play the video information.

VDO Live, a player technology, enables you to play back movies over the Internet. CUSeeMe supports bidirectional video transfer for videoconferencing. The CUSeeMe software was originally developed at Cornell University; although it has been published, it is not yet a standard.

With CUSeeMe, a specialized origin server, called a *reflector*, accepts a video stream of you from software on your computer. The reflector also provides your software with a video stream of all other participants in the videoconference. Your video stream (from your camera) is combined with the others and sent to everyone else. This is an innovative way to make things work more efficiently.

With this kind of technology, the frame rate of videoconferencing is typically slow — but it is improving. Cameras with hardware compression, and more advanced software compression are increasing the amount of information that can travel over a given network at a time, but this is still a young technology.

We've covered the basics, and behaviors, of different kinds of data for a very important reason: it helps us deal with performance and efficiency problems of our intranets and the Internet. With this knowledge, we can to avoid the pitfalls of poorly designed or deployed origin servers.

Efficiency

When using a Web browser, most of us gauge efficiency by the amount of time it takes to bring up a Web page. Several factors affect the speed of this process. One of the most obvious is the speed of our connection to the Internet. The faster the connection, the shorter the transfer time to our workstations. Remember, HTTP stands for Hypertext *Transfer* Protocol, and we are really moving data to our computers for our browsers to decode and display.

Another factor is the computing speed of our workstations. With today's advanced microprocessors, this isn't much of a problem any longer. In viewing more advanced content, such as movies and sound, the limitations of our video cards and sound cards are more likely to cause bottlenecks than is the computer's processor.

Yet another factor is the speed of the origin server with which we are communicating — that is, the speed of the attached network, and the server's capability to put data on the wire. UNIX computers are not renowned for their input/output (I/O) capabilities, yet they support more than 75 percent of the origin servers on the Internet today. An overloaded server with high-speed network links may still be slower than a lightly loaded server with slow network links.

The last major factor affecting the speed with which a Web page is displayed concerns the type, and amount, of content. Web authors have a tough time discerning who will use the information they want to publish. If the data is intended for the general public, Web authors must design their Web pages to be efficient with the links most consumers use to access the Internet. This means keeping the pages simple, without a lot of fancy graphics and sounds, because the consumer is dialed into the network with a 28.8Kbps modem. An employee of a large organization usually has fast Web-access speeds, so someone targeting corporate viewers can count on those high-speed links and include larger, more complex images, sounds, or movies.

CACHING

When we sit in front of a computer, there is a certain amount of time we'll wait for something to be displayed before we get crabby. If we don't have to wait very often during a session, we are willing to endure longer down time. There is a corollary to this: if we are constantly waiting for images to appear, our patience becomes short. In fact, a substantial amount of behavioral research has been conducted on this subject.

The most apparent affect is that we don't mind if someone, or something, else has to wait. We only care when we have to wait; if we have a slow link to the Internet, accessing information in real time can really test our patience. What would happen if we had a program to collect information, and then store it either locally, on our computers, or on the corporate network to which we have a high-speed connection? This would provide us with high-speed access to the data, which is exactly what caching technology does — it creates a local copy of the data. Some compromises must be made to use caches, however. We can't expect to know all of the information a user, or groups of users, will want to access. So, how do we create local copies of all the data they want to use?

We could collect all the data on the Internet and create locally stored copies on our corporate network. Of course, that would mean copying the entire Internet to our local network — just try this sometime.

If you want to view a particular piece of information, there is a good chance someone else in your company wants to use it, as well. When you request the information, we can cache it using BorderManager technology to make a local copy. When others request the same information, they'll get the local copy. Often, when you are requesting a piece of data, you are also getting the local copy stored after someone else initially requested it.

The point is to use technology to overcome network-speed limitations, complex-content issues, and the raw amount of data origin servers supply to move the data closer to you. This is one of the most important features of Novell's BorderManager; it's called *Proxy caching* and will be discussed in Chapter 3.

Summary

After covering all the basic Internet technologies, it's time to look at how they all fit together. How do origin servers, Internet service providers (ISPs), and the Internet work together? Where are the bottlenecks, and what kinds of opportunities are there to make life easier for users? The answers to these questions are illustrated in Figure 1.7.

The Internet is not a single backbone owned (or even managed) by any one company. It is a compilation of networks that have come together under a single protocol, and common rules of the road. Many large carriers, such as AT&T, MCI, and Sprint are also ISPs. Companies and individual users can buy access to the Internet from these large carriers. Smaller ISPs, usually regional, provide home and small-business access, but often can't buy high-speed links into the Internet. As individuals, we generally use modems to connect to our company's intranet, or the Internet. The fastest modems today are about 56Kbps — which is really slow for an intranet.

FIGURE I.7

Overview of the Internet technologies covered in this chapter and where they fit in the overall picture.

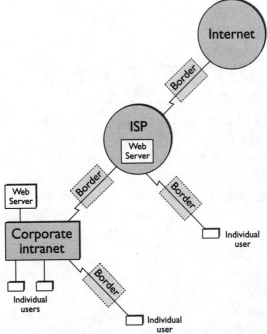

Internet content can be provided by our companies' origin servers (which are hosted by our ISPs), or just about anywhere on the Internet. Many companies use Web technologies to publish internally; these servers are not made visible to the Internet. Interestingly enough, when companies want to use the Web to improve relations with their customers, the servers on which they publish their content may not be at their site. Often, the customer-relations server is hosted by the ISP.

The opportunity for improvement exists at every link in the diagram. Each link represents the flow of information. As previously discussed, moving data closer to people improves performance. The closer that data is to the user, the less time it takes to retrieve it. Another big issue on the Internet is the lack of identity and access control. We should be able to see what we see on the Internet and our intranets based on our network user ID. If the network does not require users to identify themselves, how can it verify that users are permitted to access the specific information?

The Internet protocol suite, the Internet, and intranets are complex technologies that have evolved somewhat oddly over time. What we really need is a toolbox. The features we need to run our IP networks range from permitting or restricting specific protocols, and creating hierarchies of storage within our companies, to improving access performance over a wide range of technical levels. Each level requires a different tool. The good news is that this toolbox does exist and is, in fact, the topic of this book. Welcome to the world of BorderManager. This is the first time existing tools and exciting new technologies have been assembled into one integrated product, with centralized management capabilities. The low-level packet management tools are appropriate for controlling access, and risk, in our own networks. There, the caching technologies can be used to create distributed data highways all the way into the heart of the Internet! Enjoy your journey through the Internet tool kit, known as Novell BorderManager.

CHAPTER 2

Controlling the Borders

When companies connect their private networks to the public Internet, the borders between the two must be tightly controlled. Information Systems (IS) managers face a number of issues when controlling these borders, such as:

▸ employees who surf the Web on a daily basis, searching for nonbusiness-related items, such as the latest Dilbert cartoon

▸ significant bandwidth allocated to "pull" software running on workstations, such as PointCast

▸ outside attacks on their intranets

▸ performance complaints from employees who really do need Internet access to perform their jobs

▸ Internet-access configuration that ensures employees are using the Internet for business purposes

▸ proper setup and maintenance of multiple firewalls or proxies

In this chapter, we cover some of the problems with Internet access, including performance, management, cost, and security. We devote the bulk of this chapter to security, as it is a complex and crucial component of networks (your company's precious trade secrets may be at risk!).

By the end of this chapter, you should understand how to keep your borders fairly secure using off-the-shelf solutions (including BorderManager, of course) with minimal hardware investments. In fact, you may discover you need less hardware!

Problems of Internet Technologies

When we consider the evolution of the Internet, and associated technologies, it's no wonder that security and performance issues have arisen. The Internet was designed to enable a small group of people to share information openly. It wasn't designed to handle commercial traffic or protect trade secrets.

PERFORMANCE

The information superhighway is looking more and more like a dirt road. You already read a brief history of the Internet in the first chapter, so if you weren't already aware of it, you now know that the Internet was never designed to be the commercial village that it has become. Not that this dream isn't possible, mind you, but relying on existing infrastructure and technology won't get us where we need to go.

Most people who surf the Web aren't fortunate enough to work at high-tech companies that provide T1 (1.544Mbps) access to the Internet. If you work at a small-, or medium-sized company, chances are you don't have T1 access. In fact, you may be using dialup lines that only reach 56kbps when the wind is blowing in the right direction! Performance, therefore, becomes paramount if the Internet is going to be useful, at all. Providing a secure system and maintaining performance becomes even more vital.

At the risk of stealing our own thunder early (writers call this foreshadowing), BorderManager provides a way to increase Internet-access performance — even over a relatively slow dialup line. This even makes slow access to the Internet bearable; Chapter 3 explains how BorderManager accomplishes this task.

BorderManager also accomplishes layered security on top of the performance characteristics (rather than having security added on). This means having your cake and eating it too — providing security *and* performance to the Internet.

MANAGEMENT AND ADMINISTRATION

Imagine that you are the administrator of a large system (keep in mind you have a plethora of interns to help you). The company wants an "onramp" to the information highway. How are you going to build one? How are you going to manage it? Moreover, how can you establish the security of the system, and ensure it applies to *all* the access points? As previously stated, even if one access point permits an undesired entry, the rest might as well not exist.

One option is having *one* access point to the Internet via a high-speed router. Administrators like this solution because having one access point means having only one box to configure properly. It is, however, common for employees to bring up their own Internet-access points using Microsoft RAS or something similar, in effect bypassing all security. This is a perennial problem for any intranet manager that can only be solved by providing good intranet security in addition to Internet-access security.

Although the IS staff will have more peace of mind, having one box may mean that performance suffers. All these fat network pipes are channeling into one skinny Internet access pipe. The traffic out to the Internet can't be balanced between two pipes because there's only one way out. Whether or not this is an issue depends on the speed of the pipe (which translates into dollars spent). Fault tolerance is still an issue, because a loss of the pipe equates to no Internet access.

A second option is providing two or more Internet access points. This may appear as a solution to the speed problem, depending on how much money was spent on the first pipe that went in. If IS allocated for a fast Internet link in the budget, performance may not be the issue. If a lower-speed line was installed, having two or more may mitigate the lack of performance. With every box that's added comes several challenges, including the following:

▸ More access points means a greater chance that one may be misconfigured. This may mean a breach of security down the line.

▸ Each access point usually requires separate management. As each access point has its own tools to manage it, you may need to learn several tools if the border machines are all from different vendors.

NOTE **Several vendors are now producing router/Internet access points that can be managed via a browser. These provide a more intuitive interface for management than does the usual method, which is through Telnet (terminal emulation) to the router, with a character-based interface. These access points don't, however, enable administrators to manage security and configuration from *one* central database. Each router stores its own configuration instead of configuring out of a central repository of data. BorderManager's leveraging of Novell Directory Services (NDS) offers a central place to configure BorderManager access points. NDS provides a high-availability environment that administrators can access to configure a BorderManager server from anywhere they have client access.**

Getting the Best of Both Worlds

In an ideal world, we could provide sufficient access bandwidth (meaning multiple access points) with sufficient security to ensure proper usage (no playboy/playgirl.com access — at least during working hours!) and a centralized way of managing those access points (meaning a directory service of some sort). This is exactly where BorderManager comes in, as we'll see in Chapter 3.

IMPLEMENTATION COSTS

Now that you have Internet access points set up, what is the cost of maintaining them? Most people look only at the setup costs, but purchasing routers and software, and deploying browsers is only the beginning. Several ongoing maintenance processes will add to the total cost, including the following:

- ▸ updating the router/border software

- ▸ implementing new routers that require the same configuration as the current ones (security access/deny profiles)

- ▸ establishing new rules that provide or deny access to new or updated Web sites

- ▸ training staff to maintain the Internet access routers (if you have more than one router, and especially if the routers are from different vendors)

- ▸ logging and tracking to ensure no breach of security has occurred

The cost increases further if you maintain a Web site at your company. If they're going to be effective, Web sites need to be updated on a constant basis.

SECURITY

Unfortunately, security is a fact of life when it comes to intranets. Administrators must protect their intranets from breaches outside the border, as well as prevent unauthorized access to the Internet. To secure an intranet, some sort of control must be placed at the entry points to, and from, the Internet. These access points filter the data entering and leaving a private intranet.

Traditionally, access points are implemented one by one, rather than as a whole. Because of this, it is possible for one of the filters to be overlooked, providing enough access for a determined hacker to infiltrate. If even one border point remains unchecked, all other borders become useless. In fact, many network managers are of the opinion that hours spent protecting an intranet can be thwarted by a single person with a laptop and phone line.

There are many ways to protect the border, inside and out. They are covered in detail in the following section.

Internet Firewall Technologies and the OSI Model

Using the OSI (Open System Interconnection) model provides a view of each security technology and the level of service it provides. Table 2.1 shows the relationship between the seven layers of the OSI model and the firewall services provided at each layer.

T A B L E 2.1	OSI LAYER	FIREWALL COMPONENT
The different firewall technologies can be mapped to the seven layers of the OSI model. Mapping to the OSI model shows the extent to which each service provides security.	Application	Application gateways
	Presentation	Application gateways
	Session	Circuit-level gateways
	Transport	Packet filtering
	Network	Packet filtering
	Data-link	Packet filtering
	Physical	

As you move higher up the OSI model (to an application gateway, for example), you typically get a finer-grained capability to control the data flowing in the network — from router to router, for example. Unfortunately, because the service (a router, for instance) needs to look at more of the data being routed, there may be a performance penalty. The lower you are in the model (at a packet filter, for instance), the less time is needed to route the data, as the router service doesn't need to evaluate as much data to make a decision. We'll be discussing these various firewall technologies as we move through this chapter.

As a quick reference, Table 2.2 depicts the OSI layer again in more detail, with specific firewall technologies mapped at their appropriate layers.

T A B L E 2.2	OSI LAYER	FIREWALL TECHNOLOGY
The firewall technologies in use today can be mapped to the seven layers of the OSI model. Some of them span more than one layer.	Application	Virtual Private Networking (VPN) Internet Object Caching (Proxy Cache)
	Presentation	VPN
	Session	VPN
	Transport	VPN IP/IP gateways IP/IPX gateways Packet filtering
	Network	VPN Network Address Translation (NAT) Packet filtering
	Data Link	VPN Point-to-point protocol (PPP) Packet filtering
	Physical	

FIREWALL TECHNOLOGIES

Many Internet services have some level of security built into them. Some of the these are described in Table 2.3.

When these services were initially designed, the designers clearly had security in mind. So, why all the fuss about border managers, packet filtering, and such? Customers using the services, and connecting private networks to the Internet, determined that the security provided wasn't enough when a company linked up to the Internet. As more people joined, so did hackers and vandals who could do harm to participating companies. As you see from Table 2.3, security often depended on the UNIX security system, which is not known for its sophisticated security, or a system provided by a vendor.

Various services provided on the Internet have security inherent to each service, usually as a username/ password combination.

SERVICE PROVIDED	DESCRIPTION OF SERVICE	CONTROL
FTP — File Transfer Service	Enables a client to access and download files hosted on a machine connected via TCP/IP	If under UNIX, uses the /etc/passwd file to govern access. Under other systems, a security subsystem is provided that uses the native one through a gateway (as with Windows NT)
HTTP — Web service	Provides a variety of services: file transfer, Web-page download, execution of Web programs (via CGI or Microsoft's ISAPI interface)	May use a variety of security, such as CGI (Common Gateway Interface) or SSL to ensure security. Some use certificates from companies, such as VeriSign or Certco, to provide a user identity to the Web server.
Telnet — Terminal Emulation Service to another system host (such as an Internet router)	Permits remote terminal access to a host for purposes of administration or execution of programs	Also uses a username/password system such as UNIX /etc/passwd or provided security system (such as on a router)

Another challenge presented itself when other services on the company backbone weren't protected. A good example of this is corporate e-mail. One of the Internet e-mail standards is SMTP (Simple Mail Transfer Protocol), which doesn't have significant security mechanisms. Perhaps, the FTP service is protected, but what about other hosts that aren't? The hosts depicted in Figure 2.1 also need to be protected, which is where low-level firewall and proxy protections come in.

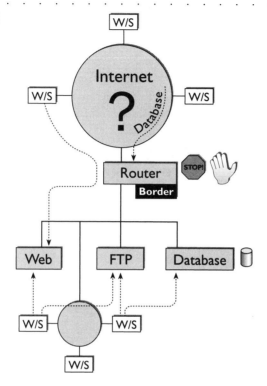

F I G U R E 2.1

Services on an intranet that provide intranet-only services need to be protected from Internet users.

FIREWALL TYPES

There are several ways to protect the intranet using traditional technologies that are available today, such as firewalls. Though many people refer to a firewall as one particular technology, it actually consists of several technologies that, together, form a protective layer between the intranet and the Internet.

Screening Routers

A screening router uses packet-filtering capabilities to distinguish your private network from the public network. Screening routers on a server can block traffic between networks, or from specific hosts on an IP-port level. You can, for example, enable the people inside your firewall to use Telnet, but prohibit anyone outside to Telnet to your inside network. Direct communication is usually permitted between multiple hosts on the private network and the Internet. Figure 2.2 illustrates how a screening router works.

FIGURE 2.2

A screening router
examines every IP header
of the packet to determine
if it is permitted to travel in
or out of the private
business network.

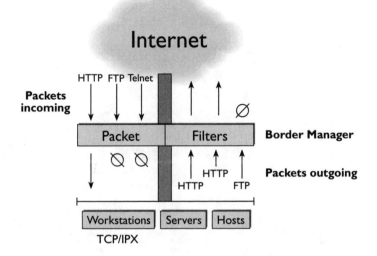

This type of firewall setup has the greatest risk of break-ins because each host on the private network is exposed to the Internet. The most common break-in is known as *IP spoofing*. IP spoofing is a way a hacker from the outside attempts to forge his/her way into your network by masquerading as a legitimate, inside address. If the router is convinced the packet is legal, the hacker now has access to the private information within your firewall.

Screening routers can be set to look at the source address in every incoming IP header, instead of the destination address. If the source address is from your private network, but the packet arrived on the public interface, the assumption must be that someone is "spoofing" an internal host and the router should automatically drop it for security reasons. The packet filter permits only internal addresses to pass the firewall to the Internet (see Figure 2.3).

Bastion Hosts

A *bastion host* is an IP host set up to prevent attacks from the Internet. With a bastion host, all access from the Internet is required to pass through the bastion host before entering your business network. By concentrating all access through a single server, it is much easier to protect your entire business network.

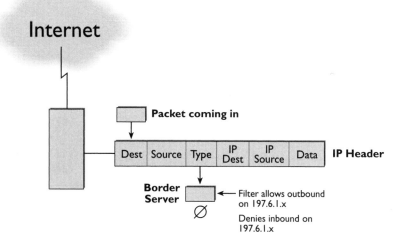

FIGURE 2.3

The packet filter examines the IP header to prevent IP spoofing; it recognizes that the packet with a correct source address is originating from the outside, and prohibits it from entering the private business network.

Bastion hosts are file servers that are stripped of all but a few services (such as Web service or e-mail). Bastion hosts usually permit logging of all activity so administrators can tell if the business network has been compromised. A bastion host may be the company "face" to an intranet, requiring Internet users to use it for a service (such as Web service). The bastion does not require authentication or host any company-sensitive data.

Screened-Host Gateways

A screened-host gateway is a combination of a bastion host and a screening router. The screening router provides even more security by configuring the router that provides outside (Internet) access to deny or permit certain traffic from the bastion host. You could, for example, set up multiple bastion hosts for each type of service, one for HTTP, one for FTP, and one for e-mail. That way, the screening router would send only the appropriate traffic to the correlating bastion host. Traffic goes to the bastion host only if it has first passed the screening router. This permits the screening host to prefilter any unauthorized traffic before it hits the bastion host (and the bastion host's hosted service). Figure 2.4 illustrates how a screened-host gateway works.

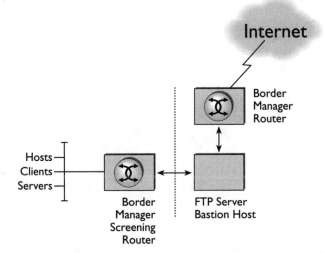

A screened-host gateway uses a screening router and a bastion host on the same private network. The bastion host is the only server that communicates to the public screening router — this way all traffic is isolated and your secure perimeter is protected.

Screened-host gateways may also use a technology called *screened subnetting.* Screened subnetting puts the bastion host on its own subnetwork by using two screening routers: one between the subnet and the private network (where the bastion host resides), and the other between the subnet and the Internet. The screening router located between the private network and the screened subnet denies all services from crossing into the subnet. The screened subnet permits only those services on the screened subnet you wish to provide (see Figure 2.5).

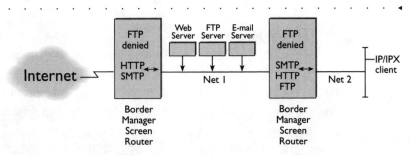

A screened subnet lets all Web and e-mail packets in and out of the network. FTP services are only permitted from the subnet to the private network

Tri-homed Hosts

A tri-homed host is considered a secure network configuration that combines some elements of a screening router and a screened-host gateway. By combining these elements, tri-homed hosts overcome the individual limitations of each technology. Figure 2.6 illustrates how a tri-homed host is used. With a tri-homed host, security is centered on screening routers by using three interfaces:

▶ an interface for the Internet

▶ an interface for the private business network

▶ an interface for secure-services subnets that house the bastion hosts and application servers

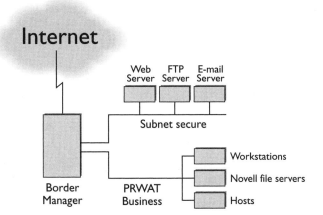

F I G U R E   2.6

A tri-homed host completely separates all incoming and outgoing points to provide a secure perimeter for your Internet services and your private business network.

Packet Filtering

Packet filtering is a fundamental way to protect an intranet from intruders. With one in place, an Internet user can't get past the router providing Internet access. Unfortunately, a packet filter can't discern users; it doesn't consider your user name. Figure 2.7 depicts incoming users with access determined by the packet filter. User names aren't a determining factor when access is calculated. A packet filter is an all-or-nothing border from the Internet to the intranet.

FIGURE 2.7

Packet filters are an all-or-nothing security mechanism. They operate at a fundamental level, but because of this, tend to be faster and less flexible in specifying access control.

Router/Firewall

Packet Filter

Packet 1 | 2 | 3 | 4 | 5

Network layer info

Yes/No?

Packet filters can filter data based on different criteria, including service type, port number, interface number, source address, or destination. With service (or RIP) broadcasts, a packet filter can permit or deny advertisements of these services on a particular interface (i.e. deny printer advertisements to be propagated from this interface to the other interfaces in the router). Filters generally do the following two things:

▸ Permit packets that match the filter and deny others, while optionally specifying some exceptions.

▸ Deny packets that match the filter and permit others, while optionally specifying exceptions.

Packet filters can permit conditions that fall outside of the general rule. For example, you may wish to restrict HTTP (Web) access to all incoming hosts except one that exists at a partner company. You can permit that exception to gain access to your intranet-only Web server.

By looking at the packet filter configured on an IntranetWare server (see Figure 2.8), you can see that any incoming host, traveling to any internal host, requesting Web service will be denied. Figure 2.9 reveals that there is one exception: user Carrie. Unfortunately, we can make this restriction based only on Carrie's IP address (137.65.157.164). We don't know if someone else sits at her workstation and uses her browser to access our Web server, which is why there are username/password restrictions on our Web server. By combining the two, we have implemented reasonable security measures to prevent unauthorized access to our Web server.

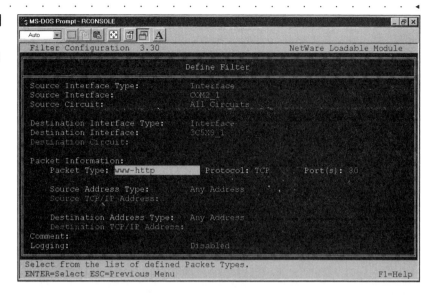

F I G U R E   2.8

Implementing a packet filter to deny access doesn't heed usernames and passwords. It is usually an all-or-nothing solution. This filter doesn't permit any external (Internet) users to access the Web server, let alone authenticate it!

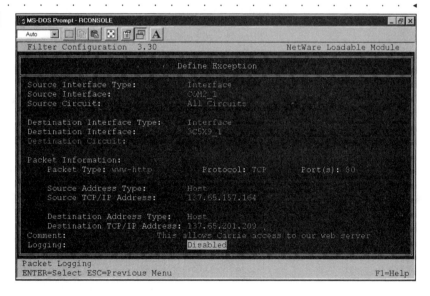

F I G U R E   2.9

By permitting a single IP address to access a particular Web server on our intranet, we can't discern who is sitting at the respective workstation. Our Web server, however, can require a username and password to ensure that the right person is given access to browse the Web server.

As you can see, packet filters can provide a first line of defense when protecting the borders. This capability is provided by the Novell Border server should you decide to use an IntranetWare server as your border router (which may be the case with a small- or medium-sized network). In a larger network, one or more network access points (NAPs) may be deployed using hardware-based routers, such as those made by Bay Networks or Cisco.

NOTE

There are many types of routers you can use for your border Internet router. Novell provides a software-based router that is included as a part of BorderManager. For higher routing performance (100,00 packets per second or higher), you may wish to use a hardware router, such as one from Bay Networks, Cisco, or 3COM. Packet filter features will vary slightly from router to router. Usually they differ mostly in their configuration and management. The newer models sport browser-based management tools to simplify the interface.

Incoming Filters   Incoming filters govern the acceptance, or denial of packets coming into the Internet or intranet router. By using incoming filters, we can keep unwanted information from coming into our intranet. For example, we can block:

▸ inbound ping (ICMP), preventing outsiders from discovering devices inside the company

▸ all inbound DNS traffic (except to the one or two DNS boxes that are needed to communicate with the Internet DNS boxes)

▸ all inbound SMTP traffic except to the SMTP gateway

▸ all Web/FTP traffic except to the BorderManager server

Outgoing Filters   As the name implies, outgoing filters discern what we publish to the outside world, including the following:

▸ all outbound Web/FTP traffic (except, from BorderManager, employees cannot bypass the BorderManager box and get direct Internet access)

▸ all outbound ACTIVE FTP

▸ all outbound NCP traffic; this blocks any information from Novell servers going out on the Internet

Selective Filtering   Incoming and outgoing filters enable you to govern the type of information that gets into, or out of, an intranet. You can get even more selective than this with a packet filter — down to where service can be provided or denied. An example of this occurs when you wish to deny any incoming FTP sessions being established in your intranet. A packet filter can be created to examine the destination-port number for each incoming packet, dropping those packets destined for the FTP port in the intranet. This can be done for any service that an outside user might attempt to use, or connect to, including Web service or DNS name resolution.

Figure 2.10 depicts a packet-forwarding filter similar to the one in Figure 2.8. In this case, we are restricting LDAP (Lightweight Directory Access Protocol) to one IP node (137.65.201.3). That node can contact any LDAP server on our network.

F I G U R E   2 . 1 0

By using packet filters, we can restrict who can access services on our intranet — or who gets to send service traffic outside our intranet.

Packet-forwarding filters aren't exclusive to TCP/IP services; services running over IPX can also be restricted. In Figure 2.11, we are restricting *all* nodes from querying server information from any server on our intranet. For example, we might have a business partner, to which we are connected via a router, but we want to prevent other users from discovering what type (and version) of NetWare/IntranetWare servers we are running.

FIGURE 2.11

Typical IPX services can also be restricted with a packet-forwarding filter. In this case, we are preventing other nodes from querying server-version information on our intranet.

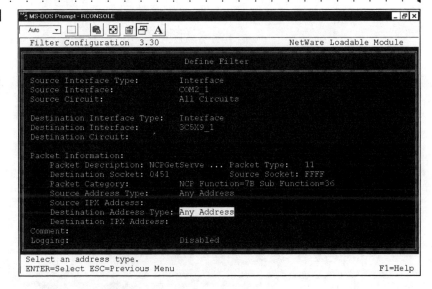

Network Address Translation (NAT)   Another useful packet filter comes in the form of Network Address Translation (NAT). This filter addresses several issues for intranet and Internet connectivity, including:

- using unregistered IP addresses on a private intranet

- preventing unauthorized inbound IP connections

- leveraging assigned IP-address ranges more effectively

- using assigned IP-address ranges more fully

In essence, NAT enables you to set up a packet filter that maps private-IP addresses to one or more public IP addresses. A good example of this is shown in Figure 2.12. As depicted, only the router has a valid public-IP address. The router between the clients and the Internet is dynamically remapping the invalid internal IP addresses to one valid external address.

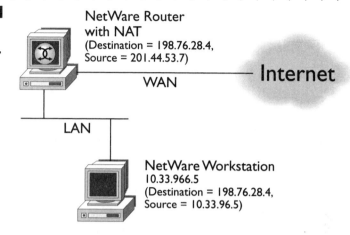

F I G U R E   2.12

Using (NAT), a private network can leverage limited, valid public-IP addresses by exposing them only at the router. The private network can legitimately use invalid Internet addresses that will be mapped to a valid public one through NAT.

NAT, under BorderManager, can accomplish this IP-address mapping two ways: dynamically and statically. The dynamic and static options are described in more detail in Chapter 3 as BorderManager-specific implementations. Request for Comments 1631 (see Appendix A) describes the concept behind NAT, and provides some sample scenarios for how it can implemented.

Another alternative to using NAT is to use a circuit gateway (discussed later in this chapter), which looks at user information to decide whether or not to provide access. The benefit of this over NAT is that we can specifically permit or deny access across a router (one that supports a circuit-level gateway) based on a user identity (such as DieterM or ThomasM). Using NAT, the best we can do is provide or deny access based on the IP address our station is using — and even that level of control is possible only when using static NAT.

In Chapter 3, you'll see two gateways that accomplish similar usage: the IP/IPX gateway and the IP/IP gateway. The difference is that the IP/IPX and IP/IP gateways can permit or deny a packet based on user information. This provides for a finer degree of access control but incurs a performance penalty (not incurred by NAT) because the permit/deny logic occurs at a higher layer in the OSI model.

A complement to RFC1631 (NAT), RFC1918 (see Appendix B) deals with address allocation for private intranets. It is a good practice to implement if you decide to use nonvalid Internet IP addresses on your private LAN — which is one of the main reasons for using NAT!

Creating One-Way Mirrors to the Internet

Many companies provide employees with outbound access to the Internet, but prohibit inbound access. A company might also have a Web site it wishes to publish, but not provide for File Transfer Protocol (FTP) or other services to be accessed. In this case, you might set up a packet filter to do the following:

▸ deny all except specifically granted exceptions

▸ enable HTTP (TCP and UDP — port 80) requests to come in from Internet users

In this scenario, any user could use any Internet services outbound, with only Web (HTTP) services permitted inbound. You can configure many permutations of this scenario based on your access and security needs.

PROXY GATEWAYS AND SERVICES

We've looked at several ways to protect the border at a fairly low level. Now we'll move up the OSI stack to define other ways of securing an intranet. As you recall, there are essentially two things on an intranet we want to secure:

▸ The routing and address information (so an external entity doesn't know our addresses — or, if it does — so we can prevent it from reaching them).

▸ The published services we are providing to the intranet (so an external entity doesn't know — or can't reach — services, such as e-mail or databases kept on an intranet).

Packet filters only go so far to protect the border. It would be nice to define a more granular access to inbound/outbound access between an intranet and the Internet. Following is a Reader's Digest-type definition of a packet filter and a proxy gateway:

A packet filter does not examine the user permitted, or denied, access. The best a packet filter can do is permit or deny based on a single address (or a range of addresses, such as network restrictions), or by service (such as Web-HTTP service). Packet filters work at the network layer of the OSI protocol model.

A proxy gateway operates at a higher layer than the packet filter. The proxy gateway recognizes the concept of an identity, as well as address. In other words, I can tell a proxy gateway, "Give access to Carrie, Eric, and Paul but no one else" or "Provide only this user with list access to FTP services from the intranet to the Internet." A packet filter uses only an address or a network address to determine whether to grant or deny access.

Providing Access Control to Intranet Services

The usual method for implementing a proxy service involves the use of a service wrapper; this external entity (such as an FTP client) contacts the wrapper directly — not the service (such as to the FTP host). The proxy then decides, based on access control, whether the external service is permitted to exchange data (with the FTP host, for example). If permission is granted, the proxy forwards requests to the service (this might be used with an SMTP gateway). You might wish to exchange e-mail with only one external entity and no one else. Using a proxy, you could govern, by entity identification, whether e-mail traffic was forwarded to your SMTP service.

Pros and Cons of Proxy Gateways   As a consequence of supporting this finer degree of access control, a proxy gateway suffers in performance when compared with a packet filter. A proxy gateway must look at more data than does the packet filter to make a decision. A proxy gateway, for example, can control access by username and password but it must take the time to determine if the username and password are permitted to access the intranet. The IP address is the closest similar criterion on which a packet filter can grant or deny access. If you have an authorized IP address, you may be permitted or denied — the packet filter cannot look at specific identity (such as a user name).

CIRCUIT-LEVEL GATEWAYS

We have already discussed NAT for mapping invalid IP addresses to the Internet. Another approach to this is to use a circuit-level gateway. Circuit-level gateways operate at the *session* layer of the OSI model — meaning, the gateway looks at more information in the packet to determine whether or not it should be denied. By looking at *session* information, access can be granted or denied based on address, DNS (Domain Name Service) — or, in the case of BorderManager, NDS user name.

A circuit-level gateway ensures that your username (or other identifying information) is granted access *before* a connection to the other side of a router (such as the Internet) is provided. In contrast, a NAT implementation looks only at the private-source IP address to govern access to the Internet. A user could easily circumvent this by walking to a workstation that has a valid NAT private address, and using that workstation to communicate to the Internet.

The downside to using a circuit-level gateway is that software must be installed at the workstation in order to use the gateway. Client-side software is required to communicate the user information to the circuit gateway so it can determine access.

When deciding which one to implement (NAT or a Circuit Gateway), you need to take into consideration the level of access or performance you require. Following are some points to consider:

▶ NAT is a network-layer service, therefore, it translates addresses with better performance.

▶ Unlike the circuit-level gateway, NAT doesn't require client-side software for implementation. As a result, NAT-enabled routers can support a variety of IP hosts (UNIX, Mac, DOS, and MS-Windows).

▶ Circuit-level gateways can provide or deny service based on username and password. Using NAT precludes this in favor of IP-address filtering.

APPLICATION PROXY

There is one vulnerable characteristic of the circuit gateway: once a virtual pipe is created between the client and the remote host, any application can run across that connection. This is true because a circuit-level gateway filters packets at the session layer of the OSI model, only. Using a circuit-gateway, for example, you may be required to authenticate before using TCP/IP to access another host. Once that is permitted, *any* application-layer program could be run, such as Telnet, Xserver, and so on. The circuit-level gateway is not concerned with the application you run as long as your initial authentication was successful. Circuit-level gateways cannot examine the application-level content of the packet they relay between the client and the remote host. It blindly relays packets back and forth across the established connection. A hacker could then deal directly with an internal server, such as a bastion host providing FTP services.

To filter the application-level of the packets generated by the client, you need a server that provides an application proxy that works in conjunction with the circuit gateway. An application-level proxy (sometimes referred to as an application gateway), intercepts incoming and outgoing packets. It runs as a proxy that copies and forwards information across the gateway. Like a circuit gateway, it functions as a proxy server, preventing any direct connection between the client and the remote host.

Because all TCP/IP applications act differently and expect different information, there isn't one application proxy acting for all applications. Thus, an application-proxy server will hold many different proxies that are specific to the application.

BorderManager offers an application proxy, such as an HTTP proxy that handles FTP, Gopher, and HTTP applications. Novell will release other application proxies in the next version of BorderManager.

Application proxies are different from pipe proxies in that they only accept the packets generated by services whose protocols the proxy can copy, forward, and filter. For example, an HTTP proxy can copy, forward, and filter HTTP traffic.

The application proxy examines the packet, and verifies the content, at the application layer. These proxies can filter particular kinds of commands or information of the supported application. You could, for example, filter FTP commands to prevent information storage. Because filtering is done at a higher level of the OSI model, it is easier to configure, creates a higher level of security, and offers a more detailed level of logging.

If no application proxy is available for the services being requested, the packet is passed through to the circuit gateway that filters and authenticates control. The business network is still protected and secure through the circuit- and packet-filter firewall services.

Packet filtering, circuit gateways, and application proxies are the technologies that create a set of firewall services. These services use security policies to define the integrity of the private business network environment and the data protected. A lot of time and effort is spent designing, implementing, and monitoring these policies, as no two companies are alike. Security risks change, thus, security policies must be flexible and easy to manage.

VIRTUAL PRIVATE NETWORKS (VPNs)

The Internet permits a relatively low quantity of content to be downloaded and used via a browser interface; however, the Internet is basically a large connected LAN. As such, businesses may make connections over the Internet instead of building private networks over a series of leased telephone lines. The challenge is to send data securely from one office to another. Whenever you send data across the Internet, anyone equipped with a protocol analyzer can see what you're sending.

A virtual private network enables two host machines to pass data between them using a secure channel. The secure channel, in the form of an encrypted data stream between each host, reduces the security risk. Even though the traffic can be "seen" on the wire, the data stream is totally encrypted, rendering the data useless to anyone but the receiving host.

Today, virtual private networking is mostly a vendor-specific technology; there aren't any RFCs (Requests for Comments) available on generalized VPN. There *are*; however, several implementations available, including the BorderManager VPN and Microsoft's VPN in NT version 4.0 (PPTP or Point-To-Point Tunneling Protocol).

CONFIGURATIONS OF VPNs

VPNs can be configured as point-to-point or as one-to-many connections. A point-to-point connection might be used to connect two offices and create one network over an Internet connection (see Figure 2.13). A one-to-many connection, on the other hand, might be used to connect several branch offices, creating one secure private network over public Internet lines (see Figure 2.14).

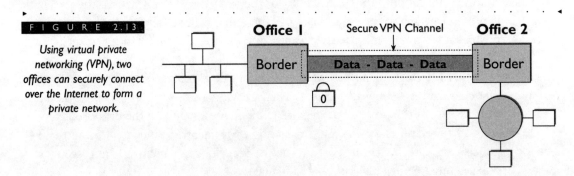

FIGURE 2.13

Using virtual private networking (VPN), two offices can securely connect over the Internet to form a private network.

F I G U R E 2.14

A virtual private network (VPN) can also span multiple points to integrate two or more branch offices into one large private network over public Internet connections.

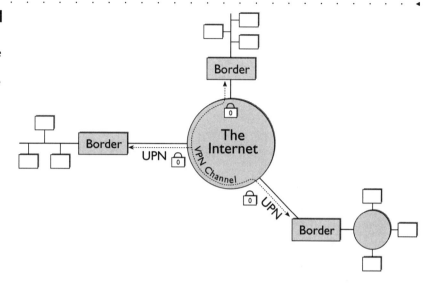

Encryption and VPN Networks

In order to secure the VPN channel from end to end, some form of encryption must be used — again, this is largely vendor specific. In the case of BorderManager, a set of public/private key pairs are generated and used from one end to the other to ensure privacy. The only stipulation is keeping the key pairs confidential to the company. For more information on BorderManager VPN and encryption, see Chapter 3.

Material Rating and the World Wide Web

One of the greatest aspects of the Internet is that there are no rules. Conversely, one of the worst things about the Internet is that there are no rules! Everything we've covered in this chapter deals with controlling access by packet, user, or service. One of the things we haven't covered is filtering content.

Whenever a public forum is available for people to speak their minds, there are times when one person speaks and someone else doesn't want to listen. In other words, there are times when it would be nice to filter based on content, rather than service.

Suppose you have an Internet connection for your company. As discussed, there are ways to prevent employees (or kids) from accessing sites, such as `http://www.playperson.com`. Using your newfound knowledge of application-level gateways, you restrict the URL. Unbeknownst to you, there is another site, called `http://www.funperson.com`, with equally undesirable content.

This is where a content filter comes in; using content-filtering technology, you can screen out all material not to your taste — as long as the material has been rated. This is similar to the movie industry with its rating of G, PG, PG13, R, and X. In order to accomplish this, you *do* need a content-filtering program.

CYBER PATROL AND SIMILAR TECHNOLOGIES

Cyber Patrol (from MicroSystems) is one such product. Novell includes a free 90-day evaluation of Cyber Patrol with BorderManager. Note that to be effective, several precautions must be made, including:

▶ You must have control of the browser and workstation to ensure that Cyber Patrol is installed (if a workstation is connected to the intranet with a browser and no Cyber Patrol software, content filtering will not occur).

▶ The firewall should be configured to permit only the proxy across the firewall.

▶ A list of authorized sites must already be set on the proxy server. The content filter is merely caching all the sites (URLs) that you don't have in your deny list.

Summary

We've covered a lot of technology! There are several technologies available that enable the management and control of Internet traffic in your intranet. Before any secure Internet/intranet project is deployed in your company, a good deal of consideration should take place to ensure that borders aren't left wide open once all the connections have been completed. A bad way to discover that you have security holes is by having a hacker make off with company secrets *and then tell you so!*

With this in mind, we'll now take a look at Novell BorderManager and how it combines several of these technologies to enable deploying and managing a secure intranet-Internet border.

CHAPTER 3

Novell's BorderManager

A new category has emerged in the IS industry — the border. The *border* describes the space between a private corporate network and the Internet; it's the infrastructure that connects the two worlds together.

Novell's BorderManager provides intelligence in this infrastructure. It delivers firewall services, centralized management of security, relief for performance bottlenecks, and services for connecting WAN sites and remote clients (see Figure 3.1).

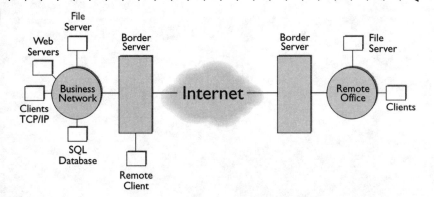

FIGURE 3.1

The BorderManager server secures the private business network from the global public network by adding security, performance and management in the infrastructure; it is placed between the Internet and a private network.

Until recently, firewalls were the only solution available to keep networks secure. But now that companies are extending their corporate networks to the Internet, a mere firewall is not enough. Companies are scrambling to provide solutions, and BorderManager provides answers to many of their concerns. The components of BorderManager include the following:

- ▸ firewall services, including:

  - ▸ packet filtering

  - ▸ network address translation table

  - ▸ circuit gateways (proxies)

  - ▸ application proxies

- centralized management for security

- caching mechanisms for performance

- virtual private networking technologies

- advanced routing provided by the Novell Multi-Protocol Router suite

- remote-access services

Firewall Services

When an organization is faced with security issues, it needs to evaluate the associated risks and how they affect business. Then it must determine what needs to be done to secure the environment. When connecting their private corporate network to the Internet, an organization's resources, data, and reputation are at risk.

This is where firewall services come into the picture. Firewall services are a combination of hardware and software solutions that are intended to reduce the risk of intrusion on an organization's private network. In Chapter 2, we discussed general firewall services available to the networking industry. At this point, you should feel somewhat comfortable with firewall services. In this chapter, BorderManager's firewall services are covered in more detail, including the additional value it provides to the intranet.

PACKET FILTERING

BorderManager offers several different packet-filtering services you can implement. These services, described in detail in Chapter 2, include the following:

- screening routers

- bastion hosts

- screened-host gateways

- tri-homed host

BorderManager provides the capabilities of all four types of packet-filtering services in the base product. BorderManager adds value by combining the base packet-filtering services (described in Chapter 2) with advanced features, such as hierarchical proxy and directory-based access control.

PROTOCOL PROXIES

Beyond the packet-filtering services, BorderManager offers other solutions to protect your company data from becoming public knowledge. An overall firewall solution must implement security in a three-tiered model comprising packet filters, circuit-level gateways, and application-level proxies. BorderManager provides these services, which offer tremendous security benefits to organizations. BorderManager offers the following services to provide your business network with protection throughout the entire OSI Reference model:

- ▸ Network Address Translation (NAT) tables

- ▸ IP-IP and IPX-IP circuit gateways

- ▸ Application proxy

Network Address Translation

Network Address Translation (NAT) provides security by keeping your private network-addressing scheme hidden from the public network. BorderManager's NAT is an extension of RFC 1631 (see Appendix A), adding several more features than were originally defined in the RFC. Refer to Chapter 2 for general information on NAT. BorderManager's network address translation tables offer the following benefits:

- ▸ enable businesses to keep their current addressing infrastructure while providing valid Internet access

- ▸ are compatible with an existing IPX/SPX addressed network

Addressing Schemes Although business networks can use any IP addresses they wish, if they want to connect to the Internet, or other remote networks, they must use legal Internet addresses for everything to function properly. By employing a NAT, a business can use its current nonlegal IP class-addressing scheme to increase the number of hosts that need IP. This way, a company has to maintain only a small set of legal IP addresses.

BorderManager provides both dynamic and static IP and IPX network address translation tables. The BorderManager administrator defines the tables with public sets of IP addresses, which are then used to remap the source address of the packet headed for a destination outside of your firewall.

The Dynamic IP network address translation in BorderManager maps all source addresses to a single legal IP address. This type of translation works by receiving a request from the client for some type of TCP/IP service that is Internet bound. This client could either be an IPX client or IP client. When the NAT receives the packet, the source address is extracted and compared with an internal table of existing private and public translations. If the source address does not appear in the translation table, a new entry is created for the host. This assigns a globally unique legal IP address, from the pool of available addresses, and replaces the original private-source address with the new public-source address.

BorderManager's Static IP translation maps individual source addresses to fixed legal IP addresses. It is commonly used for accessible resources outside firewall services (for example, a Web server, anonymous FTP server, or an e-mail gateway). These addresses do not timeout in the NAT table.

IPX/SPX: Support and Compatibility Using NAT   BorderManager's NAT provides benefits for the millions of business networks built on IPX/SPX. Internet technologies are built on TCP/IP, which makes IPX/SPX networks incompatible. There are also many sites that don't have the knowledge to take on the management overhead of implementing and maintaining TCP/IP. The BorderManager IPX Network Address Translation table enables business networks to maintain one set of legal IP addresses, and leave the IPX/SPX addressing infrastructure in place.

For IPX/SPX clients, BorderManager maps the intranet-internal IPX address to an external IP address. Because the differences between the original and translated versions of the packet are known, the checksums are efficiently updated with a simple adjustment (rather than a complete recalculation). This makes the process extremely efficient. After a configurable timeout period (during which there have been no translated packets for a particular host), BorderManager removes the entry, thereby freeing the global address for use to another inside host.

NOTE With TCP/IP there is always the chance for an Internet hacker to gain access to any system, running TCP/IP, that is accessible on the Internet. There is little (if any) chance that a hacker using TCP/IP on the Internet can access the data on your NetWare file servers, or workstations, that are using IPX/SPX connections. Using the IPX network address translation table, you have the best of both worlds — managing only TCP/IP addressing, on only one segment and being completely secure on business LAN with IPX.

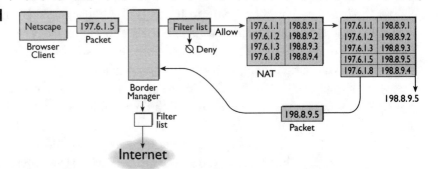

F I G U R E 3 . 2

The Network Address Translation table provides private IP addresses with access to a public IP address for security out to the Internet.

Figure 3.2 illustrates how BorderManager's NAT table works:

1 • The PC requests access to Web service.

2 • The packet is intercepted by BorderManager Server.

3 • Server either permits or denies — if denied the packet is dropped; if permitted the packet will be transferred to the NAT table.

4 • Server examines the IP header looking at source address, and checks the source address against the NAT table.

5 • The source address is not located in the NAT, so one is assigned from the IP address pool, and the IP header source address is replaced with the new public address.

6 • The final packet is then verified through the packet filter and sent out to the Internet.

IPX-IP AND IP-IP CIRCUIT GATEWAYS

BorderManager includes two circuit gateways, IPX-IP and IP-IP. The circuit gateway works with the NAT to keep the public world *public* and your private world *private*, adding an extra layer of security. A gateway mediates traffic between the private business LAN and the Internet. Circuit gateways have access-control functionality that makes them more intelligent than the NAT tables.

BorderManager's circuit gateways support both IP-IP and IPX-IP protocols. Because the circuit gateway relies on packet information from the session layer of the OSI model, it provides better protection than just a packet-filtering solution.

When an IPX or IP client requests a TCP/IP service (such as HTTP for Web services) from a host inside or outside the firewall, BorderManager's circuit gateway intercepts the request. It then consults NDS to verify that the user has the authorization to initiate a session. This authentication could be based on type of service and time of day. The user is then authenticated at a container, group, user, or server level.

Once verification is validated, packet filters are verified and the circuit gateway initiates a connection to the requested destination. All packets from this point on appear to have originated from the gateway, preventing direct contact between the client and the remote host.

In some cases, you will see a circuit gateway referred to as a *proxy*. This is because the circuit gateway is acting on the behalf of the client. This proxy feature keeps your private business network protected, as the circuit gateway usually contains two IP interfaces (one connected to the private business network and the other to the public network). Figure 3.3 illustrates how a trusted virtual pipe connects the circuit gateway and the remote origin host.

In this scenario, the two hosts, the circuit gateway, and the remote host exchange handshaking through SYN (synchronize) or ACK (acknowledge) packets. The first packet is flagged SYN, indicating a request to open a session. This packet contains a random initial-sequence number (for example, the circuit gateway might transmit a SYN packet with 500 as the initial-sequence number). The return packet from the distrusted host is flagged ACK, acknowledging the receipt of the SYN packet. The ACK packet contains a number that is next in the sequence established by the circuit gateway. In this example, the ACK packet from the remote host would be numbered 501. The remote host then sends a SYN packet with an initial-sequence number for itself (for example, SYN 1,000). The circuit gateway then acknowledges with an ACK packet numbered: 1,001. This marks the end of the handshake, and the circuit gateway now accepts the remote host as trusted. The circuit gateway will determine that the request is trusted only if the SYN and ACK flags and sequence numbers involved are logical.

F I G U R E   3.3

The steps involved in producing a trusted virtual pipe between the circuit gateway and the remote origin host.

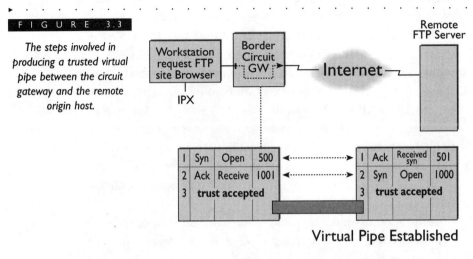

Virtual Pipe Established

Packet ◄────► Flow through pipe
until end of session I

Once the trust is completed, the circuit gateway establishes a connection. From this point on, the circuit gateway simply copies and forwards packets between the client and the remote host. The packets are no longer put through any packet filtering because the circuit gateway has built a virtual pipe between the two hosts. The circuit gateway builds a table with entries similar to the NAT table, but this is a table of active connections. While the packets are being passed, the circuit gateway matches the session information to the table and, when the packet session is completed, the circuit gateway removes the entry from the table and closes the session.

BorderManager's circuit gateway requires that your clients run the latest version of the IntranetWare client software, and that the service of the gateway be loaded at each workstation (see Chapter 5 for details on the installation of the client components). The service at the client replaces the WINSOCK.DLL with a special WINSOCK.DLL that provides the authentication services to NDS. It also enables IPX clients to perform TCP/IP services without loading TCP/IP protocol at the workstation. Internal clients do not use a local IP stack, but instead use the server's IP stack directly. They also use the server's port-management services for their applications, such as Web services. Basically, the clients become an extension to the server's IP stack. For IPX clients, rather than building tables of internal and external IP addresses and ports, the circuit gateway builds a table that maps internal IPX addresses to external IP addresses and port numbers.

There are limitations to using a WINSOCK implementation of a circuit gateway. BorderManager's circuit gateway supports only WINSOCK 1.1 or higher applications. Applications that don't use WINSOCK (such as a UNIX workstation) cannot use the circuit gateway — no WINSOCK on UNIX!. There are also some legacy applications that clients still use, such as early versions of print utilities and older terminal-emulation packages that may not work with the circuit gateway. For this reason, BorderManager includes a *switcher* that enables you to disable, and enable, the circuit function. In this case, your clients would have both an IPX and IP protocol stack.

Because the circuit gateway is a WINSOCK implementation, other clients (such as Macintosh, OS/2, UNIX, and Windows NT) are not supported. Instead, these clients would use the NAT table for address translation. This would still protect your private business network but they would lose the functionality of securing the services through NDS.

Novell is working on an implementation of the circuit gateway that uses a protocol, called *SOCKS,* for authentication and encryption services (instead of WINSOCK). This version of the client should be available in the next release of BorderManager. SOCKS version 5 will then permit any client (going through the circuit gateway) to use NDS services for security.

Even with the limitations of BorderManager's circuit gateway, Novell business networks gain many advantages using this technology to protect and connect Internet services. The biggest advantage is lower cost of ownership, as described in the following points:

- ▶ Organizations do not have to manage TCP/IP stacks on every system, and can implement a single shared WINSOCK.DLL on a NetWare server for all Windows clients.

- ▶ Organizations do not have to maintain Domain Name System (DNS) or Dynamic Host Configuration Protocol (DHCP) for every system on the network.

▸ Duplicate IP addresses don't have to be tracked down, and all other management tasks incurred from running full IP stacks on every desktop is eliminated.

Another huge advantage is the security features of NDS. Now you can manage your Internet services the same way you manage all your other network resources — without learning a new security model.

ACCESS CONTROL

In the past, businesses protected their data by keeping it in a centralized fortress and instituting strict access policies that were overseen by the security administrators. These policies used packet filtering to prevent unauthorized IP traffic from reaching certain sites. If you base access control on TCP/IP addressing schemes, however, your ability to control and maintain integrity on a private business network is limited.

For example, let's assume that certain segments of an organization are restricted from accessing a site on the Internet. An employee on the restricted segment logs on to his workstation as John. He then executes the browser and tries to access the site. The security policy is applied and John is denied access. However, John notices that Mary in IS had access to the site, so he leaves his desk, walks over to Mary's area, and logs in on Mary's workstation as John. John then executes the browser and gets to the site. Why? Because TCP/IP security policies are based on IP addresses, or segments. The security is applied to the segment to which the workstation is connected, rather than the individual employee — very easy model to break.

Novell's BorderManager provides robust access control while giving security administrators flexibility. NDS extends the policy dimensions of access control in a fundamental way — resource identity and consumer identity. Access control with Novell's BorderManager enables administrators to do the following:

▸ configure access control for outgoing, incoming, and Internet traffic

▸ organize Internet/intranet access based on users, groups, organizations, organizational units, IP address or range, subnet address, or DNS names

- ▶ configure access-control policies that discriminate among Internet content based on industry-standard ratings, protocol service port, and URL patterns

- ▶ configure access policies that deny or permit by time and day

- ▶ deny specific URL patterns or protocol service ports to specific IP addresses, subnets, or DNS names

- ▶ create enterprise polices using NDS, which are applied to all other services based on the distribution policies of NDS; the hierarchical nature of NDS enables rights to flow down through NDS containers

Following are some example policies to give you a better understanding of how access-control policies can be used:

- ▶ grant IPX nodes access to Internet resources between the hours of 8:00 a.m. and 2:00 p.m.

- ▶ deny access to sports and leisure sites to the entire organization (this rule is created once at the "Organization" level and gets applied to every BorderManager server under the container)

- ▶ provide unlimited access to the Internet from 5:00 p.m. until 10:00 p.m.

- ▶ deny access by user, or group, or let the rights flow down to every object within an organizational unit

For more detailed examples of policies and how they can be used, refer to Chapter 7.

Using Novell Directory Services to manage your security gives it a great boost. Security is much tighter now, and users are being held responsible for their actions. The security model has changed from being machine- or IP segment-centric to being user-centric.

Consider the previous example, John logs into his workstation, executes the browser and types in the URL site that is not permitted, access control is applied and the URL site is denied. Now, John logs in at Mary's workstation, executes the browser with the URL site, and is still denied access to the site — access control follows the employee.

Access-Control Lists

With BorderManager, access rules define which source can access which destination at what time. Rules may be contained at a server, on an organizational unit, or at the organization level in the NDS tree. Each access rule (in the listed order) is applied to each access request. When an access request matches the specifications in a rule, that rule is applied immediately, and the rest of the rules are ignored. Because rules can be stored in different areas of your NDS tree, you must understand the flow of effective rights as described.

To determine effective rights, control lists are checked at the server object, and then the organizational unit that holds the server object is checked, up to the root of the NDS tree. The combination of lists moving up the tree represents the effective rights of the object requesting these resources. Figure 3.4 shows a control list at a server object.

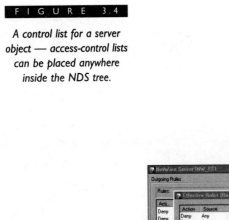

F I G U R E   3 . 4

A control list for a server object — access-control lists can be placed anywhere inside the NDS tree.

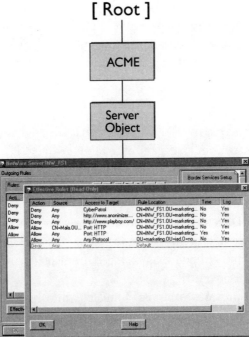

Centralized Management for Security

The goal of any administrator is to protect the data and preserve the integrity of the network. In order to provide the best security, you must be able to implement all of the different services available in a three-tiered model — packet filters, circuit-level gateways, and application gateways. These technologies are abundant throughout the industry, but if you evaluate all of the solutions available, not one vendor offers all three services — except Novell's BorderManager (see Table 3.1).

T A B L E 3.1	OSI DATA MODEL	VENDOR	FIREWALL SERVICES
Leading firewall services, vendors, and the services they provide	Application Presentation	Microsoft, Netscape, NOVELL	Application Proxies
	Session	Cisco, Microsoft, TSI, NOVELL	Circuit Gateways
	Transport		NAT Table
	Network	TSI, CheckPoint, Cisco, NOVELL	Packet Filtering
	Data		
	Physical	Ethernet, FDDI, PPP, SLIP	Physical connections

If you use products other than BorderManager, you could employ a packet-filter router from vendor A, but you would then have to buy the circuit gateway from vendor B — and if neither vendor provided application services, you would have to buy another product from vendor C. Not only will you buy several different products, you'll have to spend time learning and maintaining each product, separately.

Novell's BorderManager offers something that none of the others do — Novell Directory Services. With NDS as a central point of administering access control, you gain the following:

▶ the power of a secure environment

▶ a globally central administration model

▶ single login for your clients to private, and public, network resources

You can also use components of Novell's BorderManager to enhance your current firewall environment. For example, if you are using Vendor A's router for packet filtering, you could use Novell's BorderManager for the circuit and application functions. By doing this, you keep your packet filtering in place, and you get the benefits of using NDS for the rest of your security model.

 For more information on security policies and procedures check out the following URLs: `http:\\www.ncsa.com, http:\\www.iss.net`

NOTE

Performance-Caching Mechanisms

Besides security, performance is also a major concern on the Internet. Internet services, such as FTP, Gopher, and the World Wide Web, have evolved so rapidly that their designers and implementers postponed performance and scalability in favor of easy deployment. What can we do to ease this traffic bottleneck? What is causing the problem? Who knew the Internet would become as popular as it has?

WHY CACHING IS NECESSARY

In your own private business network, you control the flow of traffic by using segment and load balance activity when needed. With the Internet, you are connecting into the wild frontier! The Internet is made up of dumb routers and thin pipes — no single entity has control over it. Some of the issues that have created performance problems are as follows:

- ▸ The lines connecting to the Internet are typically much slower than those connecting local networks.

- ▸ Internet traffic patterns are changing — we are demanding more from it, such as timely contact among employees, vendors, and customers.

- ▸ Internet users are accessing vast amounts of information.

▸ A huge amount of replicated information is being carried over the network.

▸ More and more Web sites contain large graphics, video, and audio clips, which slow download time.

▸ New Web-based services, such as real audio and video, are being created at Internet speeds; by increasing our demands for bandwidth, the overall performance of the Internet suffers.

The following issues must be resolved so consumers can retain transparency, as well as backward compatibility with existing Internet standards:

▸ Document retrieval times must be decreased.

▸ Availability of data on the Internet must be increased.

▸ The amount of data being transferred must be reduced.

▸ Network access must be redistributed to avoid peak-usage times.

Novell's BorderManager addresses these issues by providing advanced-caching technologies. Following are three distinct caching methods offered by BorderManager:

▸ Proxy cache

▸ Reverse proxy (HTTP acceleration)

▸ ICP hierarchical caching

HOW CACHING WORKS

Caching was first implemented in the 1960s, when CPU cycle times began to outstrip the speeds of the increasingly large main-memory banks. To optimize performance, a faster — but smaller — auxiliary memory, or *cache*, was introduced. This provided a buffering capability so that main memory could interface with the processor-cycle time more efficiently.

Caching minimizes access times by bringing the data as close to the user as possible; it relies on locality of reference. This principle assumes that the most recently accessed data has the highest possibility of being accessed again in the near future. Once the data has been loaded into memory where it is cached (stored), the next request for it can be fulfilled directly from the cache memory. All caching systems rely on explicit replacement policies to decide which items should remain in the cache. Caching algorithms specify that the least-recently used documents will be removed from the cache when memory space is needed.

PROXY CACHING

One of the most absurd things happening on the Internet is the replication of information being downloaded. For example, XYZ Company has just connected to the Internet using some type of packet-charged service. The company installed a browser on all 100 workstations in its organization. Everyday, many of the employees bring up the browser (possibly at the same time and through the same pipe), they call up Mountain View, California, and pull down the exact same information. XYZ Company pays for the same information to be downloaded many times. The worst part is that the users cached the data to their local hard drives and didn't share it with any of the other users!

For XYZ Company, performance and security both suffer. More than likely, the employees pull down the information around the same time, so our "pipe" becomes full, slowing the download for everyone.

If the data is stored on the local hard drive in cache, it is not secured. Let's say Mary is authorized to access salary information from an internal Web server. Mary logs on to a workstation, executes the browser, types in the URL to the database, and receives the information. The browser has now cached that information locally to the hard drive. Mary walks away, and John sits down at the workstation, logs in as himself, and executes the browser. He then accesses the same data because the data is still local — the information is retrieved from cache, even though he really does not have access to this information.

BorderManager proxy cache eliminates the need to do caching at the workstation. Once the information is retrieved, the data is cached at a proxy server. The next time a browser requests the same information, the browser client receives the information from cache, rather than from the Internet.

The proxy cache works with Novell Directory Service's access-control policies to verify that the browser client is authorized to access the data. If not, the browser client is denied access to the information even though the server has the data in cache (this is illustrated in Figure 3.5).

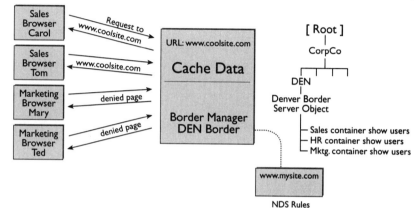

How the Proxy Cache Server Works

Novell's BorderManager proxy cache server acts as an HTTP proxy. When a client is configured to go through a proxy, the following process takes place:

1 • The client sends an absolute URL to the proxy server.

2 • The proxy server then acts as a client based on the method requested.

3 • The proxy server invokes the requested client method and accesses the origin server.

4 • The header fields (passed from the client) are then passed on to the origin server. The proxy server does not modify them before passing them on.

The BorderManager proxy server supports HTTP (versions 0.9, 1.0, 1.1), HTTPD, FTP, and Gopher. SSL requests are sent as HTTP requests to the proxy server. The proxy server caches the following:

▸ URLs

▸ HTML pages

▸ FTP files

Proxy caching with NDS access controls enables you to place multiple caches around your private business network (closer to the browser clients). In addition, it ensures that even though the data is replicated in different areas, only the authorized user will see the data. Proxy caching is illustrated in Figure 3.6.

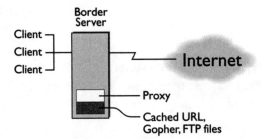

FIGURE 3.6

Using proxy caching at the border provides faster access to browser clients by intercepting the browser request and supplying the requested pages from cache.

NOTE

A browser client will get better performance by going through a proxy server, rather than going directly to the origin Web server. When a client browser requests information from a Web server, most browsers will intentionally slow the data transfer to allow time to render the Web pages they are downloading. When BorderManager is used, the BorderManager proxy will attempt to negotiate the largest TCP segment size possible (up to 64K). The size of the segment depends on the Web server to which the proxy is talking. The browser can then download the pages quickly. Because the proxy server doesn't need to render the pages, it can put them into cache as fast as the link permits. This means the proxy server will almost ALWAYS be ahead of the browser as the pages are requested. This translates into a significant increase in performance at the browser.

Once the proxy server receives the information, it breaks the packets into smaller increments and sends the information to the client. By using the proxy server, slow downs on Internet pipes are eliminated because the client receives the smaller packets at LAN speeds.

Determining Document Freshness Caching was added to firewall services in Novell's BorderManager to reduce network and Web server loads, and to improve performance. One problem with caching, however, is determining the freshness of a document. BorderManager uses different ways to determine a document's freshness, including the following:

- Time-to-live information

- HTML methods that support obtaining the latest, modified information

The time-to-live information is sent as part of the HTTP header. Currently, all major browsers support caching at the local machine, and are already using these same HTTP headers to determine how long the page can be cached. The proxy cache server uses this same information. In addition, it lets the administrator configure additional cache-aging policy information. This configurable information is accessed through NWAdmin, which is covered in detail in Chapter 6. The following HTTP headers are used in determining cache aging:

- Date

- Last-Modified

- Expires

- Cache-Control

- Age

- Max-Age

In addition, the Cache-Control header has a number of additional values, such as No-Cache, Revalidate, Private, etc. The Web server uses these headers to tell public caches (such as the Novell Proxy Cache) and private caches (such as the local cache maintained by Netscape Navigator or Microsoft Internet Explorer) whether the page can be cached. Using these headers, the Web server can specify that the page is not cacheable, that it must be revalidated everytime, or that it can be cached for a specified time before refreshing it. The time period before refresh can range from a few seconds to hours, days, or even weeks.

HTML   When it is time to revalidate or refresh a cached page, the proxy uses HTML methods to determine the latest, modified information. The proxy sends an if-modified-since query to the origin Web server. If the page has not changed, the Web server responds with a Not Modified reply and does not need to retransmit all of the page data. Novell's BorderManager proxy cache does not cache the following types of information:

▶   objects that are password protected

▶   dynamic data

▶   any objects with /cgi-bin/ in their URLs

▶   objects larger than a configurable size (this is set through NWAdmin)

▶   objects associated with protocols other than HTTP, FTP, and Gopher

▶   any HTTP header that has "Pragma:no-cache," "Cache-Control:Private," "Set Cookie," "WWW-Authenticate," "Cache-Control:no-cache"

Passive and Negative Caching   Novell's BorderManager supports two kinds of caching: passive and negative. *Passive caching* is also referred to as "on-demand" caching. When the proxy server gets a request for an object, it checks on whether the object is in the cache, whether or not it is fresh, and returns the object — if available. If the object is not available, a *negative cache* entry is created. The request is sent to the origin server, and retrieved and placed in cache before being sent on to the requesting client. Negative caching can be defined as a consequence of a stale passive cache.

In the event of HTTP error conditions, such as 403 (forbidden request) and 404 (URL not found), or if you get an error condition because the origin server you tried to attach to is too busy and has no more TCP connections available, the requests are negatively cached, and subsequent requests are denied. However, if a cached page exists, even if this page is considered stale (it needs to be refreshed) and the origin Web server is down, the proxy will return the stale page.

For example, a browser client requests a URL site that is no longer available. The proxy server will try for up to a minute to contact the host in question. If it cannot contact the host, the proxy server returns an error page to the browser client. At the same time, the proxy server caches this information. This way the next browser client that tries to access the same URL site receives an immediate response from the proxy server indicating that this site is no longer available. This saves time, frustration, and unnecessary traffic.

If a browser client contacts a URL site whose server is too busy to grant an open connection, the proxy server will try to get an open connection for approximately one minute. If it is not successful, it returns the error condition to the browser client. During this time, if another browser client attempts to access the same site, the proxy server automatically returns the error code. In the meantime, the proxy server continues to try to get an open connection to the requested URL for up to ten minutes. Once connected, the proxy server caches the information that was requested, so when the browser client tries again, the data will be delivered out of cache.

The goal of negative caching is to tell the client as quickly as possible that the object is not available without tormenting the Internet with repeated, unsuccessful requests. Expiration time for negative caching is also configurable.

REVERSE PROXY (HTTP ACCELERATION)

Reverse-proxy caching acts as a front end to publishing servers. By using the reverse-proxy caching included with BorderManager, you improve the performance, security, and accessibility of your Web sites — all crucial assets, as Web publishing platforms face many problems today.

Performance

The bottlenecks of common Web platforms differ from the bottlenecks of IntranetWare platforms. Most Web publishing servers are running on UNIX or NT platforms. These platforms are inefficient at handling many open connections and servicing files at the same time. Every time an open connection is requested of the Web publishing server, a little piece of CPU cycle time is also taken to manage the connection.

A Web page typically consists of 90 percent static data and 10 percent dynamic data. Static data is information that does not change, such as text, JGPs, GIFs, Java applets, and forms. Typically, static data is public information that wouldn't be extremely damaged if it were hacked.

Dynamic data represents data that changes, such as information from a database, stock information, or weather information. Typically, dynamic data is important information that — if hacked — could cause damage to your business.

On the common Web publishing platforms mentioned, not only is the CPU being used for open connections, it also spends 90 percent of its time fetching the dynamic data. No wonder these types of platforms reach bottleneck stages so quickly! A lot is being asked of that CPU — it must handle connections *and* send data at the same time.

The percentage of CPU cycles required to fetch dynamic and static data is illustrated in Table 3.2.

TABLE 3.2 *Web page data and the percentage of CPU cycles required to retrieve the data*	PERCENTAGE OF TYPE OF WEB DATA ON A TYPICAL PAGE	CPU PERCENTAGE OF CYCLES TO FETCH DATA
	Static Data — 90%	10%
	Dynamic Data — 10%	90%

As open connections increase, the CPU becomes saturated. At this point the bottleneck becomes the processor. Even when you add more processors to the server, you eventually have to break down and buy another platform to represent your busy site. This presents a problem because the equipment is expensive, and once it's in place, you have to maintain two hardware platforms.

Security

In addition, you are broadcasting two IP addresses to the global network, which poses a security risk because you now have two servers holding duplicate information (see Figure 3.7).

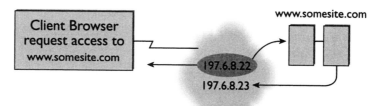

Web publishing servers open themselves up to security risks by broadcasting their IP addresses to the Internet.

In Figure 3-7, a client requests a connection to www.somesite.com. In order for the packet to be sent, a DNS resolve must be made first to obtain the IP address of the Web server target (exposed outside the firewall or on the intranet border). After that, an ARP (Address Resolution Protocol) request is made to either the local machine or to the designated gateway. The essential point to this is that *two* Web servers (or points of access) need to be secured instead of just one.

BorderManager to the Rescue

BorderManager's Reverse-Proxy Cache Server acts as a front end to one or more publishing servers. These publishing servers could be UNIX, NT, Macintosh, AS/400, or even another NetWare server.

The reverse-proxy server is essentially an automatic firewall to your publishing servers; it sits in front of the publishing server and becomes the DNS entry to your Web site. The reverse-proxy server caches all the static information, leaving the dynamic information in place. Now the publishing server has to handle only one request — opening connections — providing more time to deliver dynamic data to the reverse-proxy server. This provides three benefits:

- ▸ Security is no longer compromised.

- ▸ You don't have to mirror your expensive platform to another expensive platform — you can use Intel-based platforms to fix the bottlenecks.

- ▸ Your Web site can handle many more open connections than previously.

When you place a reverse-proxy cache in front of your Web server or servers (it supports virtual hosting), the proxy cache will cache all the static information from the origin server. Remember that this could be up to 90 percent of the publishing data.

When a client requests information from that Web server, the request is diverted to the proxy server, which responds to the request with its IP address. Typically, this IP address is different from the segment that the origin servers are on, thus protecting your origin servers. (For even more protection, the origin servers would then only permit requests from the reverse proxy, ignoring all other packets.) The proxy server supplies the cached static information to the browser, and then makes a request to the origin server for the dynamic information. The origin Web server returns the information to the proxy server, which then passes the information to the browser client. This process accelerates access and takes the request load off the Web servers, enabling them to handle more users while being protected behind the firewall, as illustrated in Figure 3.8.

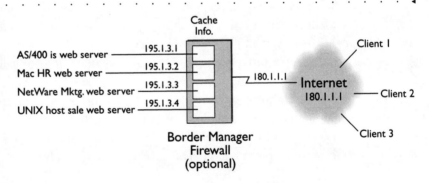

FIGURE 3.8

The BorderMangager proxy server acts as a front end to one or more Web publishing servers by caching all the static data from those servers. By centralizing the cache, access control and traffic loads can be managed globally.

ICP HIERARCHY CACHING

Novell's BorderManager enables administrators to set up a network of hierarchical proxy cache servers to reduce the WAN load and resolve misses. Novell's BorderManager bases this technology on Internet Cache Protocol (ICP) and Harvest Squid caching.

NOTE

The Harvest project, funded by ARPA, involved a research project concerned with the issues surrounding object caching, searching, and replication in the Internet space (among other things). The Squid cache was an implementation based on this research created by NLANR (National Lab for Applied Network Research). NLANR was created in 1995 and funded by several of the National Science Foundation Supercomputing Centers.

ICP is based on a project developed by the Internet Research Task Force Group on Resource Discovery (IETF-RD). The Harvest Squid project started in 1995 with the goal to develop a technology that would help relieve the congestion on the Internet backbone. Typically, the normal mode of the World Wide Web keeps information isolated to a single publishing server. Harvest Squid introduced the ICP protocol for cooperation between individual caches. The original project ended in early 1996, and two groups, the Harvest Developers Group and the National Laboratory Advance Networking Research (NLANR) group, have done subsequent development. Both include staff of the original project.

How Hierarchical Caching Works

Hierarchical caching accomplishes the following:

▶ distributes server load away from server hot spots caused by globally popular information objects

▶ reduces latency

▶ protects the network from erroneous clients

The Harvest Squid cache enables individual caches to be interconnected hierarchically in a way that mirrors the topology of an internetwork, resulting in additional increases in efficiency. In a hierarchical cache, misses at one level are passed to caches located at higher levels.

The hierarchical cache supports parent-child relationships as well as peer relationships. Peers could be CERN proxies or caches at the same level in the hierarchy. Each cache in the hierarchy independently decides whether to fetch the reference from the object's home site or from its parent or peer caches. Figure 3.9 illustrates ICP hierarchical caching.

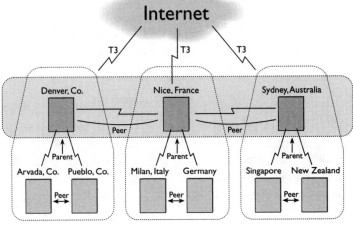

FIGURE 3.9

With ICP hierarchical caching, you can relieve physical infrastructure bottlenecks, as well as increase access to Internet sites.

* dotted lines represent different neighborhood caches.

ICP hierarchical caching works as follows:

1 • A browser client requests a URL.

2 • The proxy server intercepts the request and acts on the client's behalf.

3 • The proxy server first tries to resolve the request from its own cache. If the proxy server does not contain the information needed, it notes a "miss" and executes a simple resolution protocol (ICP). The cache then sends a "hit" message to the UDP echo port of the object's home machine. When the object's home echoes this message, the cache treats it like a hit generated by a remote cache that had the object. This option enables the cache to retrieve the object from the home site if it happens to be closer than the remote origin server.

A cache resolves a reference through the first peer, parent, or home site to return a UDP hit packet or through the first parent to return a UDP "miss" message. If all caches return a UDP miss and the home's UDP hit packet fails to arrive within two seconds, the proxy server will go out onto the origin Web server to retrieve the requested information. The cache doesn't wait the two seconds for a home machine to time out; it begins transmitting as soon as all of the parent and peer caches have responded.

If any of the parents or peers report a hit, the cache that reported the hit would then transfer the data requested to the proxy server, which then sends the data to the browser client. The goal of ICP is for a cache to resolve an object through the source that can provide it the most efficiently.

NOTE **When designing hierarchical caches, keep in mind that hierarchies as deep as three caches add little noticeable access latency. Specifications recommend a limit of five neighbors, including parents and peers, per proxy server.**

During a retrieval using ICP, three different responses can occur, as listed in Table 3.3.

TABLE 3.3	TYPES OF ICP RESPONSES	DESCRIPTION
ICP responses during retrieval of objects	ERROR	This can occur if some internal error exists or if for some reason the cache won't retrieve the specified object.
	HIT	If the first level of cache does not have the object in its resident set, the data object is simply supplied to the client.
	MISS	If the first level of cache does not have the object in its resident set, the proxy server might go up the hierarchy or contact the specified origin server.

General information about the Harvest Squid project can be found at HTTP://harves.cs.colorado.edu.

A technical briefing on Novell's implementation of ICP caching is located at HTTP://irache.nlanr.net/Cache/Workshop97/Papers/Tomlinson/tomlinson.html.

IDENTIFYING CACHE SITES

When you implement proxy servers within your private business network, you must identify which sites will benefit from which caching mechanisms. The following list offers some guidelines to help you determine the best scenarios for each caching mechanism. Use proxy caching (client acceleration) for the following:

- Sites with multiple clients — in almost all cases, operating these clients through a proxy server will dramatically improve performance. (This is especially true if groups of employees are accessing the same Internet or intranet sites.)

- Sites including remote locations that all route through the corporate location to access the Internet.

- Sites requiring user-level access control.

- Sites that need to globally maintain multiple firewall services.

Use Reverse Proxy (server acceleration) for the following:

- Sites that have Internet or intranet Web servers with high levels of usage.

- Sites that need to centralize access control on all intranet Web servers.

- Sites with intranet publishing servers that contain both company public and private information. You can maintain all security rights through NDS, instead of managing each server's access control separately.

- Sites with a variety of Internet or intranet Web server platforms. By using a reverse proxy you can consolidate and secure your environment globally.

Use ICP hierarchical caching (network acceleration) for the following:

- Sites with slow links to the Internet.

- Sites with multiple LAN segments that enable you to push the data to the users.

- Sites with congestion and delay problems at LAN points within WANs.

CACHING BENEFITS

Novell has been a leader in caching technology. The IntranetWare communication engine dramatically improves performance and scalability of proxy caching. IntranetWare is a real-time OS built from the ground up to be optimized to handle many requests and deliver services quickly without tapping into processor cycle time. An IntranetWare server can easily handle more than 1,000 connections accessing files.

Novell's BorderManager proxy cache plays off the strengths of IntranetWare and is implemented in a multithreaded fashion, which is much more efficient than a server application. The proxy cache exploits actual and virtual memory. If the administrator configures it to do so, the cache may keep hot objects in memory for fastest service. Otherwise, the vast majority of the cache is serviced from virtual memory on disk. The BorderManager proxy cache uses file cache buffers directly, eliminating the need for a separately managed application-layer RAM cache.

By caching the data on your private business network, you can reduce your WAN traffic up to 40 – 60 percent. Organizations can realize two and half times as much throughput over the same physical WAN connection without purchasing expensive, higher-bandwidth WAN connections.

When business networks were designed for wide-area connectivity to their remote sites, they configured the WAN links based on the type of traffic that would be generated. Historically, this traffic was either server-to-server communications (NDS replication traffic), or host-to-terminal traffic. For this type of traffic you didn't have to spend a significant amount of money on large "pipes," so many businesses used low-speed, low-cost solutions.

Today, with Internet traffic these "pipes" have become the bottleneck. Businesses have to look at restructuring the WAN. This can be very expensive. With BorderManager caching, you can place the data closer to the end users, and you can network your cache to create a type of "virtual cache network" to eliminate Internet traffic bottlenecks. In Chapter 4, we provide you with examples of ways to implement proxy caching.

Virtual Private Networking

Novell's BorderManager Virtual Private Networking (VPN) uses server-to-server tunneling. This means traffic transmitted between the two servers is encrypted. The encryption makes sure that no internal information is available beyond an organization's Internet gateway. BorderManager VPN enables clients on one remote intranet to communicate with services (such as a Web server) on another remote intranet without the client having any special knowledge of VPN or encryption. Although BorderManager enables a client to dial in and attach to an intranet, intranet-to-intranet VPN support is a more flexible solution.

Table 3.4 shows the information that needs to be collected to set up a VPN between two IntranetWare sites.

TABLE 3.4	SITE 1	SITE 2
Information that needs to be collected to set up a VPN between two IntranetWare sites.	Site 2 IP address	Site 2 IP address
	What networks are reachable by Site 2	What networks are reachable by Site 1
	A shared secret with Site 2 (described in the following text)	A shared secret with Site 1 (described in the following text)

MASTER VPN SERVERS

Once this information is collected, one of the servers must be chosen as the master VPN server. The following guidelines can be used:

▸ The master server should be the server that most of the VPN connections will be made on.

▸ The server is usually at the corporate location where most of the key system administration is located.

Generating Shared Secrets

Once the master server is assigned, it generates encryption information. The master server generates the RSA public and private keys and Diffie-Hellman (DH) shared secret keys, stores the private RSA and DH keys securely, and then performs a message digest (MD5) technique to distribute information to the slave servers. The distribution file contains the RSA public key and the DH shared-key parameters. The master server information gets added automatically to the server's VPN database table. The master server then distributes the master server encryption information to the administrator of each slave server.

Once the slave server gets the distribution files, it verifies the master file with a code. This verification should be done "out-of-bound," meaning that the network administrator of the slave location usually calls the administrator of the master server to verify that the file came from the master server. Once certified, the slave server generates a DH key pair using the parameters from the distribution file generated in the above step. The slave server stores its private key securely, and then builds a distribution file for the master server. This distribution file uses a Message Digest technique again to store the DH public key and the public IP address of the slave server. The distribution file is then sent to the master server administrator.

NOTE

MD (Message Digest) algorithms are used in many security-based application to ensure secrecy. There are several MD algorithms that can be used. The specific one used in VPN is MD5.

The master VPN administrator takes the new distribution file and verifies that it is from the slave VPN server. Once verified, the VPN administrator takes the information from the file and adds it to the VPN database table. Table 3.5 shows a sample VPN table.

TABLE 3.5	VPN NAME	PUBLIC IP ADDRESS	DH PUBLIC KEY	STATIC ROUTES
A sample VPN table	Master	1.1.1.1	DH1	Not required
	Slave	2.2.2.2	DH2	Not required

For each slave VPN server, the master VPN server would add the distribution file information to the VPN database table.

Once the information is added to the VPN table, the master VPN server synchronizes the VPN table to the slaves. Each slave will know all the information that the VPN table holds on each server, the DH public key, the public IP address, and any static routes. When the slave VPN server receives the update, the update will be digitally signed to ensure authenticity. The master server uses MD5 with the RSA authentication key to generate the signature. By enabling all servers participating in the VPN to recognize all other servers, pure connectivity is built in a mesh format so all traffic does not have to go to the master server. Once all the servers in the VPN have this information, it is all verified by distributing the shared secrets, and a VP tunnel is created to form connections to the sites it knows about. Bindings are generated for the VP tunnel automatically. You now have a secured, encrypted tunnel connecting your sites together. Figure 3.10 shows how a VPN works.

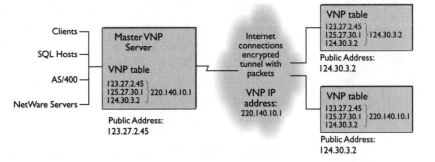

F I G U R E   3.10

Virtual Private Networking provides an encrypted IP tunnel through the Internet to the sites it knows about. VPN creates a table for each site so each server knows who is participating in the virtual network.

ADDITIONAL SECURITY FEATURES

BorderManager provides extra security on top of the VPN encryption on the fly. As described in the previous section, two communicating servers know a shared secret that enables them to create an encryption key. They also use timestamps to prevent replay attacks.

For example, a customer goes into a bank and makes a deposit of $100. Outside, a friend uses a LANalyzer to capture the transaction. The customer leaves the bank. The friend plays back the captured packet over and over again. If there was no timestamp on the packet, the bank customer looks as if he is continually making deposits of $100. Using timestamps, Novell's BorderManager can prevent these types of replay attacks.

With VPN, a different key is used for sending data than for the one for receiving data, providing another useful security feature. Using a technique called jittering, the key is changed every so often by a user-configurable field. For instance, the user default is 1,000 packets. Jittering will change the key sometime before 1,000 packets have passed between the VPN. No one can predict when the keys actually get changed. This provides an extra level of security: if one of the keys was somehow compromised, a hacker's chances of breaking into your packet and decrypting the data are very slim, as the key has probably changed many times.

BORDERMANAGER VPN ENCRYPTION METHODS

Table 3.6 summarizes the encryption methods used with BorderManager VPN.

T A B L E 3 . 6 *BorderManager VPN Encryption Methods*	ENCRYPTION METHOD	USED FOR
	RC2 key-based encryption — considered symmetric algorithms	Key-based encryption ciphers public key
	RSA encryption — considered asymmetric algorithms	Key-based encryption for public and private key generation
	Diffie-Hellman	Create shared secret
	MD5, Message digestls — considered a HASH function	Creates a packet of information for distribution to slave servers for configuration that is impossible to decrypt
	RSA digital signatures	Provides data integrity

Key-based algorithms encrypt the data so it cannot be read by anyone without a secret decryption key. Algorithms are divided into classes depending on the cryptography methodology they directly support. Symmetric algorithms are used to encrypt and decrypt a private key. Novell's BorderManager uses RC2 symmetric algorithms to create the public key. RC2 has the following features:

- ▸ encompasses 64-bit block cipher and variable key sizes

- ▸ runs approximately twice as fast as Data Encryption Standard (DES)

- ▸ operates in different modes, including:

  - ▸ Electronic Code Book (ECB), using two distinct algorithms

  - ▸ Cipher Block Chaining (CBC), in which the encryption of each block depends upon the encryption of the previous block

▸ Output Feedback (OFB), used as a random number generator

▸ Cipher Feedback (CFB), used for message authentication codes

▸ triple encryption, uses DES cipher three times and has three 56-bit keys

▸ uses confidential algorithm proprietary to RSA data security

▸ is strong under all attacks

Asymmetric algorithms are used by asymmetric (public) cryptosystem methodologies in order to encrypt a symmetric (private) session key. The symmetric key is used to encrypt the data. The symmetric key is then encrypted using an asymmetric key and transmitted, along with the encrypted data, over the network. BorderManager uses a combination of RSA and Diffie-Hellman encryption methods. RSA creates the private keys, whereas Diffie-Hellman creates a shared secret code as described in the previous discussion on shared secrets. Features of these types of asymmetric algorithms are as follows:

▸ RSA:

  ▸ Very popular computer encryption algorithm, security depends on the difficulty in factoring large intergers.

  ▸ Used to encrypt small amounts of data, such as digital signatures and encryption keys; supplements the symmetric algorithm. The sender creates a hash of the message, and then encrypts it with his private key. The receiver uses the sender's public key to decrypt the hash, hashes the message himself, and compares the two.

▸ Diffie-Hellman:

  ▸ Enables exchange of a secret key over an insecure medium by two users without any prior secrets.

  ▸ Cannot be used to encrypt or decrypt messages.

▶ Is based on the difficulty of taking logarithms in finite fields. If the elements are carefully chosen and are large, then the discrete logarithm problem is computationally unfeasible.

▶ Is patented by Public Key Partners (PKP).

Hash functions are central to key-based cryptosystems. They are relatively easy to compute but almost impossible to decrypt. A hash function takes a variable-size input and returns a fixed-size string, called a message digest, usually 128 bits. Hash functions are used to detect modification of a message and provide digital signatures. Novell's BorderManager uses MD5. This type of hashing function includes the following features:

▶ the most commonly used of the message digest family (MD2 and MD4)

▶ optimized for 32-bit machines

▶ contains strong security features

▶ provides data integrity

A digital signature provides data integrity but not confidentiality. A digital signature is attached to a message along with a timestamp to provide a limited form of identity verification. Novell's BorderManager uses RSA, which has the following features:

▶ Patented RSA digital signature proves the contents of a message as well as the identity of the signer.

▶ The sender creates a hash of the message, and then encrypts it with the sender's private key. The receiver uses the sender's public key to decrypt the hash, hashes the message himself or herself, and compares the two hashes.

To provide a complete security trust, VPNs include the features summarized in Table 3.7.

TABLE 3.7	FEATURE	TYPE OF SERVICE
Features of VPN that provide complete security trusts	Confidentiality	Encryption technologies
	Authenticity	Public key cryptography techniques
	Integrity	Message digest algorithms

VPNs ON A PRIVATE NETWORK

Using the Internet for connectivity can save your business anywhere from 20 to 60 percent of current WAN costs. VPNs offer a lot of flexibility in the type of Internet connection they can use, whether it be dial on demand, frame relay, ISDN, or even a 28.8 modem. VPNs can even be used to secure information within a private network.

If you use the Internet for WAN connectivity, the VPN servers involved have two NIC cards installed, one designated private and the other designated public. The private segment creates a VPN with another private segment, and all data sent between the two VPN servers is encrypted through an IP tunnel. IP tunneling is simply a routing function, so the data enclosed in the "wrapper" doesn't have to be all NetWare data.

For example, a VPN is created for a company with the following configuration: One segment in New York has an SQL database running on a UNIX host, and another segment in Kansas City has a workstation that wants to query the SQL database in New York. The client requests the information, and the packet is routed to the VPN server. The VPN server realizes that the destination address is located on a segment destined to another VPN server, so the data is "wrapped" and sent down the encrypted tunnel. Once it reaches New York, the VPN server verifies the packet, decrypts the packet, and sends the packet to the UNIX SQL host. The host retrieves the requested information, sends the data to the VPN router (server) that checks to make sure the destination is a VPN site, and "wraps" the packet. The packet is sent through the IP tunnel, arriving at the Kansas City VPN server, which verifies the source, decrypts the packet, and sends the information to the requesting client.

Advanced MPR Routing

Novell's BorderManager includes the entire Novell MultiProtocol Router (MPR) v3.1 suite. The MultiProtocol Router is a software-based router that operates on IntranetWare platforms. MPR provides concurrent routing of IPX, TCP/IP, AppleTalk, and SNA protocols and supports a wide range of LAN and WAN connections.

Software-based routers provide customers with a cost-effective alternative to proprietary hardware routers. MPR is fully integrated with the IntranetWare platform. All certified LAN cards work with MPR, so all LAN topologies, including Arcnet, Ethernet, Token Ring, and FDDI, are supported. Novell's BorderManager MPR suite includes one WAN connection license.

MPR can provide customers with a very cost-effective solution to Internet access. VPN services will work over any type of MPR connection that the server can support. Chapter 5 will detail the installation of MPR.

Table 3.8 provides a summary of the features and benefits of MPR.

T A B L E 3 . 8

Features and benefits of the
Novell MultiProtocol Router

FEATURES	BENEFITS
IPX routing	IPX routing provides NLSP support, support for on-demand and permanent routes, RIP, SAP, and NLSP dynamic routing over on-demand and permanent connections, static routing over on-demand and permanent connections, and IPX header compression.
IP routing	IP routing provides static, RIP, and OSPF dynamic routing, IPX and Apple-Talk data transport over IP, and TCP/IP header compression.
AppleTalk routing	AppleTalk supports AURP routing and is suitable for enterprise networks and configurable RTMP update intervals.
Source route bridging	This is used in Token-Ring environments. Bridges both routable (IPX, IP) and nonroutable (NetBIOS, LLC) data traffic. Compatible with IBM source-route bridges, it provides the capability to configure the source-route bridge to support 1-13 hops.
WAN call management	This provides ISDN, sync, and async PPP dial backup for any permanent call, dial-on-demand, and permanent connectivity for IPX, IP, AppleTalk over ISDN, sync and async PPP, ATM and X.25.

(continued)

T A B L E   3 . 8

Features and benefits of the
Novell MultiProtocol Router
(continued)

FEATURES	BENEFITS
MPR filtering	MPR filtering provides IPX, TCP/IP, AppleTalk, IPX RIP and SAP, NCP, and AppleTalk zone-filtering.
Point-to-Point Protocol (PPP)	PPP includes low-speed to high-speed support and ensures multivendor interoperability between sites. It provides ISDN support using BRI or PRI adapters with AT-ISDN or Common ISDN-API (CAPI) WAN ODI drivers and enables synchronous or asynchronous connections over dedicated links using DSU/CSUs or modems. It supports circuit-switched links with AT Command, DTR dialed, or V.25bits DSU/CSUs or modems and uses IPX WAN support for third-party PPP routers, and enables PPP data compression up to a 4:1 ratio.
MPR management	MPR management supports SNMP, X Windows, Telnet, and remote configuration. It provides remote installation through NetWare INSTALL and FTP; server-based WAN diagnostic trace tools for PPP, frame relay, and X.25; Ping tools for IP, IPX, and AppleTalk; and server-based SNMP consoles.
ATM	ATM supports high-speed links, LLC encapsulation, and VC multiplexing. It provides ATM LAN interconnection for IPX, IP, and AppleTalk routing, and source-route bridging over PVC's and SVC's.
Frame relay	This provides remote location connection via private or public services; IPX, IP and AppleTalk routing; source-route bridging using PVC's, Annex D (ANSI T1.517), LMI R 1.0, and Frame Relay Forum UNI implementations. It interoperates with frame-relay routers that support IPXWAN, up to 992 PVC's per port and is certified by AT&T, BT North America, CompuServe, MCI, Pacific Bell, US West, US Sprint, WilTel, and others.
X.25	X.25 supports remote location connection via private or public X.25 services and includes configuration profiles for the major X.25 public data networks worldwide. It supports user-definable profiles and provides modular 8- and 128-frame sequencing and packet sequencing. X.25 supports window sizes from 1 to 127 frames; 1980, 1984 and 1988 standards; and facility options. It is certified by AT&T, US Sprint, and Net2.
SMDS	SMDS allows switched Multimegabit Digital services.
SNA extensions	This supports Ethernet and Token-Ring attached SNA and NetBIOS stations and offers TCP/IP or TCP/IPX. It uses NDS for DLSw objects and security groups and supports scalable SNA internetworks and SNA/NetBIOS stations with DLSw and source-route bridging. SNA provides LINK/SNA, IPX, IP, and AppleTalk routing over LU6.2 connections. It acts as an APPN LEN attached via SDLC, Token-Ring, and Ethernet and enables software base compression up to a 4:1 ratio.

For more information on the features of MPR, check out the following link: `http://iamg.novell.com//iamg/products/mpr/specs/mprspec.htm`.

Remote-Access Services

Novell's BorderManager includes the entire NetWare Connect product, including ConnectView. NetWare Connect provides solutions for dial-in, dial-out, and modem sharing.

NetWare Connect lets remote users of MS Windows, DOS, and Macintosh computers dial in and access all resources available on your NetWare network. It also enables users to dial out from the network and connect to remote control computers, BBS, X.25, ISDN services, and the Internet. NetWare Connect consolidates communication resources, enabling them to be shared by more users.

Using NetWare Connect, businesses can maximize their investment in modems and telephone lines by centralizing them in a pool of shared network resources. NetWare Connect also provides strong security by supporting the following:

▶ NetWare Challenge Authentication Protocol (NWCAP)

▶ NDS authentication

▶ Password Authentication Protocol (PAP)

▶ Challenge-Handshake Authentication Protocol (CHAP)

NetWare Connect includes extensive management utilities, one of which is ConnectView. ConnectView is a Windows-based monitoring console that gives the administrator tools to manage the modem pools, connections, and security. Additionally, ConnectView provides an accounting package that enables network supervisors to bill for modem usage on a user or department basis. Billing rates can be based on connection type, speed, port, or the time of day.

Novell's BorderManager includes support for up to two ports. However, the full NetWare Connect product will support up to 128 sessions.

NetWare Connect has implemented a set of NetWare Loadable Modules (NLMs) that run on an IntranetWare platform. The installation of NetWare Connect is covered in detail in Chapter 5.

Summary

BorderManager is a suite of technologies that addresses customers' concerns with security, management, performance, and remote services when connecting their business network to the outside world.

As you can tell by the length of this chapter, the entire BorderManager package can be a bit overwhelming. However, the benefit of having these technologies bundled together means that organizations are given the choice to implement the right technologies for their particular environment. The best part of this is the technologies that are available are plug and play.

For example, if you have already implemented packet filtering within your organization, you can use the other technologies to enhance your current environment. In Chapter 4, the practical scenarios provide you with many different examples of how these technologies are commonly implemented in business environments. Chapters 5 and 6 cover the installation and configuration of these technologies.

CHAPTER 4

BorderManager
Solutions Scenarios

As shown in Chapter 3, BorderManager offers many technologies that can secure your intranet, help you manage it, and enhance its performance.

This chapter provides you with practical scenarios to help you determine how best to implement BorderManager in your organization. These scenarios are based on real-world businesses and provide you with examples of how BorderManager's "plug-and-play" technologies can be implemented. This chapter contains the following eight examples:

1 • A small accounting firm wants desktop Internet access.

2 • A corporate office is providing Internet access to all its employees. Performance is suffering at the remote office sites, so administrators are looking for ways to improve it.

3 • A law firm needs more than one workstation with access to the Internet so law assistants can use Internet-based law libraries simultaneously.

4 • An IS department wants to centralize intranet Web-server administration and reduce the traffic loads across the private business WAN.

5 • A private school would like to have Internet access at its six locations.

6 • A travel agency has opened up two additional offices and wants to connect the sites together.

7 • The payroll department in a medium-sized firm is concerned about security on the LAN. It wants to isolate its network segment to assure that the data is safe.

8 • A small business owner wants Internet access and use at her home office. In addition, she wants to set up a Web server promoting the company.

Scenario #1: Small Accounting Firm

This scenario highlights a company that wants to provide desktop Internet access to their employees.

Company Profile

Grifith and Guidry is a small accounting firm in Lafayette, Louisiana, that provides financial services ranging from tax returns to investment counseling.

Since the partners have implemented their network, they have seen an increase in production, but they are looking for even more ways to stay competitive. They feel that by providing Internet access to their employees, they will be able to accomplish the following:

- access financial information that will make them more competitive

- learn which services the competition is offering

- keep up on the ever-changing IRS laws

The firm believes that the employees will spend approximately 10 to 15 percent of their time accessing the Internet.

Network Profile

Grifith and Guidry's network profile is shown Figure 4.1. The existing environment consists of one NetWare file server and thirty workstations. The workstations are a combination of Windows 3.x and Windows 95.

The current server is running IntranetWare on an Intel Pentium system with 2GB of hard disk space. At least 60 percent of the server's hard disk space is still available. The server has 128MB of RAM and cache buffers are sitting around 85 percent. The topology is twisted-pair Ethernet using only IPX/SPX as a protocol. Traffic problems are not an issue. The system is fairly self-maintaining: the office manager, Shannon, is also the network administrator. Shannon spends less than four hours a week maintaining the system.

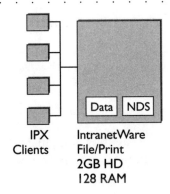

Grifith and Guidry's network before Internet connectivity

IPX
Clients

IntranetWare
File/Print
2GB HD
128 RAM

Issues

The owners have a few issues that need to be addressed for them to feel comfortable with the proposed solution:

- ▸ Cost should be kept to a minimum.

- ▸ The maintenance and implementation of TCP/IP. Shannon understands that the Internet works with TCP/IP only, and is concerned about how she will do this without training on this protocol (the company has no money in the budget for training).

- ▸ Security issues—keeping the network safe is a concern. Shannon has heard stories of people breaking into private networks via the Internet.

Before determining which solution would be best for Grifith and Guidry's environment, Shannon asked herself the following questions:

- ▸ How do we connect to the Internet?

- ▸ What kind of firewall services will we need to protect ourselves?

- ▸ Will we maintain a separate protocol for Internet access to the desktop?

- ▸ Do we have to implement proprietary hardware?

▶ What access-control policies should we implement?

▶ What changes need to occur at the workstations?

BorderManager Solution

The following BorderManager technologies were implemented to meet Grifith and Guidry's needs:

▶ Multiprotocol Router (MPR) for connecting to the Internet

▶ Firewall services: packet filtering, circuit gateway, and application proxy for security

▶ Proxy caching and reverse-proxy caching for performance

▶ Novell Directory Services (NDS) for managing Internet access control

Shannon decided to work with a local Internet service provider (ISP) for Internet access. The ISP helped her decide which type of connection she should have to the Internet. Because cost was an issue, Shannon and the ISP decided that a dial-on-demand connection using a high-speed modem would be sufficient.

To help the performance problems, Shannon implemented proxy caching. After a month of monitoring Internet access, she was able to pick the five Web sites that Grifith and Guidry employees were hitting most frequently. The hits to these sites were substantial, so Shannon decided to implement reverse proxy. The proxy server caches these Web pages at the IntranetWare file server. Whenever an employee hits one of these five sites, the employee receives the information at LAN speeds instead of waiting for the server to go out to the Internet to get the information. Shannon's proxy server will front end the remote origin servers by bringing down all the static data from those servers and caching at the NetWare file server. This system differs from a proxy cache, because with a proxy cache, Shannon caches only the pages the employees are hitting, whereas with reverse proxy the entire Web server's static data is cached.

Security was the next issue to tackle. Shannon decided that Grifith and Guidry needed to provide as many levels of security as possible within its budget. She found that by using Novell's BorderManager, she could implement packet filtering, circuit gateway, and application proxy functions. Through implementation of all the firewall services provided with BorderManager, Shannon was able to protect her network by configuring a secure perimeter around it.

Shannon did not want to maintain an IP network, and because they were going to use the circuit gateway for security features, she was able to leverage her IPX network and maintain TCP/IP only at the BorderManager server. The ISP provides Shannon with one Class-C IP address, the correct subnet mask, and a gateway address.

Because cost was an issue, Shannon wanted to use the existing NetWare platform hardware. She also did not want to have to learn and maintain any additional platforms. As it turned out, everything could be implemented on the existing IntranetWare server with the addition of a modem, more memory, and another hard drive. The new hard drive was used as the volume for the caching information. Even though 128MB was enough, Shannon found that after implementing BorderManager services her cache buffers fell to 40 percent, and she decided to add more memory to keep performance high.

Using NWAdmin, Shannon was able to provide access rights in the same way she did for files. BorderManager creates a default rule that denies access to everything, so all Shannon had to do was define rules for Grifith and Guidry. Shannon sat down with the owners of Grifith and Guidry and a human resources representative, and they decided on access control policies for the company. Based on those policies, Shannon enabled packet filtering at the server. She then enabled TCP/IP packet filtering, making sure that only the IP address of the server was permitted in and out of the network. Shannon started with the following outgoing rules:

▶ provide access to all HTTP and FTP services

▶ deny access to all nonbusiness-related categories between the hours of 8 a.m. and 5 p.m.

▶ provide unlimited access between the hours of 7 a.m. and 8 a.m. and 5 p.m. and 7 p.m.

▶ grant Shannon specific user permissions to access nonbusiness-related sites during business hours

Shannon placed all the rules at the organization container. Now that Shannon had the connection and security in place, she needed to get the employees online. Shannon installed the newest NetWare Client 32 with IPX-IP gateway support on each workstation. The new client software came with BorderManager. She then installed Netscape Communicator on each desktop and configured each browser software to use the proxy server for access. Figure 4.2 shows Grifith and Guidry's network after Internet access was added.

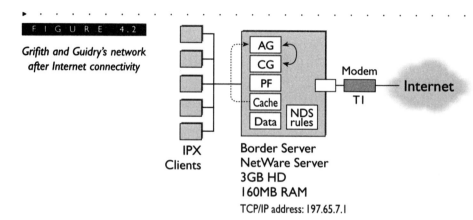

F I G U R E   4.2

Grifith and Guidry's network after Internet connectivity

IPX
Clients

Border Server
NetWare Server
3GB HD
160MB RAM
TCP/IP address: 197.65.7.1

Implementation Results

The owners and employees were very happy and more productive with the new resource. The following benefits were noted:

▸ The network was secure against outside attacks, as it used NDS as the security policy holder.

▸ Shannon was able to be flexible. She could add a new rule, for example, to grant an employee access to a site that is generally denied. Using NWAdmin, Shannon could make the change within minutes.

▸ By using caching services, employees were able to use a dial-up modem that provided cheap access to the Internet without sacrificing performance.

▸ The employees became more productive with the wealth of information to which they had access.

▸ Grifith and Guidry was able to provide customers with access to the latest financial information, tax laws, and so on.

▸ Shannon was pleased that she didn't have to learn and support another protocol suite. With the IPX-IP gateway, all the employees had access to everything they needed without increasing the time she had to spend managing the network.

Scenario #2: Corporate Office

A corporate office is providing Internet access for all its locations, including remote sites. Performance is suffering at the remote office sites, so the company is looking for ways to improve it.

Company Profile

Northwest Credit Union is a small credit union located in Fargo, North Dakota, that serves customers throughout the state. Northwest has six remote offices. Around six months ago, the corporate location decided to add Internet access services. For security it implemented a variety of third-party solutions.

Network Profile

Northwest Credit Union's network layout is shown in Figure 4.3. Northwest uses Cisco routers for packet filtering, ON/LAN technologies for circuit gateway functions, and Netscape proxy for application services. TCP/IP is maintained throughout the entire business network.

The wide-area network (WAN) consists of the six remote sites. All six sites have a Novell file server. The Novell file servers run IntranetWare and are standardized on 6GB of hard drive space and 128MB of RAM. All the sites use Ethernet for the physical LAN. The first two sites are regional offices with about 30 Windows 95 workstations. The regional offices are connected to the corporate backbone with frame relay. The other four offices are remote locations to the regional offices with 10 Windows 95 workstations each. The remote offices are connected from the site to the regional location using dial-on-demand routing.

All Internet traffic is routed through the firewall services located at the corporate location. The IS department intentionally routes all Internet traffic through this location because it doesn't want Internet access points at all locations; otherwise, it would have to place firewall services at each location (and adding and maintaining multiple remote firewalls would be cost prohibitive). The department also didn't want more than one door connecting to the global network. Northwest Credit Union has a staff of seven implementing and maintaining all the sites.

F I G U R E   4.3

The layout of Northwest Credit Union's sites and connections

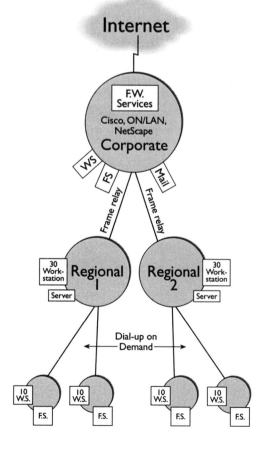

Issues

Northwest Credit Union designed its WAN around five years ago. When the system administrators designed the WAN, they asked themselves what kind of traffic patterns they would experience. At the time, traffic patterns consisted of server-to-server communications and very minimal file transfers. They decided on a hierarchical approach for the WAN layout and chose to use cost-effective connections to the sites. Since Internet access was implemented, many issues have arisen:

- ▶ Employees at the remote sites have been complaining about slow and unpredictable performance.

- ▶ The traffic load on the WAN links has increased more than 50 percent since Internet access has been in place.

- ▶ The firewall solutions the system administrators had were working great. They especially liked the application proxy because they were able to secure Internet access by username instead of by IP address. These systems, however, are not scalable so they have had to maintain two to three systems that perform the same task. The costs of maintaining these solutions are becoming apparent.

Before determining which solution would be best for their environment, the Northwest Credit Union IS department members asked themselves the following questions:

- ▶ How have our traffic patterns changed?

- ▶ What sites communicate together?

- ▶ What is the Internet being used for?

- ▶ What are the changes that need to occur to implement the solution?

BorderManager Solution

The following BorderManager technologies were implemented to meet this organization's needs (see Figure 4.4):

- Proxy caching

- ICP hierarchical caching

IS department staffers decided to monitor the traffic on their business network. They found out that the remote sites were accessing the Internet, causing an increase in traffic flow among the sites by more than 80 percent. Obviously there was a problem: the IS department either had to redesign the entire WAN infrastructure or figure out a more cost-effective way to solve the performance bottleneck.

Northwest Credit Union decided to install Novell's BorderManager Proxy Caching Service on all the remote sites. This way it would not have to replace the current WAN infrastructure. Cached data would be pushed closer to the sites, so employees wouldn't even have to access the WAN link. The only traffic generated would be from the proxy server. Because the sites had such large drives and memory, no extra hardware was needed.

The IS staff were also able to compile a list of the most commonly accessed Web sites and to ascertain which locations were accessing those sites. In doing so, they could group together sites that would benefit from ICP hierarchical caching. This permitted the IS department to set up virtual caching between the sites, which in turn enabled them to keep the traffic on the WAN links to a minimum and get the data pushed close to the browser clients.

IS staff members did not want to throw away any of the technologies they were using, but they were enticed by NDS for access control. They decided to use a proxy caching server at the corporate location. With NDS, they were able to take the rules off the Netscape proxies and centralize all access control functions in NDS. The rules that were located on each of the individual Netscape proxies were applied once through NDS, and the entire corporation security policies remained intact. Now when a new access control rule is created, the IS department creates the rule at the container level of choice, and any proxy servers that are under that container will receive the new rule. No more double entry! With this proxy server located at the corporate location, the Netscape proxy servers were capable of participating in the ICP hierarchical caching.

*Northwest Credit Union's
layout of caching
technologies*

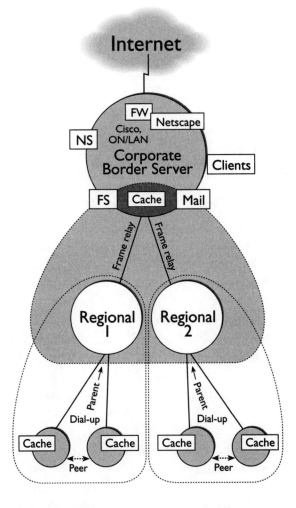

Implementation Results

With BorderManager, Northwest Credit Union was able to keep the current technologies in place and provide enhancements to make their business LAN more secure and manageable. The following benefits were noted:

> ▸ The physical WAN infrastructure did not have to be redesigned. The IS department kept the existing links in place and increased performance by 40 to 70 percent at the WAN locations.

▸ The network administrators were able to control traffic flow by defining network cache groups. This provided a more efficient way for employees to request and receive data.

▸ Security was tighter with NDS managing all of the access control.

▸ Management costs went down because the IS department had to learn only one way to apply access control.

▸ The only cost to Northwest Credit Union was BorderManager—no additional hardware was needed.

Scenario #3: Law Firm

In this scenario, a law firm is looking for ways to provide more than one workstation with access to the Internet. This will enable law assistants to access law libraries through the Internet simultaneously, which will increase their productivity.

Company Profile

Francis and Goodfellow is a small law firm in Boulder, Colorado, that uses many services to get information for their cases. Most of these services now provide that information through the Internet. A year ago, the firm implemented Internet access for the company through a stand-alone workstation and a modem. They felt this was a more secure environment that would be very easy to maintain and would keep the costs down. The law libraries are the most commonly accessed Internet resource.

Network Profile

The Francis and Goodfellow network consists of two IntranetWare file servers (see Figure 4.5). One server is a Pentium platform with 8GB of hard drive and 192MB of RAM. It is the main file server and is used for file storage, printing, GroupWise functions, and backups. The second file server is a Pentium platform with 1GB of hard drive and 64MB of RAM. It is used as a remote-access router providing remote user and dial-out capabilities for the lawyers and their clients. The network topology is Token Ring.

Francis and Goodfellow have 35 workstations. These workstations are a mixture of Windows 3.1 and Windows 95.

The network administrator is Janet Green. She has been with the firm for years and is the office manager as well.

FIGURE 4.5

Francis and Goodfellow network layout

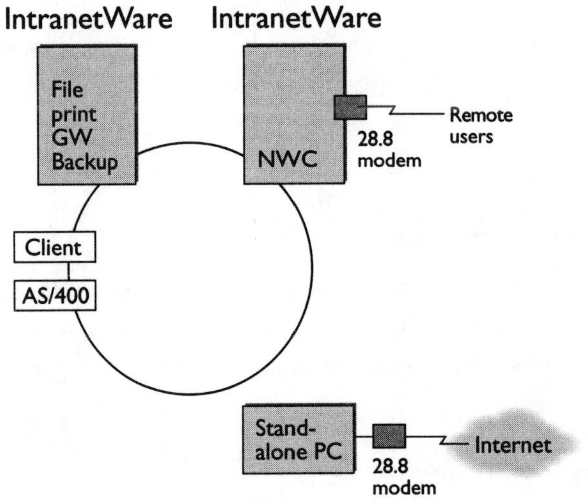

Issues

The managers have a growing list of concerns (and they don't see them going away soon, as most of the law resources are becoming Internet dependent). Their concerns are as follows:

▸ The network administrator is worried about maintaining and keeping a secure environment; the Internet is full of security holes.

▸ The law assistants stand in line to use the stand-alone workstation, which is wasting time and frustrating everyone.

▸ Management wants to keep costs down and gain more productivity.

▶ Management is concerned about implementation and costs; it doesn't want to hire another person to maintain the network.

▶ Management wants to limit access to law-related sites.

Before determining which solution would be best for its environment, the firm asked the following questions:

▶ How do we connect to the Internet?

▶ What kind of firewall services will we need to protect ourselves?

▶ Will we maintain a separate protocol for Internet access to the desktop?

▶ Do we have to implement proprietary hardware?

▶ What access-control policies should we implement?

▶ What changes need to occur at the workstations?

BorderManager Solution

The following BorderManager technologies were implemented to meet this organization's needs:

▶ MPR

▶ Firewall services: packet filtering, circuit gateway, application proxy for security

▶ Proxy caching and reverse-proxy caching

▶ NDS

The first thing Janet did was interview the law assistants to find out how they were using the Internet. She then approached other law offices to see how they were using the Internet and added their answers to her list. Janet then accessed the sites herself to find out the amount of traffic generated and the response time. She decided that an ISDN connection would work just fine.

Janet contacted the ISP that provided Internet access for the current stand-alone workstation. The ISP representative said she could use the current settings from the stand-alone system for the new BorderManager installation if she was not going to use the stand-alone anymore.

Janet decided she would not have to buy another server to install BorderManager; she could use the existing NetWare Connect server. The only purchase she would have to make would be ISDN hardware.

She used MPR to create the ISDN connection to the ISP. Traffic routed to the ISDN would be considered traffic heading for the public network. The Token-Ring card inside the BorderManager would handle all the private LAN traffic, and traffic between the segments would be routed using Novell BorderManager. Using NWAdmin, Janet was able to define access control. She started with these rules:

▸ provide access to all HTTP and FTP services

▸ deny access to all nonbusiness-related categories between the hours of 7 a.m. and 6 p.m.

▸ deny access to all services from 6 p.m. until 7 a.m.

▸ grant lawyers access to specific sites by username

▸ grant Janet specific user access to access support sites, such as Novell, Cheyenne, and Hewlett-Packard during business hours

Janet placed all the rules at the organization container. To help with performance issues, Janet enabled proxy caching at the border server. This would cache all the pages that the browser clients were accessing centrally. Then when the other network browser clients requested information, they could get it from a central cache. Because access control was maintained by NDS, Janet did not have to worry about the employees getting access to information they're prohibited from seeing.

With the list from the interview in hand, Janet used reverse-proxy caching to cache the most frequently used law libraries. Reverse proxy caches an entire Web site's static data, instead of just the pages that are being hit. This provided a performance gain to the browser clients, because they had no delays between links, as they get sometimes with just proxy caching.

Janet then installed the Netscape browser and the Novell Client 32 with gateway support on each of the desktops in the location. The browser was configured for the clients for proxy services. With the IPX-IP gateway services Janet did not have to maintain IP addresses for each workstation.

Figure 4.6 shows Francis and Goodfellow's new network layout.

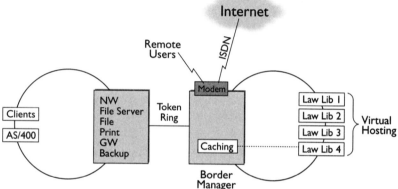

FIGURE 4.6

Francis and Goodfellow business network with Internet access to the desktop

Implementation Results

Management was happy with the results of the BorderManager implementation. The following benefits were noted:

▶ The cost of implementing Internet access was kept to a minimum.

▶ The law assistants were noticeably more productive.

▶ Janet felt secure with the firewall services that were implemented and was thrilled she didn't have to be trained on a completely different system.

▶ Janet was able to provide management with reports showing the top sites accessed from the Internet and also reports showing that security was intact with access control. Management didn't have to worry about nonbusiness-related sites being accessed.

▶ Turning off any kind of access between the hours of 6 p.m. and
7 a.m. protected the law firm from any outside attacks during non-
business hours.

▶ The law assistants were happy because they had immediate access to
the libraries from the desktop.

Scenario #4: Information Systems Department

In this scenario, a corporation's Information Systems (IS) department wants to
centralize its intranet Web server administration and reduce traffic across its
private business LAN.

Company Profile

Gariety Mining Corporation in Reno, Nevada, has six satellite facilities spread
across the western United States. The company has been accessing the Internet for
more than two years. Its network is very secure, and the departments decided that
if the Internet could provide better communications to the outside world, they
should be able to use the same technologies for communicating internally to all the
employees. Internal Web servers were being installed to post corporate information
for employees from the different company departments, such as HR, IS, and so on.

Network Profile

Gariety Mining has a Web server for the training center running on a UNIX
platform, a Web server for HR running on a Macintosh platform, and a Web server
for IS running on a NetWare platform.

The corporate office has approximately six-hundred workstations and six
remote sites. Each remote site has a NetWare file server with 6GB of hard drive
space, 128MB of RAM, and around 50 employees. The remote sites are connected
to the corporate location with 56K lines (see Figure 4.7).

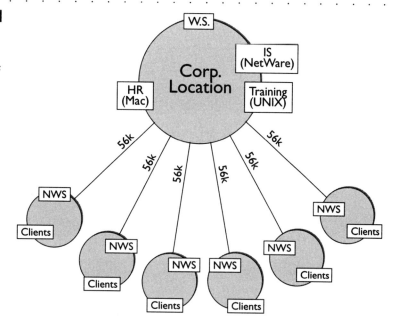

FIGURE 4.7

Gariety Mining business network, decentralized Web servers, and low latency lines

Issues

Following is a list of the many issues Gariety Mining is facing:

- Security has become a pain — each Web server is maintained separately, with completely different security policies.

- A couple of the Web servers are separate from the others. For example, the training center and the marketing department want to maintain their own Web servers because information is changing daily and they want to keep up-to-date.

- Traffic has become an issue, especially for the remote sites. The training manuals are large, and each of the workstations are downloading them separately five to ten times a day.

- The employees are complaining of performance issues—not only with accessing the Web servers, but also with the other network services that used to be faster.

▶ With all the complaints, the IS department is considering redesigning the WAN connections with larger "pipes." This would be a tremendous cost to the company as well as an implementation nightmare.

Gariety Mining had to ask many questions before deciding on a solution:

▶ Which remote locations are accessing information from the corporate Web servers?

▶ What type of information is being published?

▶ What is the administration overhead in maintaining security on the many different types of platforms?

▶ Should we centralize all Web services for maintenance?

BorderManager Solution

The following BorderManager technologies were implemented to meet this organization's needs:

▶ Reverse-proxy caching

▶ NDS

Gariety Mining started monitoring the traffic on the WAN and found that all the sites were communicating with the corporate office. The slowdown was due completely to employees using browsers to access information from the Web servers. The two most popular Web sites were the IS Help Desk server and the training center's Web server.

Employees were pulling down large files from IS to install software at their desktops. From the training center's Web server, they were pulling down courses that included manuals and sample files.

Security was another issue. With all the different platforms, Gariety Mining didn't have enough people on staff to cross-train so — on some days — security had to wait until someone who knew how to manage it arrived.

IS was having a hard time keeping up with all the necessary changes to Web sites, so departments were starting to complain that the information on the Web servers was outdated. A few departments at Gariety Mining had employees who understood HTML programming and could help with their own Web sites. The training center was one of those departments.

Gariety Mining decided to implement BorderManager's reverse-proxy caching technologies. At the corporate location, the network administrator installed an IntranetWare platform with the two-user license.

With NWAdmin, the network administrator configured the server to "front end" or reverse proxy all the corporate Web servers. Firewall servers were set up so the Web servers could communicate only with the reverse proxy. The DNS tables were changed so the Web server DNS names pointed to the reverse-proxy server.

Gariety Mining could now use NDS to administer all security policies centrally. It didn't have to maintain each platform and more than one directory for the corporation.

This configuration also enabled Gariety Mining to virtually keep all corporate Web servers hidden from everyone so that departments with the right to change Web content on their own servers could make the changes. Even though the Web servers may have been decentralized, they looked as if they were still centralized.

To relieve the performance bottleneck, Gariety Mining decided to implement reverse proxies at each of the remote locations. Through the traffic study, the IS department was able to determine which Web servers were being accessed the most, so at the remote locations the servers were configured to enable reverse proxy to the training center and IS Web servers. Each site purchased a new hard drive to serve as a caching volume.

Because access control had already been defined through NDS, no additional configuration was needed; the reverse proxies inherited the access control rules from the NDS tree. Gariety Mining's new network layout is shown in Figure 4.8.

FIGURE 4.8

Gariety Mining network with reverse proxy located strategically for security and performance

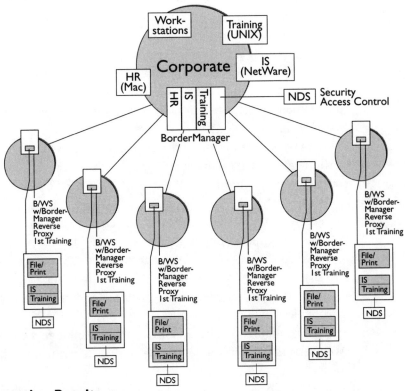

Implementation Results

Gariety Mining instantly noticed the results of implementing BorderManager. The following benefits were noted:

▸ Costs went down with this implementation because less administration was needed.

▸ Traffic loads decreased and became controllable.

▸ The remote offices had instant access to the most popular company intranet services without having the slowness of the 56K links.

▸ Other network services using the 56K lines started performing again.

▶ The training center was permitted to maintain its own Web sites and relieve the IS staff.

Scenario #5: Private School

In this scenario, a private school system would like Internet access for its six schools.

Company Profile

The Crossroads Private School in Iowa was given a large contribution to install new computer equipment and provide students with Internet access. The school has two campuses, each made up of a grade school, a middle school, and a high school. One campus is located in downtown Aurora, and another is located in Sunnytown, sixty miles away. The school computers at each campus are connected to one another, but there is no connection between the two campuses.

Network Profile

As shown in Figure 4.9, each of the campuses is using Novell IntranetWare both for administration and for the students' computer labs. The computer labs are used for homework and computer education. Each campus has one administration file server and approximately six computer-lab file servers. The lab file servers have 2GB of hard drive space, and the data files on each system are deleted each quarter. The servers each have 64MB of RAM.

Each campus is connected with Ethernet, and a backbone exists to connect the grade school, middle school, and high school. Each campus has approximately 150 computers running on Windows 95 and IPX, supporting about 800 students and 50 faculty members.

Joe manages both campuses full time. He divides his time between the two sites. For the most part, the network is self-maintaining.

FIGURE   4.9

*Crossroads Private School
business network layout*

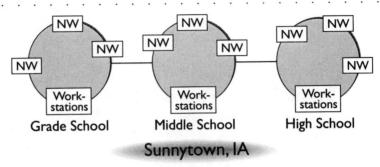

Grade School   Middle School   High School

Sunnytown, IA

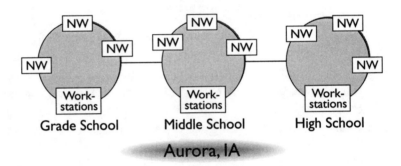

Grade School   Middle School   High School

Aurora, IA

Issues

Contributions are a great thing, but the magnitude of this project is overwhelming for Joe, who is managing the networks alone! Many concerns exist including the following:

- ▶ The school is worried about all the security risks, both for the students connecting to the Internet and for incoming Internet traffic. The school must be able to control the information that the students view.

- ▶ Even though the school was given a contribution, the contribution will not cover the costs of keeping this new network resource secure. The solution must be low maintenance and easy to use.

- ▶ The network manager has only Novell experience and is concerned about maintaining and implementing TCP/IP.

▸ Once the school began pricing out hardware needs for routing and firewall services, administrators realized that the contribution could disappear quickly.

▸ To help with the costs, the school is considering opening the schools at night and charging parents and students access to the Internet. At first this seemed like a great idea, but after weighing the benefit with the reality of more security and operation concerns, school administrators didn't know if it was feasible.

BorderManager Solution

The following BorderManager technologies were implemented to meet the school's needs:

▸ Application proxy

▸ IPX-IP circuit gateway

▸ Proxy caching and ICP hierarchical proxy caching

▸ Novell Directory Services (NDS)

The school decided that it would be safer to connect the campuses together and have only one Internet access point to secure. The school chose Cisco routers for connecting the sites together with ISDN and a T1 connection out to the Internet. The Cisco routers also provided packet filtering technologies. Joe defined the basic packet filtering on which TCP/IP addresses would be permitted in and out of the network.

To protect and secure the environment, each campus was allotted another IntranetWare server with BorderManager installed. BorderManager enhanced the Cisco solution by providing application and circuit gateway capabilities. Proxy functions made the security even tighter, because the proxy acts on behalf of all the students to access the Internet. Joe was able to provide all the access control at this level and maintain the Cisco routers without a lot of different packet filters.

Proxy caching was implemented on each of the existing IntranetWare servers. This brought the data closer to the students for faster access. ICP hierarchical caching was implemented by defining each campus as its own network neighborhood. These technologies helped with performance limitations, and Joe was able to control the traffic loads.

Because the campuses were now connected, Joe was able to merge the two directories together. This made Joe's job easier, because he no longer had to travel between the sites to support them: he could do almost all the maintenance and security control from one site.

Joe, the facility members, and the school board met to create security policies for the school. The board and the facility members were very pleased with the degree of filtering that could be implemented. Joe was able to do the following:

▸ provide or deny services by time and day

▸ deny access to TCP/IP services that could cause problems, such as Telnet and FTP

▸ use Cyber Patrol for category filtering and give the school control over which sites the students could access

BorderManager was so easy to maintain and control with NDS that the school was able to let parents and students access the Internet to help with the cost of maintaining the school computer systems.

BorderManager contains a default rule of denying access to every service. Joe created the following rules:

▸ Provide access to all school-trusted sites by category with Cyber Patrol between the hours of 7 a.m. and 4 p.m. Joe created three policies, one specific for grade school, one for middle school, and one for high school.

▸ Provide access to special sites to certain groups—for example, facility members—between the hours of 7 a.m. and 4 p.m.

▸ Joe had to create only one more rule at the top organization container. That rule opened up all access to Web sites from 5 p.m. to 10 p.m., Monday through Friday.

Rules were so easy to create and maintain that when changes did happen, Joe was able to implement the access control rule within minutes of the request.

The circuit gateway was also used to provide translation between IPX and IP. This enabled Joe to keep his IPX maintenance-free network and maintain only IP addressing schemes at the border servers. To do this, Joe had to distribute the newest Novell Client 32 with IPX-IP services. He also used this time to get Netscape Communicator installed and configured for proxy support. Figure 4.10 shows Crossroads Private School's new network configuration.

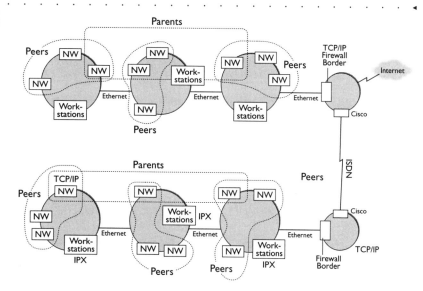

F I G U R E 4.10

Crossroads Private School business network layout with Internet access

Implementation Results

By implementing BorderManager, the school system was able to make the generous contribution go a long way, much further than originally thought. The following benefits were noted:

▸ The school system was able to control and manage Internet access with very low maintenance costs.

▸ The system was very secure, and using the IPX-IP gateway gave an even more secure feeling because IPX cannot be "hacked." Because of the strong access-control features of BorderManager, the school was able to secure access on the fly.

▸ With caching capabilities, the school was able to keep traffic loads down and controllable while the students received great performance.

▸ Joe was happy—the implementation made his job easier, as he no longer had to maintain two separate directories.

▸ Joe didn't have to receive any additional training for TCP/IP protocol management and implementation. He was able to use the best of both worlds—IPX for plug-and-play maintenance at the LAN level and TCP/IP for performance at the WAN level.

▸ The school was able to keep money coming in by charging parents a fee for access but spending very little to cover this service. The money helped maintain and buy new resources for the school.

Scenario #6: Travel Agency

In this scenario, a travel agency has opened up two additional centers and would like to securely connect all the sites.

Company Profile

Let's Go! Travel Agency in Salt Lake City, Utah, has become so successful that it opened up two more locations in the area. It decided to keep the first location central for all operations. The other two locations, with five to eight employees each, handle customer service.

Network Profile

As shown in Figure 4.11, Let's Go! uses NetWare file servers, which have special software to run day-to-day business transactions and an office suite for word processing. Novell GroupWise is installed for e-mail and scheduling. Let's Go! also uses an SQL database running on NT for customer and travel information.

Let's Go! planned to implement IntranetWare servers at each of the remote locations for file storage, printing, and e-mail but wanted to maintain only one database at the first location. Traffic loads for Let's Go! would be very light. The operations software would be loaded on each server, and files would be updated in the middle of the night to the main file server, NDS replication services, for the exchange of e-mail. During business hours, a few queries will be made to the SQL database located at the main Let's Go! location.

The main file server is a Pentium platform with 2GB of hard drive space and 64MB of RAM, using Ethernet as the topology. Windows 95 is the platform used on 20 workstations. Let's Go! has an office manager, Cheryl, who acts as the network administrator. Cheryl had to implement TCP/IP to the desktops because of the application database server that was installed six months earlier. Cheryl uses technologies like DHCP to help with the workstation implementation of TCP/IP.

For the remote sites, Cheryl is going to implement Pentium platforms with 1GB hard drives and 64MB of RAM. Cheryl is going to implement DHCP services at each site using the DHCP server included with the IntranetWare platform. Each of the remote locations will have five Windows 95 workstations.

FIGURE 4.11

Let's Go! Travel Agency's network layout

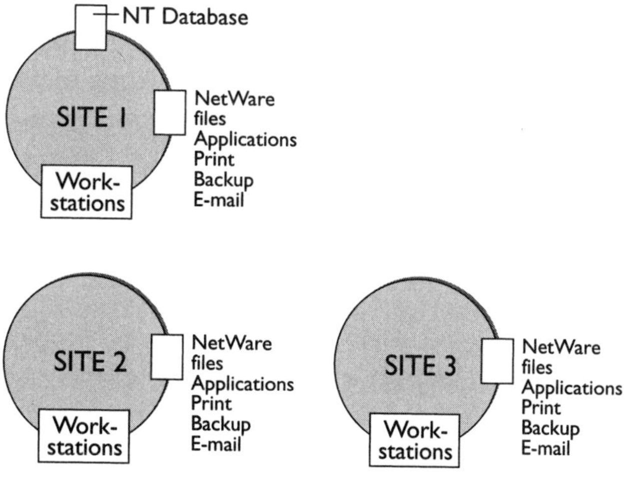

Issues

Let's Go! wanted to keep the costs down in connecting these sites. The main issues they faced were as follows:

▸ Each site had an IntranetWare server; the only connectivity needs would be for server-server operations, e-mail exchange, file exchange, and queries to the SQL database.

▸ Maintenance costs needed to be handled—Cheryl is also the office manager and doesn't have time to maintain a complex environment.

BorderManager Solution

The following BorderManager technologies were implemented to meet this organization's needs:

▸ MPR

▸ Virtual Private Networking (VPN)

The company decided to use MPR to connect the sites because each site already had NetWare servers in place. Cheryl chose to provide a PPP connection through a high-speed modem. The PPP connection would be configured for dial-on-demand operations. This means the connection would occur only when the remote sites need to communicate to the main location.

Because VPN can use the Internet for connectivity, the only thing that had to be implemented on the NetWare servers was TCP/IP addressing. The ISP provided the company with three Class-C IP addresses, a default router, and a subnet mask. Cheryl then defined the Ethernet address for the WAN links as the public network. She created her own addressing scheme for the remote sites and was able to leave the current IP addressing scheme at the main location. Cheryl then configured each server with one of the new IP addresses. Once TCP/IP was configured on all three servers, Cheryl documented the following:

▸ the IP address of each location

 ►   whether the remote Let's Go! locations needed to communicate to one another or just to the main location

Once this information was collected, Cheryl chose the main file server to represent the master VPN server. Cheryl then generated the RSA public/private keys and the shared private/public parameters for the master server. The next step was to create an encrypted message for the remote file servers. Cheryl used the VPNCFG NLM to perform these tasks. Each of these tasks are menu items in the VPNCFG utility that perform all the encryption and create the diskette for media transport for the remote sites.

Cheryl then visited each of the remote sites to generate the RSA public/private keys and the shared secret. Cheryl used NWAdmin to read the diskette. The information was completely encrypted; only the tool that was included with BorderManager can read the information. Each remote server read the configuration information and configured itself to participate in the VPN. The server then created another diskette, which contains encrypted information about its configuration.

Cheryl took the two remote diskettes back to the main location and used NWAdmin so the master VPN server could finalize the connections between the sites. Once the information was added to the VPN table, the master VPN server synchronized the VPN to the slave connections, and an encrypted IP tunnel was created across the Internet.

Once the initial configuration was set up, Cheryl did not have to maintain the VPN at all: it continued to monitor and maintain its encrypted connection. The IP tunnel automatically disconnected when traffic was not being sent. Figure 4.12 shows the new network layout.

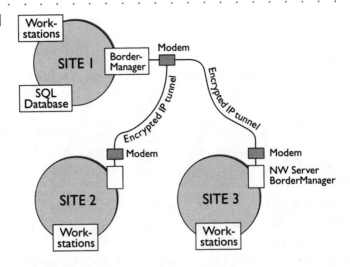

F I G U R E   4.12

Let's Go! business network layout implementing VPN technologies

Implementation Results

Let's Go! was very happy that the costs of connecting the sites was just software and modems. Using Novell's BorderManager technologies, the agency realized the following benefits:

▶ It didn't have to worry about security between the sites.

▶ VPN cut the costs of implementing a dedicated or leased solution by 50 percent.

▶ Because VPN provided IP tunneling and acted at the router level, the employees from the remote sites were able to query the SQL database, and all the resulting packets routed through the VPN for security.

Scenario #7: Payroll Department

In this scenario, the payroll department in a medium-sized distribution company is concerned about security on its LAN. Payroll employees want to isolate their network segment to ensure their data is safe.

Company Profile

Jolly's Distribution Company in Boise, Idaho distributes office supplies to retail shops throughout the states of Colorado, Idaho, and Wyoming.

Network Profile

The company had five IntranetWare file servers, one AS/400, and 230 workstations using every type of OS platform ranging from DOS to UNIX terminals. The network topology was Ethernet and was broken down into subnets by floor location. The IS provided subnets to maintain traffic loads and performance. The office building the company is located in has five floors:

- 1st floor—IS organization

- 2nd floor—Sales and Marketing

- 3rd floor—Operations

- 4th floor—Payroll and Human Resources

- 5th floor—Executives

All the servers are located in the basement with the IS department. IPX, TCP/IP, and SNA protocols are maintained in this location (see Figure 4.13).

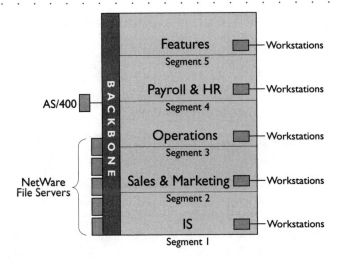

FIGURE   4.13

*Jolly's business network
layout*

Issues

Jolly's payroll staff is worried about security. They have heard that 90 percent of all security breaches happen within a company and feel that their data is very critical and needs to be protected.

BorderManager Solution

The following BorderManager technologies were implemented to meet this organization's needs:

▸   VPN

▸   Packet filtering

The IS department understood payroll's concerns, so it decided to put the payroll department on its own subnet and provide VPN technologies to this subnet.

The IS department installed a new NetWare server that had only an IntranetWare two-user license installed. This server was then designated as a master VPN server with two NIC cards installed. One NIC card was connected to the new payroll subnet and the other is connected to the LAN backbone. The payroll server is then connected to the new subnet and designated as a VPN slave server (see Figure 4.14).

The network administrator performed the five tasks on the master server using the FILTCFG utility to create the encryption keys that the two servers exchange to create a trusted environment. Once the master server was completed, a diskette was created that the network administrator used to set up the slave payroll server. The payroll server then created a diskette that the master server used to complete the encrypted IP tunnel between the two servers. This implementation ensured that any information passed between payroll servers was secure. For added security, packet filters were implemented to keep unwanted traffic off the payroll segment. It took the network administrator less than an hour to complete the configuration.

F I G U R E   4.14

Jolly's network layout implementing VPN technologies

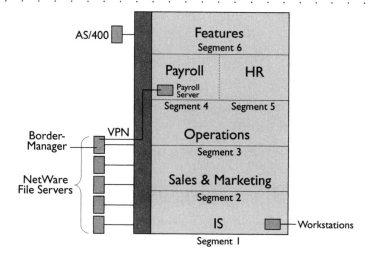

Implementation Results

Once the payroll department was subnetted to its own segment, VPN technologies provided encryption services that protected the internal payroll data between the VPN servers. The following benefits were realized:

▶ The payroll department felt more at ease knowing that critical data was protected between the servers in the VPN.

▶ The IS department spent little time in the configuration and now spends no time maintaining the VPN.

Scenario #8: Home Office

In this scenario, a home-based business owner would like to access information on the Internet and also advertise her services with a Web server.

Company Profile

Colleen Feely owns her own executive search firm based in her home office in Walnut Creek, California. She helps companies in the cable industry by providing searches for executive and high-level management positions. Colleen has built a communications network with other home businesses that provide the same services. The network has given Colleen other avenues to search for the right candidates for job openings. Colleen uses AOL to communicate with her network of peers.

Network Profile

Colleen's home environment consists of three stand-alone systems, two Pentium Windows 95 systems, and a new Pentium Pro Windows 95 system. She has a laser printer that all the systems share through a print box (see Figure 4.15). Colleen is so busy that she has hired a part-time employee, Sherry, to help enter data and distribute business literature.

Sherry is a college student who has just learned how to create Web pages. She has talked with Colleen about her desire to implement a Web site to promote Colleen's services.

Colleen finds that when she and Sherry are working at the same time, they both need access to the printer and AOL. She is also intrigued with the Web site idea.

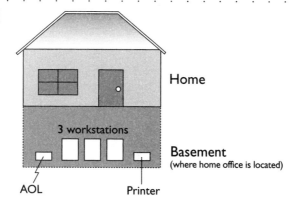

FIGURE 4.15

Colleen's home office layout

Issues

Costs are the big issue for Colleen. Bringing on Sherry helped with the backlog, but her business hasn't picked up enough to pay for the extra help. Other questions she asked include the following:

- What would provide a cost-effective platform?

- What technologies can Colleen implement to relieve the "congestion" problem?

- How can a Web site be implemented to provide Internet exposure for her company but also secure her home from outside intruders?

BorderManager Solution

The following BorderManager technologies were implemented to meet Colleen's needs:

- Firewall services, including packet filtering, circuit, and application proxies

- MPR

- Proxy caching

▸ Reverse proxy from an external ISP site of the local Web server

▸ VPN

Sherry, working with one of her friends from school, came up with a plan to implement an IntranetWare environment to network the systems and printer from Colleen's home. They were able to purchase a five-user version of IntranetWare from the local software shop. They decided that they could give up the new workstation to use it as a file server. The file server was set up with IntranetWare as a Web server. Colleen and Sherry were then able to work simultaneously and have access to the printer and e-mail from their own workstations. Sherry created a cool Web site for Colleen's business with free design tools that she had been collecting from school. Colleen then purchased Novell's BorderManager.

Colleen and Sherry contacted the local ISP to see what kind of services the ISP could provide. They needed to access e-mail and host the new Web site. The ISP was able to provide Colleen with a Class-C IP address, a gateway address, and a subnet mask.

The ISP representative proposed that Colleen keep her Web server at her house for maintenance. He offered a lease for caching her static information to his proxy cache servers. The ISP was implementing Novell's BorderManager product to offer leased caching solutions to his customers. The ISP and Colleen would create a dynamic dial-on-demand connection using her existing modem as the link. Because the ISP would be contacting Colleen's Web server only for dynamic information, and because Colleen was going to use the Internet only for e-mail and occasional surfing, a larger "pipe" was not needed.

The border server was then ready for configuration. Sherry configured TCP/IP at the server and installed MPR to create the PPP dial-on-demand connection to the ISP. Before connecting to the ISP, Sherry set up packet filters to permit her TCP/IP address out of the network and the ISP's TCP/IP address into Colleen's server. All other TCP/IP addresses would be denied. Sherry then initiated a connection to the ISP site: the ISP proxy cache communicated with Colleen's Web server and cached all of the static information. The connection was then shut down because no more traffic was being sent.

Sherry then implemented the circuit gateway and proxy caching features through NWAdmin. The circuit gateway would function as a translator between the two IPX workstations and the Internet. This way Colleen would not have to worry about maintaining IP and IPX at the workstations. Caching was implemented so performance to the Internet would be accelerated with the NetWare server.

Sherry installed the Netscape browser included with IntranetWare on both of the workstations, as shown in the configuration in Figure 4-16. They were able to use a direct connection to the Internet and to use Netscape instead of AOL for e-mail.

Once Colleen's peers found out what Colleen had implemented with little effort and cost, some of them created the same environment for their home offices. They decided that it would be helpful to create a secure connection between their sites so they could exchange secure files and database information. Again, with little effort, Sherry was able to set up VPN between the sites. VPN uses the Internet to connect the sites, and because each site was already connected to the Internet, setup was a breeze. Once the sites were connected, Colleen and Sherry felt that the information they were transferring was safe.

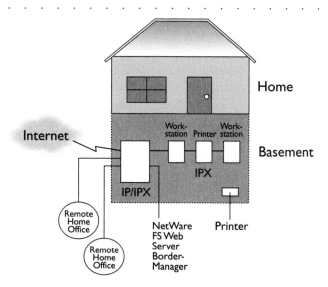

FIGURE 4.16

Colleen's home office networked and connected to the Internet

Implementation Results

The return of investment to Colleen was almost immediate. She also realized the following benefits:

▸ Colleen and Sherry were able to be more productive, because they weren't kicking each other off the systems to print or use the modem.

▸ Using a direct connection to the ISP cost Colleen as much as her monthly bill to AOL and she received more services.

▸ Colleen's Web site was a success. She received many calls from new and prospective customers in a matter of a few months. Sherry loved making daily updates!

▸ Having her peers connected with VPN gave them much more flexibility in getting files to each other and sharing database information. Before setting up VPN, Colleen would have to copy information to a disk and ship it to the partner who needed it.

Summary

In this chapter we provided you with eight real-life examples of how BorderManager technologies can be implemented. Using the examples, you should be able to determine how best to implement BorderManager in your environment. Once you have determined which technologies you will use, refer to Chapter 6 for details on the installation and configuration of those technologies.

CHAPTER 5

Installing BorderManager

Novell's BorderManager is a powerful product. It provides solutions to many of the problems that crop up when you decide to connect your company to the Internet. In this chapter we discuss the many components of BorderManager, as well as how to install them.

Before you install BorderManager, you should determine which components you will install and on which file servers you will install them. Because BorderManager contains many different components, with each component being a different technology, you may need to install some components on one IntranetWare server and other components on different servers. Refer to Chapters 3 and 4 if you are not sure which components you need to install.

What's in the Box

BorderManager includes four CD-ROMs:

> ▸ **IntranetWare platform (two-user) CD**—The two-user license, unique on each BorderManager, enables you to install many BorderManager servers in a corporation without violating the licensing agreement.

> ▸ **Novell BorderManager Services CD**—This CD contains the following technologies:

>> ▸ **IntranetWare Support Pack 3**—This is an update for IntranetWare for BorderManager.

>> ▸ **Firewall Services**—This offers packet filtering and Network Address Translation tables (you use FILTCFG to administer these services).

>> ▸ **Circuit Gateways**—These are IPX-IP and IP-IP gateways.

>> ▸ **Application Proxy**—This provides support for HTTP, Gopher, and FTP.

▸ **Proxy Caching Services** — This provides HTTP Proxy, HTTP Accelerator, Reverse Proxy Cache, ICP (Internet Cache Protocol) hierarchical caching, and CERN support.

▸ **Virtual Private Networking** — VPN provides encryption-tunneling services.

▸ **Novell Internet Access Server 4.1** — This provides Multiprotocol Router v3.32 (unlimited connections), NetWare Connect 2.XX (1-128 ports), and NetWare ConnectView.

▸ **IntranetWare Client CD** — DOS and Windows 3.1x (version 2.2), Windows 95 (version 2.2), and Windows NT (version 4.11) IntranetWare clients, along with Netscape Navigator v3.01 and Novell's Windows NT NetWare administration with Workstation Manager.

▸ **Novell Online Documentation CD** — This CD-ROM provides both HTML and DynaText documentation for Novell BorderManager and IntranetWare.

Getting Started

Whenever you introduce new technologies into an existing environment, you should always start with a testing implementation. During this testing, you are defining the scope of the implementation. You should document the test implementation and include the following information:

▸ Hardware platform, existing and future changes.

▸ Software components, including the applications that will be affected and the components you will add.

▸ Physical layout of the network.

▸ People involved with the project.

▸ Security policy definition (see Chapter 7); this typically includes a team of people ranging from telecommunications and IS administrators to Webmasters, managers, and consultants. You define what policies will be put in place, which components are needed to create the policies, and how the policies will be monitored and logged.

▸ Changes to be made to the existing environment, including who will be affected and to what extent, what changes will happen at the workstations, what changes will occur on the corporate backbone, and what changes will happen to server hardware.

▸ Testing the completeness of design; document any problems. When you implement the design in your production environment, you can refer to this list if problems occur.

You will find that the outcome of any implementation is more successful when the product and the completeness of the design are tested before the implementation. In almost every case, issues arise during the test phase that need to be resolved. It is always better to be aware of these issues and resolve them before you implement the technologies in a functioning network.

Installation Prerequisites

Novell's BorderManager must be installed on an IntranetWare platform. The BorderManager server can, however, coexist on the same network with other NetWare 4.1x servers. You can install BorderManager on an existing IntranetWare platform server or use the two-user version on a separate platform server.

The prerequisites of the hardware platform used with BorderManager depend on which components of BorderManager you will install. As we cover each component in this chapter, we will indicate when there is a change in the base hardware requirements. The base hardware requirements for a BorderManager server are as follows:

▸ An Intel platform with a 486 processor or higher.

▸ A CD-ROM drive.

▸ At least one Network Interface Card (NIC). Ideally, the system should be set up with two network cards—one for the private segment and one for the public segment—if you intend to use BorderManager as a firewall solution.

▸ The appropriate communications adapter (ISDN, frame-relay, and so on) to connect to an ISP or some type of Internet access point.

▸ Hard drive and memory as outlined in Table 5.1.

TABLE 5.1	COMPONENT	HARD DRIVE	MEMORY
Hard Drive and Memory Requirements for BorderManager	IntranetWare	25MB for DOS 90MB minimum for SYS: volume	32MB of RAM
	Online documentation	60MB	4MB
	Client Software	6MB for WIN95 15MB for DOS and Windows 3.1	At the client: 16MB for Win95 8MB for DOS and 32MB on Windows NT
	BorderManager	60MB on SYS: volume 250MB for caching 48MB of RAM	For each set of 100 concurrently open TCP connections for Novell IP gateway, you need to add 500K of RAM. For caching, add 48MB of RAM

Installing IntranetWare

IntranetWare is the base operating system that must be installed before BorderManager can be installed. This section describes how to install IntranetWare in a standard environment. Before you begin installing IntranetWare, run through the following checklist to ensure that you have everything you need to complete the installation:

▸ IntranetWare CD-ROM

▸ DOS 3.3 or later

Assemble the hardware and make sure all components are working properly.

Installing IntranetWare Server Software

To install the IntranetWare server software, complete the following steps:

1 • Create a DOS partition on the hard drive on which you will install IntranetWare. The partition should be at least 25MB in size. However, it is strongly recommended that you add the amount of RAM installed in your server to the 25MB. For example, if you have 64MB of RAM in your server, the partition size should be 89MB. This provides enough disk space to allow core memory dumps to be written to the partition in the event of an ABEND. You can do this using the DOS FDISK command.

2 • Format the DOS partition as a bootable system drive.

3 • Install DOS on the newly created partition. The CONFIG.SYS file must contain a FILES=40 statement. In addition, be sure to delete or remark the statement "DEVICE=C:\DOS\EMM386.EXE" if it exists.

4 • Install the CD-ROM software drivers. Refer to the manufacturer's instructions for details.

5 • Boot the system and verify operation of the CD-ROM drive.

6 • Insert the IntranetWare CD-ROM into the CD-ROM drive.

7 • From the CD-ROM drive, type **INSTALL**.

8 • Select the language you want to install.

9 • Select NetWare Server Installation.

10 • Select NetWare 4.ll.

11 • Select Simple Installation of NetWare 4.ll.

12 • Enter the server name in the field provided.

13 • Follow the prompts and select the correct components and information for your environment. This information will vary from environment to environment. If you require additional information, please refer to the Novell IntranetWare Installation documentation.

IMPORTANT

During this portion of the installation, the system attempts to identify any LAN and WAN boards located in your server. The drivers for these devices will be detected automatically when you install and configure the boards prior to installation.

14 • When the server has been installed, reboot your system.

Installing the Base BorderManager Product

Before you begin installing the base BorderManager product, run through the following checklist to ensure that you have everything you need to complete the installation:

▸ Make sure the IntranetWare server is up and running by logging in to the new server from a workstation.

▸ Make sure The BorderManager Services CD is mounted as a volume on the IntranetWare server on which you will install BorderManager.

▸ Be sure you have the appropriate hardware device drivers and the latest drivers from the manufacturer's technical support Web site.

▸ You need TCP/IP address information for your private segments and your public segments.

▸ You need to know the DNS domain name and the addresses of the name servers within the domain.

Base BorderManager Prerequisites

Before installing the base BorderManager product, complete the following steps:

1 • Configure your TCP/IP addressing. It is crucial that TCP/IP is working properly for BorderManager to function. To configure TCP/IP, load INETCFG.NLM at the server console.

2 • The first time INETCFG is loaded, it will prompt you with the following dialog box:
Transfer LAN driver, protocol and remote access commands?

3 • From this dialog box, select Yes. The LAN driver and address information are transferred to the Internetworking Configuration area. This is an easy way to change addresses and reinitialize your system with the changes without having to modify the AUTOEXEC.NCF file and reboot your server. Figure 5.1 shows the INETCFG main menu.

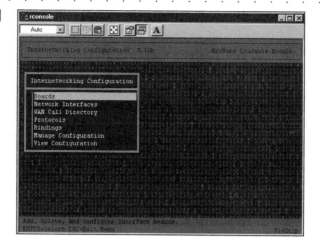

FIGURE 5.1

The INETCFG utility can be used to simplify the configuration of network addresses and protocols.

4 • From the INETCFG main menu, select Protocols.

5 • From the Protocols menu, select TCP/IP.

6 • The TCP/IP Protocol Configuration screen appears, as shown in Figure 5.2.

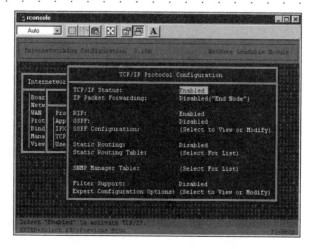

FIGURE 5.2

The TCP/IP Protocol Configuration screen is used to enable the TCP/IP Protocol and Static Routing.

7 • The TCP/IP Status defaults to Disabled. To enable it as shown in Figure 5.2, press Enter on the Disabled field. A dialog box appears with the options of Disabled or Enabled. Select Enabled.

8 • Leave the other options at the defaults, except for Static Routing.

9 • Select Static Routing and press Enter on Disabled.

10 • Select Enabled and press Enter.

11 • The selection then moves to Static Routing Table. Press Enter and a TCP/IP Static Routes table appears. This is where you define your gateway IP address.

12 • Choose the type of route your gateway will take. The options are Network, Host, and Default. For Network you need to know the IP address and subnetwork mask of the gateway. For Host you need to know the IP address of the Host. For Default Route you need to fill out the Next Hop Type, which specifies the next hop to the next router. Typically, you will choose Gateway IP address and then enter the address in the Next Hop Router on Route field, as shown in Figure 5.3.

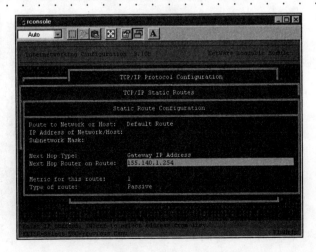

Configuring a Default Route for TCP/IP Static Routing

13 • After you've entered the Routing information, press Esc until you reach the following dialog box:
Update TCP/IP Configuration?

14 • At this dialog box, select Yes. This exits you to the main TCP/IP Protocol Configuration screen.

15 • Press Esc twice to return to the main Internetworking Configuration menu.

16 • From this menu, select Bindings.

17 • A table appears, stating the Configured Protocol to Network Interface Bindings. You should see only the IPX binding line. Press the INS key.

18 • Select TCP/IP.

19 • Select the appropriate network interface card for the address you will be defining and press Enter.

20 • A screen appears, enabling you to specify the local IP address and subnetwork mask, as shown in Figure 5.4.

▶ • ◀

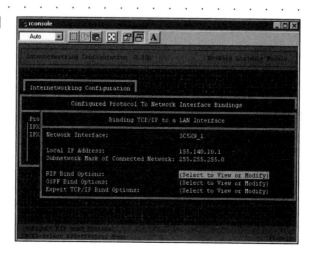

F I G U R E   5.4

Configuring the Local IP Address and Subnetwork Mask in INETCFG

21 • On the screen shown in Figure 5.4, fill in the appropriate information for your network. The rest of the fields are typically left at the default. If you need to add a secondary address to the NIC, you do this from the Sever console. If you are unsure of how, please refer to the IntranetWare Installation manuals for more information.

22 • After you have entered the appropriate information, press Esc.

23 • The following dialog appears:
Update TCP/IP Configuration?

24 • Select Yes.

25 • Press Esc twice and the following dialog appears:
Exit Configuration?

26 • Select Yes.

27 • At the server console, type **REINITIALIZE SYSTEM.** This command reads the information from INETCFG and changes the LAN configuration.

28 • Test your IP connectivity. You can do this with the PING utility that ships with IntranetWare (see Figure 5.5). Figure 5.6 shows a new host address being inserted into the PING list.

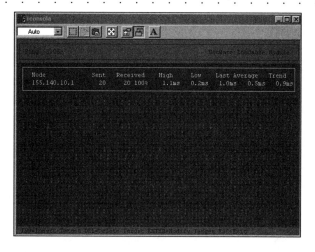

FIGURE 5.5

The PING utility that ships with IntranetWare can be used to test IP connectivity.

FIGURE 5.6

Specifying a new target to PING

29 • When you test your IP connectivity, make sure you can reach many destinations from your server. Make sure you can ping at least one site out on the Internet. You may use 137.65.1.1, Novell's DNS server, as a test.

BorderManager Base Software Installation Steps

To install the BorderManager base software, complete the following steps:

1 • Add long name space support to your server volumes. This is not a mandatory step, but it is highly recommended because most browser clients today are Windows 95 and NT, which support long names.

▸ At your server's console prompt, type **LOAD LONG**.

▸ Type **ADD NAME SPACE LONG TO SYS**.

▸ Repeat Step B, substituting the correct volume name for SYS.

2 • Begin the BorderManager installation.

▸ Make sure you do not have INETCFG.NLM loaded.

▸ At the console prompt on your server, type **LOAD INSTALL**.

▸ From the Installation Options menu, select Product Options.

▸ From the Other Installation Actions menu, select Install a Product Not Listed.

▸ To install the software, press F3.

IMPORTANT

If you are installing from a workstation running RCONSOLE, you must set MAX CACHE SIZE to less than or equal to 3MB. If this parameter is not set, you could run out of memory during the installation. To set this parameter, access the Network Control Panel on the workstation, and then choose Properties/Advanced Settings and MAX CACHE SIZE.

▸ Enter the path to the installation files. For example, if you are installing from the BorderManager CD-ROM mounted as a volume on your server, type **BORDERMGR:** and press Enter. Refer to the IntranetWare documentation for examples on installing remotely from other servers or workstations. Figure 5.7 provides an example of choosing the path to the installation files.

• ◀

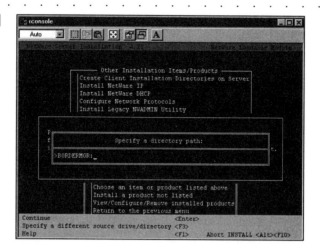

F I G U R E   5 . 7

Selecting the Path to the BorderManager Installation Files

3 • Choose the products to install.
  ▸ Choose both Novell Internet Access Server and BorderManager, as shown in Figure 5.8. Both are selected as default. Use the spacebar to select or deselect the X for the appropriate field.

NOTE

If you select Novell Internet Access Server 4.11, then MPR, NAT, Filtering, and NetWare Connect components are installed. If you select BorderManager, the Circuit Gateways, Application Proxy, Proxy Caching, and VPN components are installed. If you select only BorderManager, Novell Internet Access Server 4.11 is automatically installed.

Both products automatically install Support Pack 3. If you installed earlier versions of BorderManager, be aware that this Support Pack is different from the one originally put out as Support Pack 3 on the Novell Technical Support Web Site.

▶ . . . . ◀

Selecting the BorderManager components to install. Choosing Novell BorderManager automatically installs the Novell Internet Access Server.

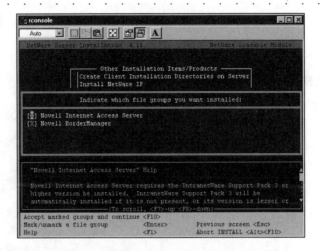

▶ Press F10 to begin the installation process.

▶ An information screen appears, stating that Support Pack 3 is required and will be installed. After the support pack is installed, a temporary copy of the Novell BorderManager files is created. These files are not installed on the server at this time.

4 • To continue the installation, press Enter. The installation program verifies that the server operating system is NetWare 4.11 or IntranetWare. Press Enter to continue.

5 • When prompted to install routing configuration files to server_name, you will typically choose No (see following note) and press Enter. If you have these files, choose Yes and press Enter.

NOTE

Routing configuration files are used to configure multiple servers without the requirement to perform all the configuration steps on each server. These files are created using the Novell Internet Access Server (NIAS) configuration utility and then exported to a file. If you

already have a NIAS server configured with these routing tables, refer to the Novell Internet Access Server 4.1 documentation for the procedure.

6 • You're prompted for licensing options. You can choose a demo license or the product license. Choose the product license.

7 • You're then asked for the path for the license. If you have the product license on diskette, enter **A:**. Insert the license diskette in drive A and press Enter. If you have the license file in another location, enter the appropriate path to the file.

NOTE If you want to install the demo license, a complete license is included with BorderManager that is valid for 45 days from the time of installation.

8 • The File Copy Status (Main Copy) window is displayed, and the installation program copies the temporary files to their permanent locations on the server. When the copy is complete, the following message is displayed:
To optimize server performance, you must complete additional installation steps. Refer to the installation manual that came with this product.

9 • You then have the option to see the installation logs. Press Enter to continue.

10 • The Other Installation Actions menu is displayed.

IMPORTANT DO NOT shut down the server at this point. The installation is not complete until the following steps are complete.

11 • Modify the server's configuration files.

    ▶ Press Esc twice to return to the Installation Options menu.

    ▶ From the installation Options menu, select NCF files options.

    ▶ From the Available NCF File Options menu, select Edit STARTUP.NCF File.

    ▶ When prompted for the path to SERVER.EXE, enter **C:\NWSERVER**.

    ▶ Add the following SET commands to the top of the STARTUP.NCF file:

```
SET MINIMUM PACKET RECEIVE BUFFERS=400

SET MAXIMUM PACKET RECEIVE BUFFERS=1000

SET MAXIMUM PHYSICAL RECEIVE PACKET SIZE=<value>
```

The value for the Maximum Physical Receive Packet Size parameter is based on the type of network card you are using in your server. Table 5.2 shows the values for each media type.

TABLE 5.2	MEDIA TYPE	VALUE
Maxium Physical Receive Packet Size for Each Network Media Type	Ethernet	1514
	Token-ring	4202
	FDDI	4530
	ARCnet	608
	LocalTalk	608

NOTE

If you are going use Point-to-Point Protocol, you need to add 10 bytes. For example, Ethernet's value would be 1,524.

▸ Press Esc

▸ Choose Yes to save the STARTUP.NCF file.

▸ Press Esc to return to the Installation Options menu.

12 • Exit the Install program.

13 • From the Installation Options menu, choose Exit. When prompted, highlight Yes to exit Install.

14 • At the server console prompt, type in **DOWN** and press Enter. After the server is down, you see the following message:
Type Exit to return to DOS

15 • Type RESTART SERVER and press Enter.

16 • When the server restarts, the message shown in Figure 5.9 appears.

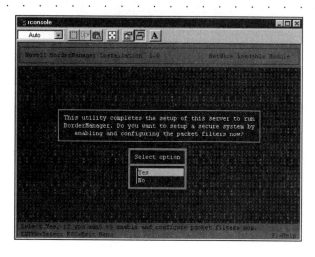

F I G U R E   5 . 9

After the BorderManager installation is complete, the server is downed and restarted. This screen appears when the server restarts. Selecting Yes at this screen launches the initial filter-configuration program.

17 • If you answer Yes at the screen shown in Figure 5.9, the initial filter configuration program, BRDCFG.NLM, will run. This utility lets you block all IPX, RIP and SAP, NetBIOS, IPX Packet Forwarding Filters, EGP filters, OSPF filters, and TCP/IP RIP and Packet Forwarding Filters, and to permit only traffic from the gateways, proxy, or VPN.

18 • If you answer No, the Novell BorderManager does not enable filtering.

NOTE

If you answer No at this time, BRDCFG.NLM can be loaded later to automatically set up packet filters. If you answer Yes at this time and need to disable the filtering, you must do so manually by loading FILTCFG.NLM and individually disabling each IP and IPX filter per interface. FILTCFG is shown in Figure 5.10.

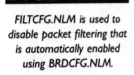

F I G U R E   5.10

FILTCFG.NLM is used to disable packet filtering that is automatically enabled using BRDCFG.NLM.

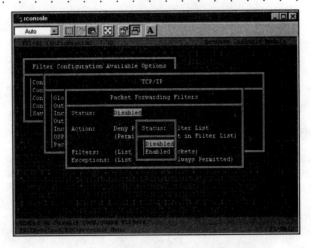

19 • When you exit BRDCFG, you are asked if you want to launch INETCFG. Answer Yes.

20 • Answering Yes takes you to the INETCFG menu. Verify your TCP/IP and IPX bindings, and make any changes if necessary.

21 • Press Esc to exit INETCFG.

22 • When you exit INETCFG, the system verifies your TCP/IP configuration.

23 • If a DNS Resolver file is found (this file is called RESOLV.CFG and is located in the SYS:ETC directory on your server), the installation of the BorderManager is complete. If there is no DNS Resolver file, you will be prompted to enter your DNS information in the form shown in Figure 5.11. Fill in the appropriate information for your environment.

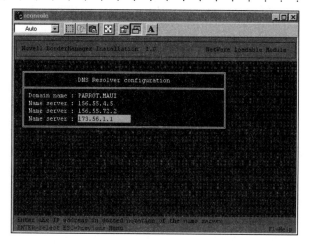

24 • Press F10 to save the file and continue.

25 • The following prompt appears:
Exit DNS Resolver?

26 • Select Yes and press Enter. This action exits INETCFG and automatically reinitializes your system.

27 • Verify TCP/IP connectivity again. Troubleshoot any TCP/IP issues before continuing.

Installing the BorderManager NWAdmin Snap-in Module

Before you begin installing the BorderManager NWAdmin Snap-in Module, run through the following checklist. The snap-ins are necessary to manage elements of the BorderManager server from NWAdmin. Once installed, several new Detail Pages will be visible under a NetWare server icon under NWAdmin.

- ▸ Your workstation should be running the latest IntranetWare client, although the one included with BorderManager will work. The latest client software can be downloaded from http://www.novell.com.

- ▸ Run NWADMIN95.EXE at least once on your workstation before installing the snap-in. This places the necessary NWAdmin parameters in the Windows Registry; the file is located in the SYS:PUBLIC\WIN95 directory.

- ▸ The BorderManager administration utility runs on the Windows 95 platform only. It does not run on Windows 3.x or NT by default (see the sidebar "Using the BorderManager Snap-ins in Windows NT" for instructions on configuring the snap-in to work with Windows NT). Novell will include the Windows NT version in a support pack after the initial release of the product. The BorderManager support packs can be downloaded from www.novell.com.

Using the BorderManager Snap-ins Windows NT

Though Novell says the snap-ins provided with BorderManager 1.0 are for Windows 95 only, with a little effort you can configure your BorderManager from NWAdmin for Windows NT. The snap-in DLLs are built to work under either version of NWAdmin. What is lacking in the first release of BorderManager is a setup program that will install the DLLs properly for Windows NT. You have to perform the setup manually.

Setting up the snap-ins for use with Windows NT requires two simple steps: copying the snap-ins to the NWAdmin for NT directory, and registering the snap-ins. Copy the following files from your SYS:PUBLIC\WIN95 directory to SYS:PUBLIC\WINNT:

BRDEXT.DLL

BSCOV.DLL

BSMON.DLL

PROXYAUT.DLL

PROXYCFG.DLL

RESTRICT.DLL

VPN.DLL

VPNA.DLL

NLS\ENGLISH\BRD_SEC.CNT

NLS\ENGLISH\BRD_SEC.HLP

NLS\ENGLISH\NBMML.DLL

NLS\ENGLISH\NWMAIN.HLP

After you copy the files, you need to create a new text file that will contain the commands REGEDIT needs to add into the Windows registry to tell NWAdmin about the new snap-in files. In Notepad, type the following text:

REGEDIT4

[HKEY_CURRENT_USER\Software\NetWare\Parameters\NetWare Administrator\Snapin Object DLLs WINNT]

(continued)

(continued)

ìBSCOV.DLLî="BSCOV.DLL"

"PROXYCFG.DLL"="PROXYCFG.DLL"

"NWCADM95.DLL"="NWCADM95.DLL"

"RESTRICT.DLL"="RESTRICT.DLL"

"PROXYAUT.DLL"="PROXYAUT.DLL"

[HKEY_CURRENT_USER\Software\NetWare\Parameters\NetWare Administrator\Snapin View DLLs WINNT]

"BSMON.DLL"="BSMON.DLL"

Then save the text to the SYS:PUBLIC\WINNT directory as BMSNAPNT.REG. From any Windows NT workstation you can now double-click the BMSNAPNT.REG file to register the BorderManager snap-ins on that workstation. You can manually enter each of the keys into the registry of each workstation, but it's much easier to create the file once and then just double-click.

Border Manager NWAdmin Snapin Installation steps

To install the BorderManager NWAdmin Snapin, you must first launch the BorderManager Setup program on your server. Figure 5-12 shows the initial install screen for the BorderManager snap-in components. Complete the following steps:

1 • At the workstation on which you will install the snap-in, log in to your server.

2 • Click Start and choose Run.

3 • In the Open field, type **F:\PUBLIC\BRDRMGR\WIN95\SETUP.EXE**, and then click OK.

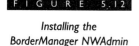

F I G U R E   5.12

*Installing the
BorderManager NWAdmin
Snapin on a Workstation*

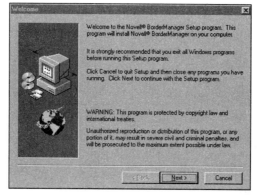

4 • Click Next.

5 • You're prompted to enter the path to where the NWAdmin utility is located. The proper path should be provided by default. If it is not, browse to SYS:\PUBLIC\WIN95.

6 • You're prompted to read the README file. If you choose No, you are finished with this part of the install. If you choose Yes, the README file will appear. When finished, exit the README file.

7 • When prompted, click Finish to complete the installation.

8 • When prompted, click Yes to restart your workstation now.

The next step is to finish installing BorderManager within NWADMIN95. Follow these steps:

I • Log in to your server as Admin.

2 • Double-click the NWADMN95 program icon on your desktop.

3 • Double-click your server's icon.

4 • Click the BorderManager Setup page option shown in Figure 5.13.

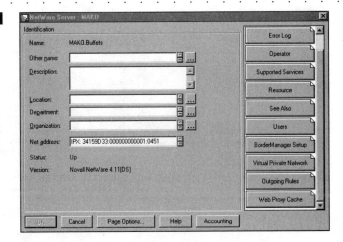

FIGURE 5.13

The final step to installing the base BorderManager product is completed through NWAdmin by selecting the BorderManager Step page option of the Server object.

5 • The first time this option is selected, you are presented with a dialog box that gives you the option to allow or deny outgoing proxy and gateway traffic. Choose Allow at this time.

NOTE

If you choose Deny at this time, any Browser client using the Proxy server will be denied access to any services. It is recommended that you choose Allow at this time so that Browser clients will be allowed access through the Proxy Server. No access control will be implemented at this time. Setting up access control manually will be covered in Chapter 8, "Administering BorderManager." If you change your mind, you can enable or disable the checkbox marked "enforce rules."

6 • From the BorderManager Setup screen, use the bottom half of the screen to configure IP addresses, described in the next step.

7 • In the Configured IP Addresses box, click the list button or double-click the table box to add an IP address. The IP addressing form shown in Figure 5.14 appears.

FIGURE 5.14

IP addresses for each LAN and WAN segment on your BorderManager server must be configured from the BorderManager Setup page.

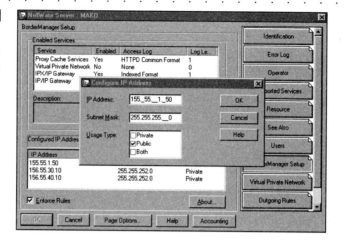

8 • In the IP address field, enter the IP address of the first LAN segment or WAN Segment to configure.

9 • In the Subnet Mask field, enter the subnet mask for your addressing scheme.

10 • In the Usage Type field, select Public, Private, or Both. *Public* defines the public interface—this could be the WAN or LAN connection that connects you to the Internet. *Private* defines the segments within the firewall to which this server is attached. *Both* is used for a BorderManager server that has only one network interface card with one IP addresses bound to it. The proxy will listen for HTTP only on the private interface.

11 • Repeat Steps 7–10 for each IP address on your server.

12 • Click OK to save changes and exit to the main BorderManager Setup screen.

13 • Exit NWAdmin.

Installing Cyber Patrol

The next step in installing the base BorderManager product is to install Cyber Patrol. Cyber Patrol is a third-party product that provides category filtering. Novell's BorderManager ships with a free 45-day Cyber Patrol subscription. For the first 45 days after installation, CP automatically downloads the latest list from the Internet. After that time the feature is disabled. To continue the subscription, fill out the registration form when prompted, and Cyber Patrol will send you a bill.

To install Cyber Patrol, complete the following steps:

1 • At your workstation, click the Windows 95 Start menu.

2 • Choose Run.

3 • In the Open field, type **F:\ETC\CPFILTER\CP_SETUP.EXE**.

4 • Click OK.

5 • Click Proceed twice to bypass the startup screen and accept the license.

6 • When prompted for the drive letter of the Novell SYS: volume, type F (or the appropriate drive letters), as shown in Figure 5.15.

IMPORTANT

At this screen, be sure to enter the drive letter only; a colon should not follow the drive letter.

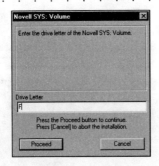

FIGURE   5.15

When installing Cyber Patrol, it is important to enter the drive letter without a colon when prompted for the drive letter of the Novell SYS: volume.

7 • Click Proceed and the installation program begins the file copy.

8 • When prompted to load SYS:\ETC\CPFILTER\CPFILTER.NLM at the server console, click Proceed to bypass this prompt.

IMPORTANT

DO NOT LOAD CPFILTER.NLM AT THIS TIME. If you try to load the NLM now, it will not load properly because you have not configured or loaded portions of BorderManager. CPFILTER.NLM should be loaded after BorderManager proxy services are configured, and loaded at the server. This should be done by adding the line LOAD SYS:\ETC\CPFILTER\CPFILTER.NLM to your server's AUTOEXEC.NCF file.

9 • Next you're prompted for registration information. Fill in the appropriate information and select either Save Settings, Save and Register, or Cancel.

NOTE

If you choose to register later, simply run REGISTER.EXE from the SYS:\ETC\CPFILTER directory when you are ready to register your product.

Installing the Online Documentation

One of the CDs included with BorderManager is the online documentation. There are three options for using the documentation:

▶ It can be viewed directly off the CD using the DynaText viewer.

▶ The DynaText viewer and document collections can be installed on a server and/or workstation.

▶ The HTML version of the documentation can be installed on a server and viewed using a standard Web browser.

Each of these methods enables you to electronically view, search, mark, and print the BorderManager documentation.

The easiest way to use the documentation is to view it directly off the CD, although this method makes it difficult for others to use the documentation. If more than one user needs to use the documentation, you may want to consider installing either the DynaText version or the HTML version on a server on your network.

If you choose to use the DynaText version, you must install two components— the viewer and the document collections. DynaText viewers can be installed on each workstation requiring access to the documentation or on a server. Although you can install the document collections on a workstation, it is more practical to install them on a server's volume.

TIP

To simplify the distribution of the DynaText viewer to workstations across the network, consider using the Novell Application Launcher (NAL). NAL's Novell Directory Servers let administrators centrally control and distribute applications on the network.

If you choose to use the HTML version of the documentation, you must have the Novell Web Server installed on the server to which you will install the documentation. In addition, a Web browser (such as Netscape Navigator) must be installed on the workstations that will view the documentation.

Each of the methods for accessing and installing the BorderManager online documentation is described in the following section.

DynaText Online Documentation

Before you use or install the DynaText version of the BorderManager online documentation, run through the following checklist to ensure that you have everything necessary to access the documentation:

▶ Windows 3.*x*, Windows 95, or Macintosh workstation

▶ Novell's BorderManager documentation CD

Viewing the DynaText Documentation from CD

The DynaText documentation either can be viewed directly from the Novell BorderManager documentation CD or can be installed on a workstation or server. To view the documentation directly from the CD, complete the following steps:

I • Insert the Novell BorderManager documentation CD into your CD-ROM drive.

2 • Run SETUP.EXE from the CD-ROM. For Windows 95 workstations, simply double-click the CD-ROM icon from the My Computer interface. You're presented with a menu allowing you to install or view the documentation, as shown in Figure 5.16. Select View documentation.

▶ · ◀

The BorderManager online documentation can be viewed directly from the CD or installed on a workstation or server.

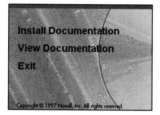

Install Documentation

View Documentation

Exit

Copyright © 1997 Novell, Inc. All rights reserved.

Installing the DynaText Viewer

To install the DynaText viewer, complete the following steps:

I • Insert the Novell BorderManager documentation CD into your CD-ROM drive.

2 • Run SETUP.EXE from the CD-ROM. For Windows 95 workstations, simply double-click the CD-ROM icon from the My Computer interface. You're presented with a menu allowing you to install or view the documentation, as shown in Figure 5.16. Select Install Documentation.

3 • From the screen shown in Figure 5.17, click the Install button on the left under the DynaText Viewer portion of the screen.

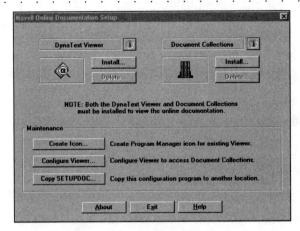

FIGURE 5.17

To install the DynaText documentation viewer, select Install under DynaText Viewer.

4 • Select the Source directory—the CD-ROM drive that contains the documentation CD.

5 • Select the destination directory—either the workstation drive or the server volume on which you wish to install the viewer.

6 • Select the viewer language you want to install.

7 • Click OK.

8 • Verify the configuration and click OK to begin the installation. A progress bar window appears, indicating the installation progress.

When the installation is complete, the viewer will be installed to the destination specified. On the Windows desktop, an icon will be created for the viewer under Novell Online Documentation. When the process is complete, you're returned to the main documentation setup screen, where you can install the documentation collections as described in the next section.

Installing Online Documentation Collections

To install the BorderManager Online documentation collections, first install the viewer as described in Steps 1–8 in the previous section. From the main documentation setup screen shown in Figure 5.17, complete the following steps:

1 • Click the Install button on the right under the Document Collections portion of the screen.

2 • Select the Source directory—the CD-ROM drive that contains the documentation CD.

3 • Select the destination directory—either the workstation drive or the server volume on which you wish to install the documentation collections.

4 • A list of documentation collections appears. By default, all collections are highlighted, as shown in Figure 5.18. Deselect any collections you do not want to install. Click OK to begin the installation.

▶ · ◀

F I G U R E   5.18

When installing the DynaText online documentation collections, all collections will be installed by default unless they are deselected on this screen.

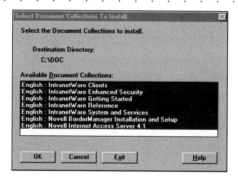

5 • When the installation is complete, exit the installation program.

To access the documentation, click the DynaText icon on your workstation desktop to display the documentation collection.

HTML Online Documentation

Before you begin installing the HTML version of the BorderManager online documentation, run through the following checklist to ensure that you have everything you need to complete the installation:

- ▶ You need an IntranetWare server with the Novell Web Server 3.0 installed. The Novell Web Server is available free from Novell and can be download from Novell's Web site at `http://WWW.NOVELL.COM/ INTRANETWARE/products/novell-web-server/`.

- ▶ A Web browser must be installed on the workstations to view the documentation. Netscape Navigator v3.01 is included on the IntranetWare Client CD-ROM.

- ▶ You need at least 48MB free on the SYS: volume for all the HTML documents.

- ▶ You need the login name and password for Admin or an equivalent user.

Installing the HTML Online Documentation

One caveat of the HTML version of the BorderManager documentation is that many of the sections in HTML refer to the documentation collection of the DynaText version. To have a complete BorderManager documentation set, you should install both formats. In addition, the HTML documentation is currently available in English only. If you require the online documentation in other languages, you should use the DynaText version.

To install the HTML version of the BorderManager online documentation, complete the following steps:

I • Insert the Novell BorderManager documentation CD into the NetWare server CD-ROM drive and mount the CD as a volume.

The online documentation can also be installed from a workstation running RCONSOLE. In this case, the CD can be placed in the workstation's CD-ROM drive.

NOTE

2 • At the file server console, type **LOAD INSTALL** and press Enter.

3 • From the Installation Options menu, select Product Options.

4 • From the Other Installation Actions menu, select Install a Product Not Listed.

5 • From the screen shown in Figure 5.19, press F3 and change the path to *Server_Name*\IW_DOC:\W2WEB\. Or, if you are installing from a workstation running RCONSOLE, press F4 and specify the path to the workstation's CD-ROM drive.

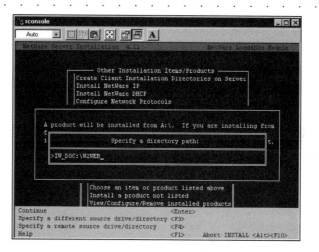

F I G U R E   5.19

To install the online documentation from the CD mounted as a volume at the server, press F3 and specify the path as shown. If the online documentation is being installed from a workstation running RCONSOLE, F4 is used to specify the path to the CD on the remote workstation.

6 • If you are installing to a remote server, you're prompted for a username and password. Log in as Admin or someone else with Supervisor rights to the root of the NDS tree.

7 • A dialog box appears, stating that the BorderManager HTML Documentation will be installed. Press Enter to continue.

8 • A dialog box appears, stating the files will be copied to SYS:\WEB\DOCS\. Accept the default or enter the desired path, and press Enter to continue.

9 • Another dialog box appears, stating where the files are being copied from. If this path is correct, press Enter to continue or enter the appropriate path.

10 • You are asked to authenticate to Directory Services. Log in as Admin or an equivalent user.

11 • The files are copied to the appropriate directories. The installation progress is indicated by a progress bar.

12 • When the installation is complete, press Esc to exit to the server console.

The online documentation can be viewed with a client running Netscape Navigator or another Web browser. To view the documents, enter the appropriate URL for the Web Server and load INDEX.HTM. You can then browse the online documentation as shown in Figure 5.20.

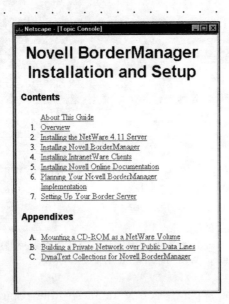

F I G U R E   5.20

When the HTML version of the BorderMananger online documentation is installed on a server running the Novell Web Server, users can access the documentation using any standard Web browser.

Netscape - [Topic Console]

Novell BorderManager Installation and Setup

Contents

About This Guide
1. Overview
2. Installing the NetWare 4.11 Server
3. Installing Novell BorderManager
4. Installing IntranetWare Clients
5. Installing Novell Online Documentation
6. Planning Your Novell BorderManager Implementation
7. Setting Up Your Border Server

Appendixes

A. Mounting a CD-ROM as a NetWare Volume
B. Building a Private Network over Public Data Lines
C. DynaText Collections for Novell BorderManager

Summary

Congratulations! Now that we've covered the installation of BorderManager, we'll move on to Chapter 6, "Configuring BorderManager Components." By and large, you shouldn't have to complete the installation steps again, unless you're adding a new BorderManager server to your NDS tree. Most of the effort from here on in involves fine-tuning your BorderManager installation. This should be simplified by leveraging NDS and your tree design.

Configuring BorderManager Components

In this chapter, we'll cover the configurations for BorderManager components step by step. Each section lists the prerequisites for the component, and then describes its implementation. For details on the ongoing administration of the BorderManager components, please refer to Chapter 8.

It is important to plan which BorderManager components you require, and on which servers. Once you determine this, you need to install BorderManager on the various servers as necessary. You can then configure the components you need on each server. This chapter provides step-by-step instructions for the initial configuration of the following BorderManager components:

▸ Network Address Translation Table (NAT)

▸ Virtual Private Networks (VPN)

▸ NetWare Connect and ConnectView

▸ Circuit Gateways

▸ Proxy Caching

This chapter covers the initial configuration of these components. For ongoing administration of the BorderManager components please refer to Chapter 8.

Network Address Translation (NAT)

The Network Address Translation (NAT) table provides the following functions:

▸ authorizes the IP clients on your private network that do not have globally unique registered addresses to access the Internet

▸ enables you to limit outside clients' access to your private network

NOTE

The IP circuit gateway provides a similar function to NAT. However, it grants or denies Internet access based on login ID. When using NAT, all internal addresses are permitted to access the Internet, or only those with a specifically configured internal IP address.

Before configuring NAT on your network, it is important to understand its limitations:

▸ NAT is not supported for most applications that embed the IP address in the packet's data. It does, however, perform special processing that enables FTP to function properly. More information about this limitation can be found in RFC 1631 (see Appendix A).

▸ NAT does not translate multicast and broadcast packets.

▸ The private and public address of each address pair configured in the NAT table cannot be set to the same IP address (unless the public address is used to access local services, such as an FTP or Web server, on the router running NAT).

▸ NAT cannot be enabled on two LAN or WAN interfaces used to reach the same private host if that host is configured in the NAT table as a static entry.

▸ NAT-enabled WAN interfaces must be configured with WAN Network Mode set to Numbered Point-to-Point or Multiaccess. The router must be configured with IP Forwarding set to Yes.

▸ If the parameter Remote Router Will Dynamically Assign the IP Address is set to Yes and the assigned address is subject to change, only dynamic mode is practical. This is what occurs when you dial into most ISPs.

In addition to understanding these limitations, you should run through the following checklist. This will ensure that you have everything you need to properly configure NAT on your network.

Checklist

▸ Registered IP addresses: one address is required for Dynamic Mode, while a pool of registered addresses is required for Static mode.

▸ You should have knowledge of interfaces located in the server, including LAN and WAN.

▸ For hosts that require static IP addresses, you must know the Host IP address and the IP address to which it will be mapped.

Configuring NAT

To configure NAT on your network, perform the following steps:

1 • From the server console, type LOAD NIASCFG and press <Enter>.

2 • Select Configure NIAS.

3 • Select Protocols and Routing; this automatically loads INETCFG.NLM.

4 • Select Bindings.

5 • Select the interface that will provide the address translation. Typically, this is the public interface; it can either be a network card, or a WAN interface. The Bindings screen shown in Figure 6.1 will appear.

6 • From the screen shown in Figure 6.1, select Expert TCP/IP Bind Options. The screen shown in Figure 6.2 will appear.

FIGURE 6.1

To configure an interface to provide address translation, select the LAN or WAN interface in INETCFG and choose Expert TCP/IP Bind Options.

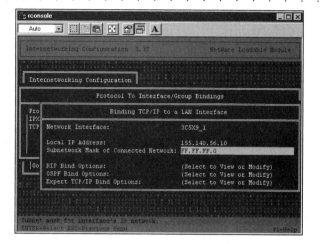

7 • From the screen shown in Figure 6.2, select Network Address Translation.

FIGURE 6.2

From the Expert TCP/IP Bind Options menu, NAT is enabled by selecting Network Address Translation.

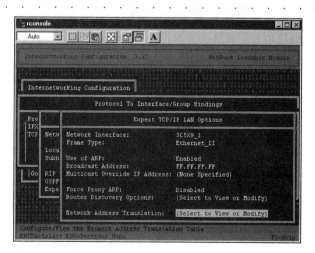

8 • From the screen shown in Figure 6.3, choose the mode in which you want the NAT to operate.

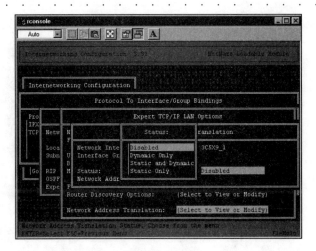

F I G U R E   6.3

NAT modes of operation

To determine the proper mode of operation, refer to Table 6.1 for a definition of each one.

MODE	DEFINITION
Disabled	This mode disables the use of the NAT function.
Dynamic only	Dynamic only enables clients on your private network to access the Internet. This provides a many-to-one mapping of numerous local IP addresses to one, public registered IP address.
Static only	This mode employs permanent one-to-one mapping of the public registered IP addresses to local IP addresses inside the private network. It is recommended for internal network service hosts, such as FTP or Web servers. This mode requires the creation of a static mapping table.
Static and Dynamic	This mode enables you to use both methods (dynamic-address translation and static-address translation) concurrently. This mode requires the creation of a static mapping table. It is used if some hosts on your network require one type of address translation and other hosts require the other.

T A B L E   6.1

Definition of NAT modes of operation

If you select Static Only, or Static and Dynamic, you will automatically be prompted to create a static mapping table. Enter the actual IP address of the host, and then the public IP address to which it will be mapped.

NOTE

9 • After selecting the mode, press <Esc> three times and you will see the following prompt:

Update TCP/IP configuration?

10 • Select Yes and the Protocol to Interface/Group Bindings table will appear.

11 • Press <Esc> to return to the main INETCFG menu.

12 • Select Reinitialize System.

13 • Select Yes to reinitialize your system; this will reconfigure your server with the new TCP/IP settings. The console screen will display the reinitialization of the configuration.

Virtual Private Networks (VPNs)

A Virtual Private Network (VPN) enables you to connect remote sites, using the Internet as your transport. It also lets you create secure segments within the firewall, on your private network. VPN uses authentication and encryption to provide secure transfer of data. Generating keys is performed at the server console, eliminating the possibility of a security breach.

We recommend that you don't generate keys using RCONSOLE. The keys are generated at the server console to avoid compromising key information by placing it on the wire when generated.

IMPORTANT

Once the keys are generated, NWAdmin is used to monitor and maintain the VPN. Monitoring and maintaining a VPN is covered in detail in Chapter 7. Before beginning the configuration of a VPN, run through the following checklist to ensure that you have everything you need to configure it properly.

Checklist

▶ An Internet connection is required if you plan to use the Internet.

▶ A high-end processor is required, such as a Pentium Pro, if you expect heavy loads of data to be encrypted.

▶ The public IP address is needed for every server that will participate in the VPN.

▶ A VPN subnet IP address is required, though it is never sent over the Internet. It can be any unregistered address (for example, 192.168.10.1 and FF.FF.FF.0 for the master server, and 192.168.10.2 and FF.FF.FF.0 for the slave server). NOTE: The master server and all slave servers must use the same subnet for the VPN tunnel IP addresses.

▶ Static routes to the peer VPN sites are necessary. This is not a requirement, but can be added to route traffic through the VPN to the remote segment.

▶ A diskette is needed to copy the encrypted information for key generation to a directory located on your server.

You must also determine the following:

▶ The file server you will use as the master server. The master server generates the first set of keys and defines how the VPN will be configured.

▶ The routing topology that the VPN will use. The options are Mesh, in which, every server recognizes every other server; Star, in which all servers will route through the master; or Ring, in which, each server communicates with its immediate neighbor.

Configuring a VPN

To help you understand how to configure your VPN, we will connect three sites through the Internet. Figure 6.4 illustrates each of these sites, the IP address information, and how they will be connected through the Internet.

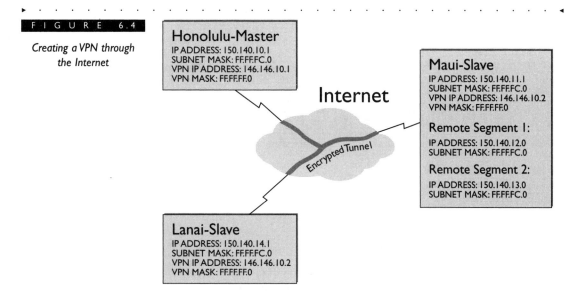

F I G U R E   6 . 4

Creating a VPN through the Internet

Honolulu-Master
IP ADDRESS: 150.140.10.1
SUBNET MASK: FF.FF.FC.0
VPN IP ADDRESS: 146.146.10.1
VPN MASK: FF.FF.FF.0

Internet

Maui-Slave
IP ADDRESS: 150.140.11.1
SUBNET MASK: FF.FF.FC.0
VPN IP ADDRESS: 146.146.10.2
VPN MASK: FF.FF.FF.0

Remote Segment 1:
IP ADDRESS: 150.140.12.0
SUBNET MASK: FF.FF.FC.0

Remote Segment 2:
IP ADDRESS: 150.140.13.0
SUBNET MASK: FF.FF.FC.0

Encrypted Tunnel

Lanai-Slave
IP ADDRESS: 150.140.14.1
SUBNET MASK: FF.FF.FC.0
VPN IP ADDRESS: 146.146.10.2
VPN MASK: FF.FF.FF.0

Configuring the Master Server

To configure a VPN master server, perform the following steps:

1 • From the server console, type LOAD NIASCFG and press <Enter>. If you prefer, you can just type LOAD VPNCFG, and skip to Step 4.

2 • Select Configure NIAS.

3 • Select Virtual Private Network. This automatically loads VPNCFG.NLM.

4 • Select Master Server Configuration. The screen shown in Figure 6.4 will be displayed.

FIGURE 6.5

When you configure a master server, you are reminded that a VPN can have only one master.

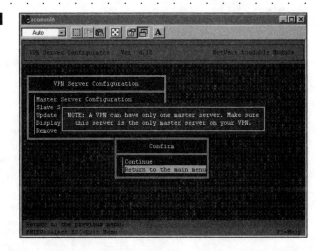

5 • Select Continue from the screen shown in Figure 6.5.

6 • Select Configure IP Addresses from the Master Server Configuration menu.

7 • Enter the IP address of the server into the public IP address field. For our example, this would be 150.140.10.1.

8 • Enter the subnet mask of the server into the public IP mask field. For our example, this would be FF.FF.FC.0.

9 • Enter the VPN IP address into the VPN Tunnel Address field. This address does not have to be a legal IP address: it can be any unique address for which all servers participating in the VPN will use the same subnet. For our example this would be 146.146.10.1.

10 • Enter the VPN subnet mask into the VPN Tunnel IP Mask field. For our example, this would be FF.FF.FF.0.

11 • Press <ESC> and Yes to save changes. The IP addresses will then be verified, and proper VPN packet filters will be put into place.

12 • Press <Enter> to continue.

13 • Select Generate Encryption Information from the Master Server Configuration menu.

14 • For the random seed, enter up to 255 characters. This can be any combination of numbers and letters. You don't need to remember the number entered: you can enter it randomly.

15 • Press Enter to continue. The system will generate the keys, and then the Diffie-Hellman parameters. This process can take anywhere from 30 seconds to 3 minutes.

16 • The following message will appear:

Generate the Encryption Information Successfully.

Press Enter to continue; this will update the VPN table and load the VPMASTER.NLM.

17 • A message will be displayed indicating that the server was successfully updated in NDS. Press <Enter> to continue.

18 • Copy the master encryption information file (MINFO.VPN) to a formatted diskette or a location on your server. To do this, select Copy Encryption Information.

19 • Enter the path where you want to save the master encryption file.

20 • Give the diskette, or file location, to the administrator of the slave server.

21 • Wait until the slave configuration is complete before you continue.

22 • Once the slave configuration is started, you will be asked to verify "out-of-band" certification. When the slave administrator contacts you to authenticate, select Authenticate Encryption Information. The Message Digest for Authentication appears as shown in Figure 6.6.

23 • Repeat the numbers of your message digest to the slave. It will then verify that these are the numbers it is also holding. If all agree, press Enter to continue.

24 • To exit NIASCFG, press <Esc> until you are asked to confirm the exit. Exit the utility by selecting Yes.

Configuring a Slave Server

To configure a VPN slave server, perform the following steps. In our example, we would complete the steps for each slave location, Maui and Lanai.

1 • Type LOAD NIASCFG from the file server console at the slave site.

Do not use RCONSOLE to perform this task—doing so would compromise the security of the VPN.

IMPORTANT

2 • Select Configure NIAS.

3 • Select Virtual Private Network. This automatically loads VPNCFG.NLM.

4 • Select Slave Server Configuration.

5 • Select Configure the IP addresses.

6 • Enter the IP address of your server into the public IP address field. For our example we enter 150.140.11.1 for Maui and 150.140.14.1 for Lanai.

7 • Enter the subnet mask of the server into the public IP mask field. For our example we enter FF.FF.FC.0.

8 • Enter the VPN IP address into the VPN Tunnel Address field. For the slave servers, use the VPN IP address subnet defined by the master server. For our example, we use 146.146.10.2 for Maui and 146.146.10.3 for Lanai.

9 • Enter the VPN subnet mask and press <Enter> in the VPN Tunnel IP Mask field. For our example, we enter FF.FF.FF.0.

10 • Press <Esc> and select Yes to save the changes. The IP addresses will then be verified and the proper VPN packet filters will be put into place.

11 • Press <Esc> and select Yes to save the changes.

12 • Select Generate Encryption Information from the Slave Server Configuration menu.

13 • You will then be prompted for the MINFO.VPN file. Insert the diskette, or specify the path to the MINFO.VPN file generated on the master server.

14 • A message screen will appear with a HEX code. This code verifies that you received this file from your master server. Contact your master server administrator and repeat the numbers to verify that they are the same. Figure 6.7 shows the message digest for the slave server.

F I G U R E   6.7

The Message Digest for
Authentication as displayed
at the slave site

15 • The following message will appear:

VPNCFG successfully saved the RSA public key file

16 • Press Enter to continue.

17 • For the Random Seed, enter up to 255 characters. This number can
be any combination of numbers and letters; it is not necessary to
remember the number.

NOTE

**This does not have to be the same random seed used for the master
server. This number is unique for each server; it can be any
combination of numbers and letters.**

18 • The following message will be displayed:

Generate the Encryption Information Successfully

19 • Press <Enter> to continue. This will update the VPN table and load
the VPSLAVE.NLM.

20 • Press <Enter>. You will see a message that the server was successfully updated in NDS.

21 • Press <Enter> to continue.

22 • Copy the slave encryption information file (SINFO.VPN) to a formatted diskette, or to the location on your server. To do this, select Copy Encryption Information.

23 • Enter the path in which you want to save the slave encryption file. The default file name will be SINFO.VPN. This file can be renamed as long as the new name is provided to the master server. In our example, the file is renamed on each of the slave servers as follows: Maui's file name is MAUI.VPN and Lanai's is LANAI.VPN. The files can be saved anywhere on the server, on diskette, or e-mailed.

24 • Give the diskette, or file location, to the master server administrator.

25 • Select Authenticate Encryption Information.

26 • Wait until the master server is done configuring the slaves. Once the slave configuration is started, you will be asked to verify out-of-band certification.

27 • When the master administrator contacts you, you will need to authenticate. To do this, select Authenticate Encryption Information.

28 • Repeat the numbers to the master administrator, who will then verify that these are the numbers he or she also holds. If all agree, press Enter.

29 • To exit NIASCFG, press <Esc> until you are asked to confirm the exit. Exit the utility by selecting Yes.

Adding Slave Servers to VPN Table

Once you complete the configuration for the master, and slave sites of your VPN, you need to add the slave servers to the master server's VPN table. To do this, perform the following steps for each slave member you need to add to your VPN (for our example we perform the same steps for Maui and Lanai):

1 • To add a slave server to the VPN table, log in to your NDS tree as Admin or an equivalent user.

2 • From your Windows 95 desktop, double-click the NWAdmin icon or run NWADMN95.EXE from the Start menu.

3 • Browse the NDS tree to find the server objects that represent your master VPN server.

4 • Double-click the server object to access the Details page.

5 • From the server's Details page, click the Virtual Private Network page option. You will see a list of VPN members, as shown in Figure 6.8. The first time you access this screen, the master server will be the only entry.

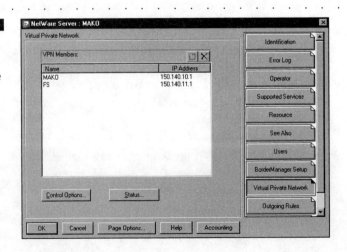

Add a slave server to the master's VPN table by selecting the Virtual Private Network option of the master server's Details page, in NWAdmin.

6 • To add a slave server to the VPN, click the Add button. This button is located in the upper-right corner of the VPN Members window, and is represented by a small box.

7 • You will be prompted for the path to the SINFO.VPN file. Enter the path to the location of the file for the fist slave VPN site. For our example, we enter the path to the first file, MAUI.VPN.

8 • Once the file is read, a dialog box appears containing the message digest numbers that must be verified with the slave administrator (see Figure 6.9).

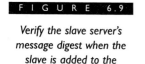

F I G U R E   6.9

Verify the slave server's message digest when the slave is added to the master's VPN table.

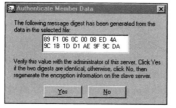

At this time, the master administrator calls the slave administrator and repeats the numbers displayed. The slave administrator verifies the numbers by accessing the Authenticate Encryption Information option of the slave configuration menu, in the VPNCFG utility (see Step 10 of the slave configuration list).

9 • If the two digests are identical, the master administrator clicks Yes to proceed. The VPN slave is then added to the table.

10 • Repeat Steps 6 – 9 for each VPN slave site. For our example, we repeat the process for the second slave site, Lanai. We enter the path to the file LANAI.VPN, contact the Lanai site administrator, and verify the message digest.

11 • Once the slaves are added to the VPN member list, the master synchronizes the VPN sites and creates the "virtual" encrypted-IP tunnel between the sites.

Please refer to Chapter 8 "Administering BorderManager" for details on managing the VPN after the initial configuration.

Removing a Server from the VPN

You can perform the following steps to remove a server from the VPN at any time:

1 • At the server console (of the server you want to remove), type LOAD VPNCFG and press Enter.

2 • From the VPN Server Configuration menu, select Remove VPN Server Configuration.

3 • A warning message will appear stating that you are about to remove the server. Select Continue. The configuration is then removed, and the NLM is unloaded.

4 • Press Enter to continue.

5 • The VPN Server is removed from Directory Services. Press Enter to continue.

NetWare Connect and ConnectView

NetWare Connect, included as a part of BorderManager, provides a solution for remote computing. NetWare Connect's remote-access software runs on an IntranetWare server; this enables multiple remote users to access the network through telephone lines including ISDN, leased lines, X.25 packet-switched networks, or direct connections. ConnectView enables you to manage the Novell Internet Access Server 4.1 remote-access software and NetWare Connect 2.0 servers.

NetWare Connect

Before installing NetWare Connect, run through the following checklist to ensure that you have everything you need to complete the installation.

Checklist

▸ an IntranetWare Server with NIAS installed

▸ communication boards and modems that are attached and functional

NOTE

When you install the Novell Internet Access Server 4.1, all previously defined groups, restrictions, and other definitions from NetWare Connect 2.0 are retained. Remote Node Services (RNS), however, are no longer supported.

Installing NetWare Connect

To install NetWare Connect, complete the following steps:

1 • At your BorderManager server console, type LOAD NIASCFG and press <Enter>.

2 • A window is displayed prompting you to move all driver LOAD and BIND commands from the AUTOEXEC.NCF file to the NETINFO.CFG file. If you have previously configured other BorderManager technologies, skip to Step 4. If not, select <Yes> to transfer the commands.

3 • When the transfer is complete, a message will be displayed indicating that NIASCFG has completed copying all the LOAD and BIND commands to NETINFO.CFG. Press <Enter> to continue.

4 • From the NIAS Options menu, choose Configure NIAS.

5 • From the Select Component to Configure menu, choose Remote Access. This automatically loads the Remote Access Configuration NLM.

6 • The Connect Object Installation Requirement menu appears (see Figure 6.10). From this menu you can extend the NDS schema to add the NetWare Connect object and associated attributes to your NDS tree.

When installing NetWare Connect, the NDS schema is extended to support the NetWare Connect object and associated attributes.

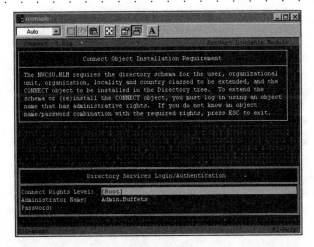

7 • From the menu shown in Figure 6.10, specify the Connect Rights Level. Accept the default of [Root], or specify the NDS container for which the NetWare Connect object should be granted rights. Users in this container, and below, can access the NetWare Connect Server remote-access services.

8 • Enter the login name and password for Admin (or equivalent) user.

9 • At this point, you are asked if you want to review the instructions. Select Yes to view the instructions, or No to continue.

10 • A message is then displayed asking if your server contains any synchronous adapters, such as X.25 or ISDN. If so, select Yes; if not, select No and go to Step 22.

11 • If you selected Yes in the previous step, you will be asked if you want to enter the MultiProtocol Router Fast Setup menu. Select No (remote access does not support Fast Setup).

12 • Choose Boards from the Internetworking Configuration menu.

13 • Press Insert and select the appropriate driver for your adapter.

14 • Enter the appropriate board parameters and save.

15 • Repeat Steps 13 and 14 for each board you will use for remote access.

16 • Press <Esc> to return to the Internetworking Configuration menu.

17 • Select Network Interfaces.

18 • For each interface you defined in Steps 13 and 14, select the interface, and the PPP Remote Access for the medium, and specify the ISDN address and ISDN subaddress (if applicable).

For examples on how to configure X.25/ISDN boards and network interfaces refer to "Configuring Ports for ISDN" in the BorderManager Online documentation.

NOTE

19 • Press <Esc> to return to the Internetworking Configuration menu.

20 • Press <Esc> again to exit INETCFG.

21 • At this point, a prompt indicates that the system must be reinitialized and gives you the option of terminating the automated setup. If you terminate the setup, you will need to repeat the setup from the beginning.

22 • If you answered No in Step 10, you are prompted to identify the communications adapters that are installed in your server. When an adapter is selected, the appropriate driver is automatically loaded with the board's default settings.

An AIO driver must be selected to continue with the installation. If you do not have an asynchronous adapter in your server, select Serial Port (COMx) to continue.

IMPORTANT

23 • The configuration program will then automatically identify ports that have modems attached. Be sure the modems are connected to the ports, and are turned on, so they can be identified properly.

24 • The automated setup program then attempts to detect the modem types attached to the ports. If it cannot automatically detect a modem type, you are prompted to identify the modem manually, as shown in Figure 6.11. If modem information already exists from a previous installation, this step will be skipped.

F I G U R E   6 . 1 1

The automated setup program attempts to detect the modem type automatically. If it is not successful, you are prompted to specify the modem type manually.

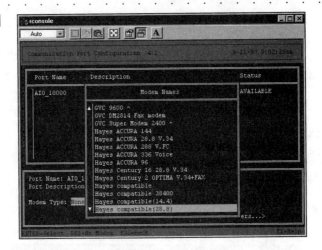

25 • Select the remote-access services that you want to load (for example, PPPRNS, ARAS, etc.). You may be required to enter configuration information at this time, depending on the service chosen. Each protocol requires different sets of information to be implemented. Please refer to the BorderManager online documentation for details.

After you successfully complete the automated setup procedure, remote access is ready for remote clients to dial in, or LAN workstations to dial out.

ConnectView

Before installing ConnectView, run through the following checklist to ensure that you have everything you need to complete the installation. Because ConnectView runs on a standalone workstation, the prerequisites for the product are different from those of other Border Manager components.

Checklist

▶ A 386, or greater, workstation with at least 8MB RAM, a VGA or super VGA monitor, and 6MB of available disk space.

▶ The workstation should be running MS-DOS 5.0 (or higher), or Windows 3.1 (or higher) with the latest version of the NetWare VLM Client, or the IntranetWare Client installed.

▶ The workstation should have a network adapter installed along with the appropriate drivers and cable to connect to the network.

▶ BSPXCOM.NLM and NCMA.NLM must be loaded on the servers to be managed by ConnectView.

ConnectView uses SNMP over IPX to monitor and manage remote access. ConnectView does not support SNMP over IP.

NOTE

Installing ConnectView

The ConnectView installation program is simple, it displays a series of self-explanatory dialog boxes that walk you through the installation. Complete the following steps to begin the ConnectView installation process:

1 • Insert the Novell BorderManager CD into the CD-ROM drive of the workstation.

2 • Run SETUP.EXE from the \CLIENT\CVIEW\DISK1 directory.

3 • Accept the installation defaults, or enter the desired installation locations.

4 • Select Continue to begin the installation.

Installing the IPX/IP or IP/IP Gateway and Clients

BorderManager includes an IPX/IP and an IP/IP gateway. The IPX/IP gateway enables the workstations on your network (that are running IPX alone) to access the Internet and other IP-based services without requiring the addition of IP. The IP/IP gateway provides a private-IP addressing scheme behind the firewall, and enables the gateway to act on behalf of the clients to hide identity and provide access outside the firewall. Run through the following checklist before installing the IPX/IP or IP/IP gateway:

Checklist

▶   You should have knowledge of interfaces located in the server, including LAN and WAN, and IP addressing.

▶   You will need to install NetWare/IP on the BorderManager server if you are going to implement the IP/IP gateway. In addition, any clients that will be using the IP/IP gateway must use the NetWare/IP client stack. Refer to the IntranetWare installation for configuration and implementation steps.

The gateways included with BorderManager do not support UDP traffic.

NOTE

Enabling the IP or IPX Gateway

1   •   Log in to your server as Admin (or equivalent) user.

2   •   Start NWAdmin by double-clicking the icon on your desktop, or by running NWADMN95.EXE.

3   •   Browse your NDS tree to find the server where you wish to enable the gateway. Double-click the server's icon.

4 • Click the BorderManager Setup page option.

5 • Verify that the IP addresses have been defined in the lower portion of the screen. If not, refer to Step 2 in the BorderManager NWAdmin Snapin Installation section.

6 • In the Enabled Services box, double-click the Gateway you wish to enable — IPX/IP gateway or IP/IP gateway. This will display the Gateway Attributes dialog box, shown in Figure 6.12.

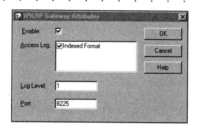

F I G U R E   6.12

Enable the IPX/IP Gateway in NWAdmin.

7 • Check the Enable box.

8 • If you wish to have logging enabled, check the Indexed Format box.

9 • Enter your log-level preference. Table 6.2 provides definitions of the various log levels.

T A B L E   6.2

IPX/IP and IP/IP Gateway log-level definitions

LOG LEVEL	DESCRIPTION
0	Does not log any information.
1	Logs Internet-access information. The server records the user's fully distinguished NDS name, the access protocol (HTTP, for example), and the destination (http://www.novell.com, www.novell.com, for example).
2	Logs error codes, such as NDS errors. Logging this information will help you determine why a user cannot access a particular service.
3	Logs debugging information. This includes internal-server communications, such as socket calls. Typically, this information is only of interest to software developers.

The information logged at each level is additive. For example, if the log level is set to 2, level 1 information is also logged.

NOTE

10 • Keep the default of port 8225 in the Port field of the Gateway Attributes dialog box. This represents the number of the port used by the gateways to transmit gateway traffic on the server. 8225 is the default for both the IPX/IP and IP/IP gateway.

11 • Click OK to save the changes.

12 • Click the OK action button at the bottom of the page. The gateway NLMs will load at the server.

The Gateway-Client Component

In order for clients to use the IPX/IP or IP/IP gateway, a component must be installed at each client. This can be done at each workstation (the most time-consuming method), or it can be automated from a central location. Of course, the latter makes the most sense if you need to enable the gateway on multiple workstations. IntranetWare includes two utilities that enable you to "push" changes down to client workstations from a central location—the ACU (Automatic Client Update) and NAL (NetWare Application Launcher). Please refer to the IntranetWare utilities reference guide for details on using these utilities.

This section provides step-by-step instructions to enable the gateway-client component on a workstation. Before you enable the gateway, run through the following checklist to ensure that you have everything you need to use the gateway client.

Checklist

▶ Currently, the gateway client supports only the Windows 3.x and Windows 95 IntranetWare Client software; however, a Windows NT client that supports the gateway is scheduled for release soon. The latest IntranetWare client software can be downloaded from Novell's Web site: (http://www.novell.com).

▸ If you are using the IP/IP gateway, the client must be running the NetWare/IP client stack.

▸ You will need Windows 95 software and IntranetWare client software available during the gateway-client installation.

▸ Browser Clients must use BorderManager as the Proxy choice in the Browser client setup to take advantage of access control through the gateway.

Enabling the Gateway-Client Component

To enable the IPX/IP or IP/IP gateway-client component on a Windows 95 workstation, complete the following steps:

1 • From the Windows 95 desktop, click the Start menu and select Settings.

2 • From the Settings menu, select Control Panel.

3 • From the Control Panel folder double-click the Network icon; you will see the screen shown in Figure 6.13.

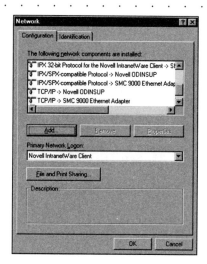

F I G U R E 6.13

The IPX/IP or IP/IP gateway-client component is enabled through the Network Control Panel.

4 • From the Network Control Panel, click the Add action button.

5 • From the Select Network Component type dialog box, highlight the Service icon and click Add. The Select Network Services dialog box will appear.

6 • In the Manufacturer's box, click Novell. The available Novell network services will appear as shown in Figure 6.14.

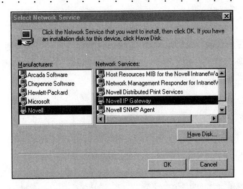

F I G U R E   6.14

Enabling the Novell IP Gateway-Client component

7 • From the Network Services box shown in Figure 6.14, select the Novell IP Gateway and click OK. (The same client service is used for both the IPX and IP client).

8 • From the Novell IP Gateway Properties dialog box, enter the preferred IPX/IP gateway server.

9 • Click OK.

10 • From the Network dialog, click OK.

11 • You will be prompted for the locations for the IntranetWare client and Windows 95 software. Enter the appropriate paths to continue.

12 • When prompted to restart your computer, click Yes; the client will then reboot.

13 • After the workstation reboots, the Novell IP Gateway Enabler screen will appear. Here, you can enable the IPX/IP or IP/IP gateway, or disable the gateway client entirely. Click the gateway you wish to enable and click OK.

Disabling the Gateway Functions at the Client

There may be instances when you need to disable the gateway client. Some legacy applications, for example, cannot use the gateway; you may also have an application that requires a true IP stack. The IP Gateway Switcher program enables, or disables the Gateway client on the fly.

To access the Gateway Switcher Program, complete the following steps:

1 • From the Windows 95 desktop, click the Start menu and choose Programs.

2 • Click the Novell menu and highlight the IP Gateway folder.

3 • Click the Switcher icon, and the screen shown in Figure 6.15 will appear.

NOTE

Once access to the Gateway is enabled you must use the Novell WINPING utility to "ping" IP addresses. (Microsoft's WINIPCFG utility won't work when the Gateway switcher is enabled. WINPING is automatically installed when the IntranetWare Client software is installed.)

FIGURE 6.15

The Novell IP Gateway Switcher program enables, or disables, the gateway on the fly.

4 • From this screen, select Disable Gateway and click OK.

To re-enable the Gateway, simply access the Gateway Switcher program again, and choose Enable.

Configuring Proxy Caching

There are three primary ways to configure Proxy Caching with BorderManager:

▶ Web client acceleration (standard forward proxy cache) — In this scenario, the proxy server makes requests to Web servers for the intranet clients and then caches URLs, HTML objects, and FTP files to accelerate future requests to the same objects.

▶ Web server acceleration (reverse-proxy cache acceleration) — In this scenario, when a client requests information from a Web server, the request is directed to the proxy server. The proxy server then supplies the cached pages to the client at high speed. This method not only accelerates client access; it also takes the request load off the Web servers, enabling them to handle more users.

▶ Network acceleration (Internet Core Protocol [ICP] hierarchical caching) — In this scenario, the WAN traffic load is reduced and available bandwidth is increased because ICP hierarchical caching permits multiple caches to cooperate.

BorderManager can perform each method of Internet object caching on one platform. These methods can also be implemented on separate platforms. Before enabling Internet Object Caching, run through the following checklist.

Checklist

▶ Plan where you will place the caches. They should be placed where you're short on bandwidth.

▶ Monitor caching statistics to add more memory and hard drive space if needed.

▶ Determine the server on which volume caching will be done. The default is SYS: (however, this is not always a good idea). If you run out of disk space on the SYS: volume, serious implications can occur.

▶ If you are using Internet Object Caching technologies for HTTP Acceleration, you must know the IP, or DNS, names of the Web publishing servers you are hosting.

▶ Understand which BorderManager servers will be performing Internet Object Caching technologies.

▶ Lay out a plan for ICP Hierarchical Caching. You need to know the IP address or DNS name of every server that will participate in the neighborhood.

▶ Browser clients must use BorderManager, as the Proxy choice in the Browser client setup, to take advantage of caching technologies.

Configuring Web Client HTTP Proxy

To configure Web client HTTP Proxy Caching, perform the following steps:

1 • From your workstation, log in to your NDS tree as Admin (or equivalent) user.

2 • Launch NWADMIN95.EXE.

3 • Browse the NDS tree to locate your BorderManager server.

4 • Double-click the BorderManager server object.

5 • From the server's details page, click the BorderManager Setup option.

6 • In the Enabled Services box, double-click the Proxy Cache Services entry. This will display the screen shown in Figure 6.16.

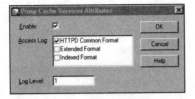

7 • From the Proxy Cache Services Attributes dialog box, select Enable.

8 • If you want to enable logging, choose the desired type of logging by clicking the box to the right of the choice. The choices are defined in Table 6.3.

	FORMAT	DEFINITION
T A B L E 6 . 3 *Proxy Cache Services Event log format definitions*	HTTPD Common Format	This format logs remote hostname, user's remote login name, authenticated username, date, request line from client, status, and length of data (in bytes).
	Extended Format	Extended format logs cached status (0 or 1), date, time, client IP address, URL method, and URL.
	Indexed Format	Indexed format logs information based on the BorderManager component from which information is being collected. For example, an access-control log for the proxy cache contains the following information: when access was granted or denied, the IP address that initiated the access attempt, the destination, the HTTP command (GET, for example), and the result of the attempt ("hit" or "miss").

9 • Enter the log-reporting level. This number, between 0 and 3, indicates the type of information logged by the server. The log reporting levels are defined in Table 6.4.

TABLE 6.4	LOG LEVEL	DESCRIPTION
Proxy Cache Services log level definitions	0	Does not log information.
	I	Logs Internet-access information. The server records the user's fully distinguished NDS name, the access protocol (HTTP, for example), and the destination (`http://www.novell.com, www.novell.com`, for example).
	2	Logs error codes, such as NDS errors. Logging this information will help you determine why a user cannot access a particular service.
	3	Logs debugging information. This includes internal-server communications, such as socket calls. Typically, this information is of interest only to software developers.

NOTE

The information logged at each level is additive. For example, if the log level is set to 2, level I information is also logged.

10 • Click the OK button; this exits you to the main BorderManager setup page.

II • Click the OK button at the bottom of the page; this exits you to the NWAdmin main screen, and then the appropriate NLMs for Proxy cache loads at the server. The NLMs, PROXYCFG.NLM and PROXY.NLM, are loaded.

12 • Verify that proxy-cache services have started on your server.

13 • At your server's console prompt, verify that the timestamp synchronization for BorderManager has been achieved. If so, the following message will appear on your screen:

Timestamp synchronization of BRDMGR.NLM is completed.

You may have to wait 30 seconds to 3 minutes for this to occur.

Verify that the Proxy Cache Service is running by pressing
<Ctrl>+<Esc>. Novell BorderManager Proxy Cache Server should
appear as one of the entries.

If the Proxy Cache Server did not load, there is likely a problem with the TCP/IP
configuration. To troubleshoot the problem follow these steps:

I • Verify TCP/IP addresses through INETCFG.

2 • Verify the TCP/IP addresses you configured through NWAdmin under
BorderManager Setup page option.

3 • Verify that the DNS Resolver file exists, and is correct. This file is
located in SYS:\ETC\RESOLV.CFG. You can edit this file with any
editor, or from within INETCFG. Select Protocols, TCP/IP, and then
DNS Resolver Configurations.

4 • Perform a cold-boot.

Configuring HTTP Acceleration

To configure HTTP acceleration, complete the following steps:

I • Log in to your NDS tree as Admin (or equivalent) user.

2 • Launch NWAdmin by double-clicking the program icon on your
desktop, or by running NWADMN95.EXE.

3 • Browse your NDS tree to locate your BorderManager server.

4 • Double-click the server's icon.

5 • From the server's Details page, click the Web Proxy Cache option.
This will display the screen shown in Figure 6.17.

F I G U R E   6.17

HTTP Acceleration is enabled by selecting the Web Proxy Cache option of the BorderManager server's Details page.

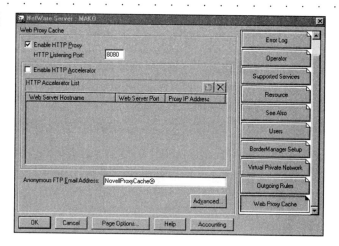

6 • Click the Enable HTTP Accelerator box.

7 • Add a Web Server location to the HTTP Accelerator list by clicking the Add button. This button is located in the upper-right portion of the HTTP Accelerator List next to the X icon. This will display HTTP Accelerator dialog box, as shown in Figure 6.18.

F I G U R E   6.18

Add a Web server to the HTTP Acceleration list.

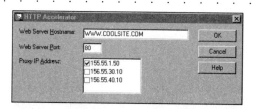

8 • Type in a Web Server Host name, or the IP address of the Web Server.

9 • Type in the Web server port of the Web site you are front-ending; the default is 80. Keep this port number unless you know that it is something other than this number.

10 • Click the IP address of your proxy server in the proxy IP address box. This address indicates the interface from which you want BorderManager to listen for requests.

11 • Click OK to save the changes.

12 • Click OK at the bottom of the page.

13 • Verify that the proxy cache server was reloaded with the new changes.

14 • At your server's console prompt, verify that the timestamp synchronization for BorderManager has been achieved. If it has, the following message will appear on your screen:

Timestamp synchronization of BRDMGR.NLM is completed.

You may have to wait a few moments for this to occur.

15 • Verify that the Proxy Cache Service is running with the new parameters by pressing <Ctrl>+<Esc> and verifying that Novell BorderManager Proxy Cache Server has an entry under Configured Services, as shown in Figure 6.19.

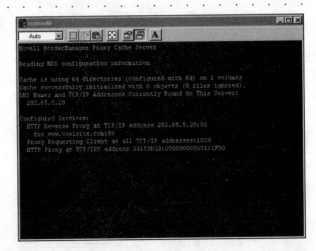

FIGURE 6.19

Verify that HTTP Acceleration has been enabled. Configure Hierarchical Caching.

To configure ICP Hierarchical Caching, complete the following steps:

1 • Log in to your NDS trees as Admin (or equivalent) user.

2 • Launch NWAdmin by double-clicking the program icon on your desktop, or by running NWADMN95.EXE.

3 • Browse your NDS tree to locate your BorderManager server.

4 • Double-click the server's icon.

5 • From the server's Details page, click the Web Proxy Cache option.

6 • Click the Advanced button.

7 • Click the Hierarchy tab. This will display the screen shown in Figure 6.20.

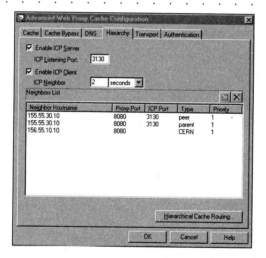

FIGURE 6.20

To enable ICP Hierarchical Caching, select the Advanced button from the Web Proxy Cache option of the server's Details page.

8 • Check the Enable ICP Server box if this server is going to participate in a neighborhood. Leave the listening port at the default value.

9 • Check the Enable ICP Client box to define your own neighborhood.

10 • To add a neighbor to the list, click the Add button. This is the button located in the upper right-hand corner, next to the X icon, in the neighborhood List box. This will display the Neighbor dialog box shown in Figure 6.21.

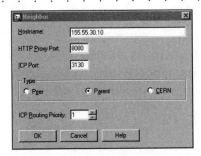

F I G U R E   6.21

*Add a neighbor to the
Neighbor list.*

11 • Enter the hostname or IP address of the other proxy cache.

12 • Keep 8080 as the HTTP Proxy Port.

13 • Keep 3130 as the ICP Port.

14 • Select the neighbor type—peer, parent, or CERN. The peer types are defined in Table 6.5.

T A B L E   6.5

*Hierarchical Cache neighbor
type definitions*

NEIGHBOR TYPE	DEFINITION
Peer	A peer cache that is located in a hierarchical manner at the same level as your own location in the hierarchy.
Parent	In a hierarchy, this is the cache above your location.
CERN	Any CERN-compatible cache located in your environment. Examples of these are Netscape Proxy, Microsoft Proxy, or any UNIX CERN proxy product.

15 • If you chose Parent or CERN in Step 14, select an ICP Routing Priority between 1 and 10—1 is the lowest priority, 10 is the highest.

An ICP cache chooses among the responding caches by selecting the one with the highest priority.

NOTE

16 • Click OK to save.

17 • Repeat Steps 10–16 for each neighborhood entry.

18 • Click OK to close the Advance Web Proxy Cache Configuration.

19 • Click OK to close the Web Proxy Cache window; this will load the new configuration at your server.

20 • Verify that the proxy cache server was reloaded with the new changes.

21 • At your server's console prompt, verify the timestamp synchronization for BorderManager has been achieved. If so, the following message will appear on your screen:

Timestamp synchronization of BRDMGR.NLM is completed.

You may have to wait a few moments for this to occur.

22 • Verify that the Proxy Cache Service is running with the new parameters by pressing <Ctrl>+<Esc> and verifying that Novell BorderManager Proxy Cache Server has an entry under Configured Services (see Figure 6.22).

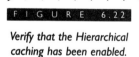

FIGURE 6.22

Verify that the Hierarchical caching has been enabled.

Summary

The installation and configuration of each of the BorderManager components (covered in this and the previous chapter) are just the beginning. Chapter 7 will help you establish policies for security on your intranet, and Chapter 8 will explain how to administer BorderManager.

Defining and Setting a System Security Policy

Keeping a system secure used to mean that you kept your username and password a secret. Now, setting and implementing security policies requires hours of meetings and pages of documentation. Systems have become very complex, as have the ways in which people use them. In fact, systems have become so complex that securing a system is almost considered a black art, practiced by acolytes in long robes with hoods, in dark rooms with pixie dust and dead chickens.

The number of resources available in your company, the various ways you can access those resources, and the policies you use to secure your data all contribute to this complexity. For example, consider a file on a NetWare server. You can access it from your PC using the Novell Client software. You can get to it using your Web browser if the NetWare server is also running the Novell Web server. You can use FTP or NFS, and even the Macintosh computer can directly access the file using AppleTalk. Each access method was developed with its own security system, and some—the Web, for example—had no security system at all. As a result, each access method must be managed separately. Even if you secure one access method, someone may still get to the same data via another access method that you haven't yet locked down.

Fortunately, unwanted access doesn't occur in the NetWare environment, because NetWare security is automatically applied to all access methods and completely protects the data stored in it. But what about all those other systems and the data that isn't stored on NetWare? Can we export Novell's excellent security model to other systems, particularly the Web? The answer is yes. This chapter covers the why and how of using Novell's BorderManager to secure your Web-accessible data.

Can Systems Be Totally Secure?

A totally secure system is one that nobody can log in to. If you take a computer, lock it up in a vault, and grant access to no one, you have a totally secure system. Even if you let only one person, your administrator, use the system, you are still dependent on the honesty and integrity of that person. People who work in computer security must learn to deal with the reality that you can't trust anybody. There is no such thing as a totally secure system.

If you are tasked with securing data and programs within your organization, and you really don't want to trust anybody, how do you do your job? The answer is that you must rely on not only the technology to secure your data, but also the policies and procedures for using it. The real challenge lies in creating the policies. Even a really good technology can be completely neutralized by bad usage policies. You wouldn't take your car skydiving. Although the car will probably protect you adequately in a variety of crashes on the ground, it will do a particularly bad job of protecting you from a 200-mph impact with the ground. We'll say it again: The most important tool in preventing misuse of systems and data is a good security policy.

Security Policies for an Intranet

The word *policy* has acquired, quite unjustly, a rather negative connotation in modern lexicon. When asked to read a policy document, an employee will often follow with the question, "What idiot wrote this?" Lack of communication between the author of a policy document and the subjects of the document is usually the cause for this negative connotation. What's in a security policy, and how do you create a good, useable one?

The Role of a Security Policy

Security policies are about the battles you choose to fight, not how you fight them. You might have a policy stating that you want to control and secure all external access to your networks. This statement says nothing about how you will go about it, yet it clearly states that you want to have ways to access your internal data and systems from other locations. This statement also leads you to believe that a set of rules exists that tells you which technologies you may use to access your data and how those technologies may be used to keep your content secure.

The security policy is a guideline for those implementing solutions in their organizations. It may also be dependent on available technologies. The example of wanting to secure external access to your networks is a global statement. If there are no ways to effectively secure external access to your networks (usually because the technology doesn't exist to do what you want), you may issue a rule that says,

"In order to secure all external access to our networks, I will not permit any external access to our networks." This is a strategy as well as a tactic.

If the technology becomes available to secure external access to your networks, you may change the strategy statement to "I will permit external access to the networks, and the tactical methods will be to use only dial-up modems secured with a username and password, authenticated to NDS." The policy of securing access to your network didn't change — how it will be accomplished changed. The security policy is a guideline. It tells what the company is concerned about but not how to accomplish the security goals. Developing a security policy is often a long and involved process, and whole books have been written on the subject. There are a few things to consider.

A Few Guidelines on Writing a Security Policy

Everyone needs to live with the security policies within an organization. This implies, of course, that staff members and administrators actually read and adhere to the policy. This also implies that everyone understand the policy. The following offers a few guidelines for creating your own policy.

Explain Everything

Make sure to include why a policy is in place. This helps in the future as the policy changes. A policy document is a living thing and is subject to review. Explanations of each policy help during the re-evaluation process simply because you may not remember why you did things. Perhaps the people who created the policy no longer work for the company. Also, as a company grows, its need for information technology changes, as does its security policies.

Plain Language

Remember that you need to understand this document. The lawyers will want you to use precise legalese, but this is often about as readable and as voluminous as programming source code. Also, you want your employees to understand their responsibilities. They are not likely to read anything that weighs more than they do! Don't be afraid to create short versions to give to the employees.

Responsibilities

Everyone needs to know what to do to make the security goals realistic. Administrators and employees alike are members of a team, and they need to know the positions that each person will play. An example might be that employees must protect their passwords and never give them out to anyone, including other people in the organization.

Authority

This is crucial. Who has the authority to take action when the rules aren't being followed? State the actions that may be taken — revocation of access, reprimand, censure, demotion, fine, dismissal, cattle prod, forced listening to disco tunes, and so on. In most corporations, the manager or the person with authority over whatever network resource (confidential information, an entire file server that houses that information, and so on) the policy was put in place for determines punitive action. In larger companies, this list of actions can be quite large and unwieldy, and lawyers are often intimately involved in its creation. What fun!

What to Consider Including in Your Security Policy

This section covers the kinds of things you probably want to include in your policy. Because almost all computer systems share some common features, a few things in a policy document will be standard from company to company. Each of us, however, has special cases that must be addressed. You will need to get opinions and input from many people in your company, including administrators, staff members, and managers. Consider the following list a starting point:

- ▸ Who gets accounts on your systems? Employees, contractors, family members?

- ▸ Who may use accounts on your systems? The account owner, the account owner's secretary, and so on?

- ▸ What can be connected to your network?

- ▸ What rules must be met for connecting a host to your network? What about a client?

► What are the rules for connecting to the Internet?

► What are the rules for the information that will be published on the Internet?

► What are the rules for connecting remote users to your network?

► What are the rules for connecting partners to your network?

► What are the rules for connecting customers to your network?

► What are the rules for using e-mail on the network—personal mail, mailing source code, and so on?

► What will the rules be for protecting really confidential information, such as company secrets, financial information, source code, and so on?

This list is the tip of the iceberg; however, it ought to get your creative juices flowing. Now that you have some idea of what is in a policy, the next question seems logical. How do you go about creating a policy?

Creating Your Security Policy

This is where the fun starts. Creating a policy is usually a big job. It's also a continuing process. Don't expect the policy that you created back in the days when the computer was locked up in a glass room to work today. Now we have data that employees insist on storing on the most insecure of systems—personal computers and laptops. The same rules just don't apply.

You don't have to schedule monthly meetings to perform complete re-evaluations of your security policies, but it is a good idea to get administrators or executives together and go over new technologies as they are introduced into the company. In fact, it is a good idea to evaluate the security risks of new technologies before they are installed.

The following is a rough guide for creating your own policy:

- Learn as much as you can about security policies. Documents are available from INTERNIC.NET and NCSA, and you can find books on the subject. This is a battle best entered well armed.

- Categorize the types of applications and data in your company, such as accounting, financial, production, e-mail, and so on.

- Determine what types of data need to be protected and what is publicly available. Also determine what is public within the company and what can be public outside the company.

- Determine the relationships that your company currently supports and those it wants to support. For example, does your company enable, or want to enable, customers to look up their own order information? This implies a network relationship with your customers. What about your suppliers? Do you have any current or future plans to include automatic technology relationships with your suppliers? The relationships outside the company have a direct effect on the direction of your policy document.

- Create categories of employees who need access to the applications and data. For example: everyone gets e-mail, accounting gets access to the general ledger system, payroll gets access to the payroll system, and so on. You will probably need to break it down further and specify what kind of accounting staff will have access to what modules of your accounting system—an accounts receivable person may not be permitted access to the accounts payable module.

- Run this list by all the departments that run the systems and own the data on your list. Get input from employees on what will help them. Ask what they need to access to do their jobs. Do they need to retrieve this data from places other than the office, such as at home, in hotels, on the plane, or in the car? This input will have a really big impact on which battles you choose to fight and what access is considered important. Be prepared to make some concessions. If employees could really use access to the accounting application from the road, but you don't think you can make that access as secure as you would like, make a compromise in the name of productivity if you can. Specify what your security technology should do if it fails — remain wide open or cut off all users. This may vary from system to system. For example, if security for an order-entry system should fail, is it better to place no orders or to risk a few bogus orders during the time the security system is down?

▶ Develop a policy for enhancing your security policy. As new applications, technologies, and user requirements come into existence, how will they be incorporated into the company? How will you measure it against your security requirements? Consider legal input. Are any of your policies opening the company to unacceptable liability?

▶ Publish the policy. Make sure staff members, administrators, and policy makers all understand their responsibilities in keeping your data safe from misuse or damage. Don't be afraid to make quick reference versions that are easily understood. In the quick reference versions, cover the basic roles and behaviors expected of everyone.

▶ Enforce the policy. The best policies in the world are worthless if you don't ensure that your employees follow the rules you have laid down.

▶ Build systems that follow the policies. Remember that your policy document shouldn't say anything about what technology will be used to achieve the type of security desired. Once you have a set of guidelines, use it when adding new systems and applications to your environment.

▶ Review the policy regularly or at least every time a new technology is introduced. The policy should be a living document that always reflects the current policies of your company. As the company grows and creates new technology relationships, the security policy will probably need to be updated.

This list is a good start, but good research is your first step. The more you know about your users and the functions they would like to perform on your network, the more complete the security policies will be. Remember that there is no such thing as a totally secure system, but with good planning you can reduce the risk of hostile invasion and still have a productive network for your users.

Building a Policy

Up to this point we've talked about some of the things that are important in creating a security policy, but we haven't covered what a policy looks like. In this section we are going to use the process described in this chapter to create a security policy for a fictional school district.

Upper Mudwhomp Flats School District has decided to connect to the Internet. In an unprecedented strategic move, the school board will graduate the school district into the Internet age. "Connection to the Internet will open up vast vistas of research and educational information to our students, giving them the edge they'll need to compete in today's technology-driven society," said the school board president. "We will make Upper Mudwhomp Flats the premier primary school system in the world with this bold investment in technology."

Although the board president's pontificating is rather overstated, it provides an item of the security policy that we are about to create: "We will connect to the Internet." There is also an implied statement in "We will allow our students and teachers access to the Internet." Wow, we have two of our policy statements already! This might be easier that we thought.

You know that the foundations for the Internet and the Web are rooted in sharing research information, largely among educational institutions conducting research. You also know that the Web seems to run on a principle of unexpected destinations. When you're browsing the Web, you don't know where the link you are currently following will lead you. How many times have you gone to the Web looking for, say, a NetWare driver, and found yourself looking at a Web site dedicated to the hard science of alien autopsies? It's easy to trip over *controversial information*, and there is a clear need to control this. Okay, another policy statement: "We want to control the type of information that students and teachers can access."

Connecting the school system's network to the Internet may have an effect on the security of the current data. What data must be protected versus the data you don't mind being public? Table 2.1 shows a matrix of the types of data that we have and who we want to have access to it.

TABLE 2.1

This table describes what types of data and what types of access are desired in our example.

DATA TYPE	PUBLISH TO INTERNET	PUBLIC USER	SCHOOL ADMINISTRATOR	TEACHER	STUDENT
Accounting	No	No	Yes	No	No
Student Records	No	No	No	Yes, only of their students	Read only their own
School Financial Information	No	No	Yes	No	No
Internet	NA	NA	Yes, restricted by school board policy	Yes, restricted by school board policy	Yes, restricted by teacher
Student Work and Assignment Information	No	No	No	Yes, only of their own students	Yes, only of their own

There are a few policy statements in this chart:

▸ Although we currently have no interest in publishing any data to the Internet, we may someday want to put up a school district Web site. Currently, we won't publish any information on the Internet, but publishing information may be permitted as long as it meets approval of this policy and the school board.

▸ We will provide Web access to the employees and students of each school district but will restrict access to any Web sites that the school board and the community deem inappropriate.

▸ We want to protect private information. Financial and accounting information and student records and assignments are not to be available to unauthorized users.

In a meeting with the teachers, we discover that they want individual control of the sites their students can access. In fact, they want the students to access only the sites that the teacher has approved for specific assignments. The teachers also want access from home to control the rules and be able to complete their lesson plans remotely. This implies, of course, some form of remote access for the teachers.

Now let's meet with our students; the students want access to anything on the Internet. They argue that the Internet is about discovery, and they don't want to be restricted from accessing a site that could be important to an assignment. Because no one really knows everything that's on the Internet, how can the students be sure the teacher has given them access to all the information that may be available for their current assignment? Of course, we don't want to curtail innovation and creativity in our students.

We now have enough information to perform a first pass on our security policy. This is just a first pass and applies only to our fictional school district.

Mudwhomp Flats School District Security Policy

This document contains the policy guidelines by which Mudwhomp Flats School District will secure and maintain security on school district data and access to and from school district networks.

1 • Mudwhomp Flats school district networks will be connected to the Internet.

2 • Each school in the district will be connected to the district network and permitted access to the Internet.

3 • Currently, no school district data will be published; however, it is the intention that information about the school district eventually will be published on the WWW. All requests to publish information on the WWW must be approved by the security committee.

4 • Access will be permitted from the school district networks to the Internet for administrative personnel, teachers, and students.

5 • Carte blanche access will not be granted to any school district user. Content will be restricted according to policies set by the school board that apply to all users. More detailed restrictions are the responsibility of the teacher.

6 • At this time, no remote access for teachers or administrative personnel will be permitted; however, it is the intention of the school district to permit remote access for teachers and administrative personnel at a later time. The policies for remote access will then be included in this document.

7 • The school district will implement procedures to protect access to school district financial information as well as student academic and medical records.

8 • If any of the security technologies used to implement this policy should fail, all Internet access should be disabled automatically. The default for a failure in any other security system should provide no access to the data it protects until the system can be repaired.

9 • Administrative personnel, teachers, and students will be given accounts on the school district networks.

10 • Teachers will be permitted access only to the records of their students.

11 • Students will be permitted access only to their own records.

12 • Passwords are the keys to school district computers and networks. As a result, users are responsible for keeping their passwords safe and known only to themselves.

13 • If a student is caught using another person's account, that student will be subject to parental notification and possibly suspension. The decision to suspend will be at the school principle's discretion with input from the teacher and the student's parents.

14 • If a teacher or administrative user is caught using another person's account, the offender will be subject to reprimand at the minimum, up to dismissal at the maximum. The decision to dismiss will be at the discretion of the school board with input from the school principal or supervisor.

15 • As new technologies and requirements for data access on the school districts networks (or the Internet) are discovered, this document will be updated to include policies that incorporate the new desires of the network users.

16 • To make sure that the needs of all users of the school district's networks are being met, there will be representatives from each category of user. The security committee will consist of one school board member, the principals of all schools in the district, and a teacher and student representative from each school in the district.

Now that we have that out of the way, let's review our policy. Does it contain the basics? Everything is explained in rather plain language, as far as policy documents go. It includes the responsibilities of teachers, students, and administrators, and also includes who has the authority to take action when a policy is inadequate or has been compromised. In the real world, this document would be run through several iterations and by a few lawyers before it goes into effect, but for our purposes, this is as complete as we need. We'll look at Mudwhomp Flats School district again later, but now it's time to look at the tactics that we can use to implement our security policy.

Technologies for Implementing the Security Policy

Now that we have defined the need for a security policy, we can begin to implement specific technologies that carry out the terms of the security policy. As noted earlier, the two are always changing on an intranet. You may change an edict in the security policy (we enable personal Web pages to be exported), which in turn forces a change in deployed technology (we *must* install Novell's

BorderManager!). We won't go into gory detail, because installation was covered in Chapter 5, and Chapter 8 will cover the day-to-day administration.

Over the years, as new technologies have been added to our intranets and the Internet, we've built up quite an array of methods to implement various security policies. We will go through these methods, explain the merits of each, and then discuss how each might help the Mudwhomp Flats School district. For each method we will also, of course, talk about the technology in Novell BorderManager that can be used for each security method.

Many of these technologies are not new. As a matter of fact, some (such as proxies and firewalls and application gateways) have existed for several years. BorderManager combines these technologies into one comprehensive location, where they are centrally configured (via NDS).

Chapter 2 described many of these technologies as general-purpose options for controlling the border. We hope you now have a better understanding of what these technologies can offer your intranet. As we move forward here, you can gain a better understanding of how they apply to Mudwhomp Flats High School.

Packet Filtering

As we explained earlier, the packet filter was one of the first security tools to emerge for the Internet. In simple terms, the packet filter is a guard on a moat. If you want to cross the moat, you first have to get past the guard. If the guard doesn't like your looks, too bad—you won't cross the moat. The problem with this type of filter is that your identity isn't even looked at to determine whether you pass the guard. The filter looks only at the protocol (such as HTTP) and either permits or denies access.

In the case of Mudwhomp Flats, using packet filters enables us to carry out several parts of our security policy:

> ► **Currently, no district data will be published (Policy Number 3).**
> Using one or more packet filters, we can prevent financial
> information, student records, and so on from being available via our
> Internet connection.

▶ **No remote access will be available (Policy Number 6).** We may want to prevent any access over the Internet, such as Telnet or FTP. Using a packet filter can prevent such access.

▶ **Protect access to school district financial information and records (Policy Number 7).** Again, access can be blocked from the outside using one or more packet filters.

As the needs of the security policy document change, so can our packet filter configuration. Bear in mind that because packet filters operate at such a low level in the hierarchy of protocols, they are an all-or-nothing protection. We cannot screen based on any type of identity, only by the type of data that we request.

Application Proxies

As engineers created advanced application environments using Internet technologies, we moved from protocol-oriented to application-oriented security models. Application proxies were developed to perform more advanced functions than we could with just protocols. A great example of the difference between protocol security and application security is HTTP.

As we already know, HTTP is used between a Web browser and a Web server to transfer information. With protocol security (such as a packet filter), we could shut off HTTP. Unfortunately, this is an all-or-nothing solution. No HTTP means no Web browsing. Application proxies enable us to be more specific: We can restrict HTTP to certain sites or by content.

Application proxies work at higher levels in the protocol stack than protocol filters. You've already learned a bit about application proxies in Chapter 2. In Chapter 8 you'll see how they are configured and set up using NWAdmin and BorderManager.

In the case of Mudwhomp Flats, we can use an application proxy to carry out more specifics of our security policy document:

▶ **Access from the district networks to the Internet (Policy Number 4).** Using an application proxy, we can govern, by user, who can and cannot access information on the Internet. In addition, we can decide which types of services (such as WWW or FTP) the individual can use.

▸ **No carte blanche access (Policy Number 5).** Using an application proxy, we can limit how much an individual can do on the Internet (similar to the last policy).

▸ **As new technologies and requirements appear, access may be expanded (Policy Number 15).** We can easily expand this Internet access through BorderManager and the graphical administration tool (NWAdmin).

In addition, content filtering of the scope provided by Cyber Patrol also enables us to further carry out the intent of our security policy. Because Cyber Patrol enables us to screen by content rating, we can further restrict undesirable Internet access.

Circuit Proxies

What has astounded almost everyone is the rate at which Internet technologies are being adopted. This rate has caused a well-known problem with connecting to the Internet — the dearth of IP addresses. As a result, we have circuit proxies.

Usually employed to help translate between IP and other protocols, circuit proxies have a unique side effect that can enhance the security of our networks when connecting to the Internet or other public networks. BorderManager includes several circuit proxies, such as the IP/IPX and IP/IP gateways.

The circuit gateways can also help us implement our security policy by limiting access to the district intranet. By masquerading as valid IP addresses, the circuit proxy prevents an unauthorized user from pinging internal addresses that might be hackable. Specifically, these policy statements could benefit the following policies:

▸ **No district data will be published (Policy Number 3).** An IP/IP or IP/IPX gateway can prevent unauthorized access to internal resources by putting on the appearance that valid IP addresses exist inside the firewall.

▸ **Access will be permitted from the district networks to the Internet (Policy Number 4).** A circuit gateway will permit access to the Internet while restricting what an outside user can contact inside the firewall. If an Internet user sees a district person's address and tries to FTP to it, it will get back an invalid address.

▶ **The district will implement procedures to protect the financial information and records (Policy Number 7).** A circuit gateway is another layer to protect the internal data while still providing availability internally.

▶ **If any security technologies should fail, access should be disabled automatically (Policy Number 8).** If the circuit gateway fails, no mapping of addresses will occur. Hence, the outside and the inside users will be cut off from each other. This means that if the circuit gateway fails, we go to a more secure state rather than a less secure state.

You may notice that several of these technologies will overlap with each other to form a layered approach to securing the system. This means that if one layer fails (such as the circuit gateway in the last example), we will lose only part of our protection. Extra layers maintain a majority of the security policy.

Virtual Private Networking (VPN)

With every major carrier—AT&T, MCI, Sprint, and the Baby Bells—becoming ISPs, it has become trivial to get Internet access anywhere in the United States. Companies maintaining lots of private lines to small branch offices are wondering, "Could we use the Internet instead?" One option for these companies is to buy a line from their branch office to the local Internet hookup, called a *point of presence* or POP. This is much cheaper than the same kind of WAN line back to the corporate offices. The big problem with buying a line is that your company data could be going places you'd rather it didn't.

Virtual private networking deals with this issue by creating an encrypted channel for your company across the Internet. BorderManager lets you build VPNs in your company during installation (see Chapter 5). In addition, we will cover some additional administration in Chapter 8. If you're looking for more descriptions of VPN, see Chapter 2.

VPN as a standard isn't much to look at these days, only because there aren't any pervasive standards yet. As another technology for our security policy, VPN has a lot to offer in cost savings and in extending our ability to connect. Using VPN to connect multiple district sites together, we can get security and connection at the same time.

Because we are connected to the Internet and we need to be connected to each other, a VPN to each site can enable us to carry this out securely and over the Internet.

Remote Access

Now that we have so much information available on our intranets, our users have this irrational desire to get at it from anywhere. Most companies feel uncomfortable with allowing that information to travel via the Internet, so few of them enable employees to retrieve it via their ISPs. Most companies want to control the access points into their networks; we'll spend some time talking about BorderManager and its capability to control remote-access solutions.

Remote access is different from normal dial-up access, which is usually accomplished via an ISP. You may, however, wish to provide direct dialup access to your own internal networks using your own modems. This is where remote access becomes involved with our security policy. We get several advantages when we implement it because:

▸ We don't permit remote access yet (Policy Number 6) but intend to in the future. Using remote access to dial directly into the district reduces security issues by coming in over the Internet.

▸ Administrators need to have access to the district networks regardless. This provides a high-speed option that they can use. No one can guarantee the speed of the Internet at any given time. Using our own modems, we can be assured that we'll go faster than a crawl when performing remote administration.

▸ We can require authentication as well as gain the security of coming in over a dial-up line instead of the Internet. Authentication standards are supported in BorderManager's remote dial-in feature set (such as CHAP and NWCAP).

Summary

In this chapter we've had a chance to see a little more of what's needed to provide a secure system tied to the Internet. Instead of just looking at technologies, companies and organizations need to look at how the Internet will be used and connected to maintain a secure yet productive environment.

When using BorderManager, there is a wealth of technologies included to secure all aspects of the border. Creating a security policy for that border should be one of the first actions a company takes to ensure a workable deployment. That security policy should be one that caters to the needs of the users while keeping the borders around the corporate or organizational data reasonably secure. If the policy is too strict, it will not be followed; if it is too loose, there may be significant risk.

Once created, technologies (such as BorderManager) can be used to enforce the edicts of the security policy. As such, the policy will (or should) be a living document that changes to fulfill the needs of the corporation or organization connected to the Internet.

With all that in mind, in the next chapter we'll take a look at how to manage day-to-day, the technologies provided by BorderManager.

CHAPTER 8

Administering BorderManager

In the preceding chapters, you learned about the many components contained in BorderManager, as well as the purpose of each of them. This chapter provides a basic reference for administering the components with examples of configuring BorderManager for several typical uses.

The purpose of this reference is not to reproduce the information provided in BorderManager documentation but to provide a concise explanation of which administration options are available with each of the tools.

Depending on which part of BorderManager you are managing, you will use one of two platforms. Options that are stored in NDS are configured through a set of snap-ins to the NetWare Administrator (NWAdmin). Options that only affect the server on which they are set can be configured through various utilities run from the server console.

Administering BorderManager Through NWAdmin

Many of the tasks necessary for administering BorderManager can take place from the NWAdmin console. This is usually the desired interface, as administrative tasks can be accomplished anywhere NWAdmin is available and the snap-ins have been installed.

Ideally, even the snap-ins can be centrally available on NetWare/Border servers, making day-to-day administration fairly flexible. One good way to ensure this is by using NAL (Novell Application Launcher) to deploy NWAdmin to administrators, thereby ensuring that the snap-ins and registry changes are always intact before NWAdmin is launched.

In this section, we are assuming that you have already installed BorderManager snap-ins for NWAdmin for Windows 95 and that you are familiar with administering NDS objects using NWAdmin. Refer to Chapter 5, Installing BorderManager, if you haven't already installed the snap-ins. This section will walk you through the new pages provided for Server, Organizational Unit and Organization objects, User, as well as the new monitoring view.

Administering Servers

The BorderManager snap-in set adds several new pages to server objects. These pages enable you to set up general BorderManager options and to configure the

Proxy, VPN, and Outgoing Rules. Although the pages show up on all servers, any server that does not have BorderManager installed will show the message "BorderManager is not installed or is not available on this server."

NOTE

NWAdmin enables the detail pages to be reordered so you can place the most-often-used detail page buttons at the top. If someone has already reordered the pages, the following detail pages may appear in a different order. In addition, if any snap-ins for BorderManager haven't been configured or could not be loaded, you won't see all of the described detail pages. The remedy (if you are the administrator) is to revisit Chapter 5 and install the snap-ins properly.

BorderManager Setup

The first of the detail pages in NWAdmin is the BorderManager Setup page. This is where you configure general BorderManager settings (see Figure 8.1).

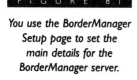

F I G U R E   8.1

You use the BorderManager Setup page to set the main details for the BorderManager server.

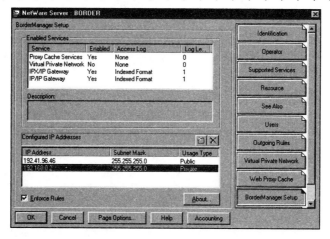

Enabled Services The top section of the page provides a list of available BorderManager services, showing whether the service is enabled and the logging options are selected. When you double-click any of the services in the list, a dialog box appears to configure the selected service (see Figure 8.2).

F I G U R E   8 . 2

Select a service from the list under the BorderManager Setup detail page to configure services, such as the IPX/IP Gateway.

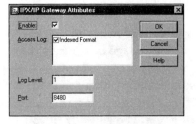

All services have a check box to enable the service, a list of available access-log formats, and a log-level edit box. The IPX/IP Gateway and IP/IP Gateway services also provide an edit box for setting the port number on which the gateway will operate. Proxy Cache Services permit the access log to be recorded in HTTPD Common Format, Extended Format, and Indexed Format. The other services only permit logging in Indexed Format. Refer to Chapter 5 for a description of the different log formats and log-level options.

The checkbox to enable the Virtual Private Network service is disabled unless you have configured VPN at the server, as described in Chapter 6. When you enable any of the services and close the detail pages, the snap-in will notify the server that the new service should be started. The first few times you turn services on from inside NWAdmin, you will likely feel the urge to watch the console and make sure the service is starting; over time this urge will diminish.

Configured IP Addresses The lower section of the page lists the configured IP addresses. For each entry, the list shows the IP address, its subnet mask, and its usage type. When you double-click an entry, or blank space, in the configured IP addresses list, the snap-in shows a dialog box (see Figure 8.3). This enables you to edit the elements of the selected entry or to configure a new entry.

F I G U R E   8 . 3

When configuring the BorderManager server, you can choose an address that is seen only internally (private), one that is seen externally (public)— or both.

Make sure the information you enter in the IP Address and Subnet Mask fields is correct. The snap-in does not validate incorrect masks. For the usage type of each IP address, you can select Private, Public, or Both. Private addresses are known only to hosts within your private internal network or intranet. Private addresses do not need to be valid or globally unique IP addresses. For added security, however, follow the guidelines described in Chapter 2 concerning RFC 1918, and regarding Network Address Translation (NAT) for private addresses.

Public addresses are globally unique, valid IP addresses registered by the InterNIC and assigned to you. This is the address exposed to the Internet for your server. Select Both if your server is known by the same address internally and on the Internet. Defining which interface is the private (or internal) side is important because the proxy server listens for requests only from the private interface(s). New addresses can also be defined by pressing the Insert key or clicking on the ⬚ button. You can delete addresses from the list by selecting the address and pressing the Delete key or clicking the ✗ button.

At the bottom of the page, you can select whether or not to enforce rules with the circuit gateways and proxy server. If this option is checked, the rules (defined in the Outgoing Rules pages of the selected server and containers in its tree) will be applied to requests for data through the gateways and proxy. Otherwise, all the rules will be ignored. To learn how to configure rules to apply to data requests, refer to "Outgoing Rules" later in this chapter.

The About button opposite the enforce rules option shows a dialog from which you can get information about the versions of the snap-in DLLs for BorderManager. This comes in handy when you're checking the revision levels of the snap-ins to make sure you have the latest updates.

Once the BorderManager components have been activated from the BorderManager Setup page, you can configure each service in more detail from the Web Proxy Cache, Virtual Private Network, and Outgoing Rules pages, as described in the following section. If you just configured IP addresses for this server for the first time, you will need to close the detail pages so the IP address information is written to NDS before you configure the active services.

Web Proxy Cache

The Web Proxy Cache detail page (see Figure 8.4) enables you to administer all aspects of the proxy server, including Internet Caching Protocol (ICP) hierarchy and reverse-proxy acceleration.

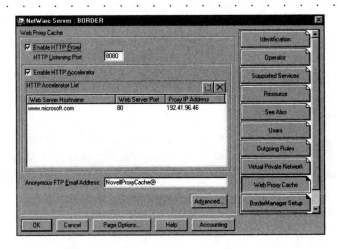

FIGURE 8.4

You can configure the Border Proxy from the Web Proxy Cache detail page in NWAdmin.

At the top of the page, you can Enable HTTP Proxy and set the HTTP Listening Port. The HTTP Listening Port is the port to which Web browsers will be configured to make proxy requests. When configuring your browsers, this will be the port used to contact the proxy server (BorderManager). Leave the listening port set to 8080 unless you have a conflict or other compelling reason to change it.

Just below the Enable HTTP Proxy box, you can enable and configure reverse proxy. Checking the Enable HTTP Accelerator causes the proxy server to act as a reverse proxy to cache specific Web servers.

Once you have enabled HTTP acceleration, the snap-in activates the HTTP Accelerator List. Each entry in the HTTP accelerator list displays the Web server host name, Web server port, and proxy IP address for the site being accelerated. When you double-click an entry, or blank space, in the HTTP accelerator list, the snap-in shows the dialog box that appears in Figure 8.5. This enables you to edit the elements of the selected entry or configure a new entry.

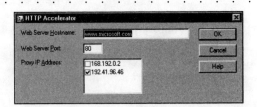

FIGURE 8.5

This dialog box enables you to enter information when adding a Web server that will be part of a reverse-proxy configuration.

In the Web Server Hostname field, enter the DNS name (or IP address) of the Web server you are accelerating. If possible, use DNS names so you won't have to come back and change your accelerator definition if the Web server providers change the IP host address.

The Web Server Port, usually 80, is where the Web server listens for HTTP requests. This is also the port on which your BorderManager proxy server will listen for requests for this Web site.

The Proxy IP Address list shows all IP addresses configured for the selected BorderManager server. Note that the list contains both public and private IP addresses. If you select only a private address, the acceleration will only be available within your private intranet. If you select only a public address, the acceleration will only be available to the Internet. To make the new HTTP accelerator available both internally and on the Internet, either select an IP address configured as both public and private, or select one public and one private IP address.

The proxy server can only accelerate one Web site on each proxy IP address/Web server port pair. If you want to accelerate more than one Web server operating on the default port 80, you must have one IP address configured for each accelerator you wish to define. The IP addresses must be configured through the BorderManager Setup page and bound to an existing network interface in your server, using INETCFG. For details of binding multiple IP addresses to network adapters, refer to the INETCFG documentation included with BorderManager.

NOTE

You can easily devise mirror Web sites by setting up an HTTP accelerator that specifies the origin Web server and port in the "Web server hostname" and "Web server port" fields, and then selecting one of your public IP addresses as the "Proxy IP address." The DNS entry that refers to the selected IP address can then be listed by the origin server as a mirror site for the accelerated host. Novell's mars.novell.com **is a good example of the advantages of a BorderManager-based mirror server.**

New accelerators can be defined by double-clicking blank rows in the HTTP accelerator list, pressing the Insert key, or clicking the ▓ button. You can delete accelerators from the list by selecting the accelerator in the list and pressing the Delete key or clicking the ✖ button.

At the bottom of the page, you can set your anonymous FTP e-mail address and display the Advanced configuration dialog box. The Anonymous FTP E-mail Address field enables you to specify an e-mail address, within your domain, that will be used for anonymous FTP requests from the proxy. This address is the password provided by the proxy's FTP client when making anonymous connections to remote FTP sites.

Advanced Web Proxy Cache Configuration Now we leave the realm of the ordinary administrator and enter the Advanced Web Proxy Cache Configuration dialog box. Fear not! This is where the fun begins. From the Advanced Web Proxy Cache Configuration dialog pages (see Figure 8.6), you can configure all the gory details of the proxy's advanced features: the proxy's cache, cache bypass, DNS, hierarchy, transport, and authentication.

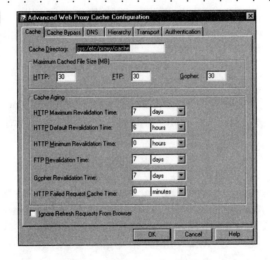

FIGURE 8.6

In the Advanced Option, under the Web Proxy Cache detail page, you can set a variety of options. The first tabbed option is the Cache page option.

▶ Cache

The Cache page enables you to set the location, size limits, and aging of the cache, and to deal with browser refresh requests. In the Cache Directory field, specify where the proxy will store the objects it is caching. If you have added a new volume for your proxy cache, specify that volume here. In the Maximum Cached File Size section, set the maximum file size you will cache for each of the supported protocols.

BorderManager 1.0 supports caching of HTTP, FTP, and Gopher files. Files smaller than the maximum specified for the protocol will be stored in the cache; files larger than the limit will be stored in the cache just long enough to fill the immediate request for the file. After this time, it will be removed from the cache.

The *Cache Aging* section is used to set several parameters. These specify how long data stays in the cache.

HTTP Maximum Revalidation Time specifies the maximum number of hours (or days) that any HTTP object can stay in the cache, even if the origin server specified a longer Time to Expire for some pages. Once a page has been in the cache for the maximum revalidation time, it must be reloaded from the origin server. If you want the origin server's Time to Expire settings to apply for all pages, set this value to a large number of days.

HTTP Default Revalidation Time sets the number of hours or minutes that a page with no Time to Expire set by the origin server is permitted to live in the cache.

HTTP Minimum Revalidation Time specifies a minimum time, in hours or minutes, that a file is kept in the cache, even if the origin server specified a shorter Time to Expire for a page. This setting will not apply to dynamic pages that the origin server has flagged with a No Cache or Must Revalidate directive.

FTP Revalidation Time sets the days (or hours) that FTP files are kept in cache before requiring a reload from the origin server. Because FTP does not provide any Time to Expire or related directives, this setting applies to all FTP files. There is no need for maximum or minimum override values.

Gopher Revalidation Time sets the days or hours that Gopher files are kept in cache before requiring a reload from the origin server. Because the Gopher protocol does not provide anything like a Time to Expire, this setting applies to all Gopher files.

The *Ignore Refresh Requests From Browser* option is used to specify whether browser reload commands should affect the proxy's cache. If the checkbox is set, the proxy will fill refresh requests from the cached data; otherwise it will clear the requested page from the cache and reload it from the origin server.

If your Web surfers are impatient, set this to ignore refresh requests. When they are loading a graphics-intensive page from a slow server, they can press the browser's stop button once most of the text is already loaded. The proxy will continue to load the page into its cache.

After they read all the text that made it to the browser before they got impatient, they can press the reload button. With the proxy set to ignore the reload request, their requests will be filled immediately. If the proxy was set to accept refresh requests, it would dump the page it had worked so hard to load after the Web surfers pressed stop and load the page again from the slow server.

▸   Cache Bypass

Many Web servers have a similar method of naming directories, or aliases, from which scripts are accessed. Because the HTML code resulting from a script request is usually dynamic, you don't want to cache pages loaded from script objects. The Cache Bypass page, shown in Figure 8.7, provides an easy way to exclude all pages that are addressed by similar patterns from your cache.

FIGURE 8.7

Under advanced options of the Web Proxy Cache detail page, another tabbed option is the Cache Bypass page. This enables custom URLs to bypass cache when necessary.

The cache bypass page contains a single list of *Non-Cacheable URL Patterns*, listing the access type and pattern to exclude from the cache. When you double-click an entry or blank row in the list, the snap-in shows the Non-Cacheable URL Pattern dialog box.

Access Type enables you to specify whether the pattern applies to HTTP, FTP, or Gopher requests. In the Pattern field, enter the text of the pattern that indicates a non-cacheable request. For example, to prevent all NetBasic scripts from being cached, specify /netbasic/ as the pattern.

New non-cacheable patterns can be defined by double-clicking blank rows in the pattern list, pressing the Insert key, or clicking the  button. You can delete patterns from the list by selecting the appropriate pattern in the list and pressing the Delete key or clicking the ❌ button.

▸ DNS

In order to find the files requested by clients, a proxy server needs to resolve DNS names to IP addresses. On the DNS page you can specify how your proxy server obtains DNS information and how long it will cache that information (see Figure 8.8).

F I G U R E   8.8

Another advanced option concerns DNS settings. This page enables protocol and Time-To-Live (TTL) options for DNS lookups.

In the *DNS Transport Protocol* section you can specify whether the proxy will make DNS requests over TCP or UDP. Unless you know that your DNS server is configured for TCP requests, leave this option set to UDP.

In *DNS Resolver Timeout*, you can specify the number of minutes (or seconds) that the proxy's DNS requester will wait for a response. After this time has elapsed, it determines that the request is not available and returns an error message to the client.

From the *DNS Time-To-Live* section, you set parameters for caching DNS information. Negative DNS Lookup specifies the number of minutes or seconds that a lookup timeout will be remembered. Instead of attempting to resolve each request for an unresolved DNS name, the proxy will simply return an error message to any subsequent request that comes within the negative DNS lookup time.

Maximum DNS Entry TTL sets the maximum time-to-live (TTL), in days (or hours) that any DNS entry will be kept in the proxy's cache. DNS entries that come from the origin server with TTL settings larger than the maximum DNS entry TTL value will be expired from the cache when the maximum DNS entry time expires. Entries with TTL values shorter than the maximum will expire according to their TTL value set at the origin.

Minimum DNS Entry TTL specifies the minimum number of seconds (or minutes) that a DNS entry is kept in the proxy's cache, even if the entry's TTL is set to a shorter time.

Maximum DNS Entry Threshold sets the maximum number of DNS entries that your proxy server will keep in cache. When this number of live entries is reached, the oldest entries will be expired to make room for new entries.

▸   Hierarchy

In earlier chapters you learned about BorderManager's support for Internet Caching Protocol (ICP)—based hierarchical caching (see Figure 8.9). This section describes the options that are available to configure your ICP neighborhood.

▸ . . . . ◂

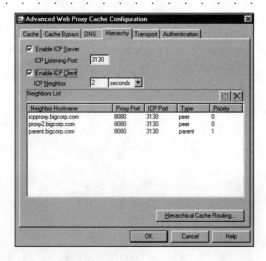

FIGURE   8.9

The advanced option, labeled Hierarchy, enables you to add one or more servers to the ICP list.

Enable ICP Server sets your cache up as an ICP server. Once it is enabled, you must also specify on which port it will listen for requests. ICP Listening Port sets that port.

Enable ICP Client permits your cache to make ICP requests of other servers. When selected, it enables the rest of the ICP options.

ICP Neighbor Timeout specifies the time your ICP client will wait for a reply from a neighbor before moving on to the next neighbor in the list (which is described next).

Neighbors List lists the hostname, proxy port, ICP port, type, and priority of each ICP server configured as a neighbor of your ICP client cache. These entries are created or edited by double-clicking a row in the Neighbors List. This brings up the Neighbor dialog box shown in Figure 8.10.

In the Neighbor dialog box, you can enter or edit information about an ICP neighbor:

▶ Hostname specifies the DNS name of the ICP neighbor.

▶ HTTP Proxy Port sets the port on which the neighbor services HTTP proxy requests.

▶ ICP Port identifies the port your ICP neighbor has set to service ICP requests.

▶ Type specifies whether the neighbor is a Peer, Parent, or CERN proxy.

▶ ICP Routing Priority can be set for parent and CERN proxies.

The *Hierarchical Cache Routing* button, at the bottom of the Hierarchy tab, brings up the Advanced ICP Cache Routing dialog shown in Figure 8.11.

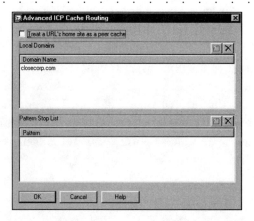

F I G U R E   8.11

Under Advanced Web Proxy Config, in the Hierarchy page, you can enter Web servers that will skip proxy. You can enter a pattern that, if matched, permits the request to bypass proxy cache.

From the advanced ICP cache routing dialog box, you can identify Web servers and request patterns that should not be retrieved through the cache hierarchy. You can also configure how BorderManager will deal with special types of origin servers.

Treat a URL's home site as a peer cache tells the proxy to pass requests on to the origin server as if it were specified as a peer to your cache server. Because this option potentially cuts off the parents and all of the cache hierarchy above them, you should leave this box unchecked.

Local Domains provides a list of origin domains that are closely connected on the logical network to your proxy server. These high-bandwidth links lie between Web servers on these domains and your proxy cache. The high-capacity link enables you to fetch requests to the listed domains quickly—directly from the origin servers—rather than searching the cache hierarchy. Double-click an entry or a blank row to edit an existing entry or create a new one.

If a pattern occurs in a URL, the *Pattern Stop List* enables you to list these patterns. The URL should be requested directly from its origin, rather than the cache hierarchy. Double-click an entry or blank row to edit an existing entry or create a new one.

▶   Transport

From the Transport page (shown in Figure 8.12), you can set TCP timeout values for the proxy server.

▶ · ◀

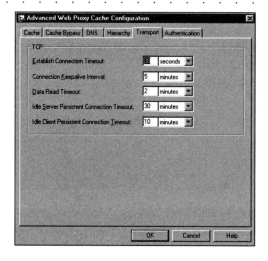

F I G U R E 8.12

Under Advanced Web Proxy Cache options, you can also specify how to handle TCP connections from the Proxy server to the connected Web servers.

Establish Connection Timeout sets the number of minutes (or seconds) that the proxy will wait when attempting to establish a new connection before timing out.

Connection Keepalive Interval specifies the interval (in hours or minutes) at which your proxy server will check in with the servers. It does this to verify which of those connections the server should continue to keep active.

Data Read Timeout sets the amount of time the proxy server will wait for data it has requested before abandoning the request.

Idle Server Persistent Connection Timeout sets the number of minutes (or hours) that your proxy will maintain persistent connections to browser clients before dropping them. The *server* part refers to the proxy acting as a server to the client connections.

Idle Client Persistent Connection Timeout sets the number of minutes (or seconds) that your proxy, acting as a requesting client, will maintain persistent connections to origin servers before dropping them.

▶ Authentication

The Authentication page provides settings to configure proxy authentication on your proxy server (see Figure 8.13).

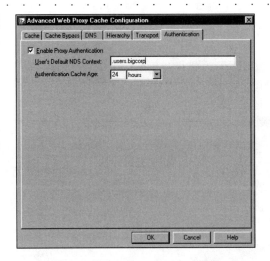

Users attempting to use the proxy server may be forced to identify themselves; this dialog box (under Advanced Web Proxy Cache Configuration) enables the administrator to require this authentication and a default NDS context to look for users attempting to authenticate.

Enable Proxy Authentication enables users, who are accessing the proxy server, to identify themselves to the server as NDS users. Without an NDS user to associate a connection with, user- and group-based restrictions cannot be enforced. Enabling proxy authentication causes the proxy server to present users with a login prompt when they establish a session with the proxy server.

User's Default NDS Context specifies the NDS container in which most users accessing the proxy server belong. Users in this context can log in to the proxy with a simple user name. Users that are not in the specified context must provide a fully distinguished NDS name to log in to the proxy.

Authentication Cache Age sets the number of minutes or hours that a user's authentication to the proxy will remain in the cache. After this time expires, the user will have to re-log in with the next proxy access.

Web Proxy Cache Summary Whew—That's a lot to cover at once! As you have now discovered, you have a *lot* of options when you're configuring the Proxy Server part of BorderManager. Ideally, you won't have to modify many of these parameters on a day-to-day basis, but you should be aware of your options.

Virtual Private Network

Unless you have already installed your VPN master server, as described in Chapter 5, this is going to be a boring page. If the master server has already been installed, the Virtual Private Network page (see Figure 8.14) enables you to configure your VPN, including adding new slave servers to the network.

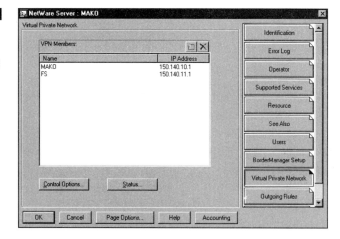

F I G U R E   8 . 1 4

Virtual Private Networking (VPN) partners and status information can be entered from the Virtual Private Networking detail page under NWAdmin.

VPN Members The VPN Members list contains the name and IP address of each server currently configured to participate in the private network. Initially, the list will contain only the master server. You can add new slave servers into the VPN by pressing the ▨ button.

All configuration of the slave server was performed at the slave server's console using VPNCFG. Thus, clicking the ▨ button just brings up the open file dialog box to locate the configuration file created by VPNCFG. If you haven't yet set up the slave server, refer to Chapter 6. It explains how to set up a VPN slave server and generate the file required by the snap-in.

Once the file is located and read, the snap-in displays a dialog box containing the message digest data generated by the slave server (see Figure 8.15). The numbers on this screen should be verified with the numbers displayed on the slave server's console, by running VPNCFG and selecting Slave Server Configuration Authenticate Encryption Information. If the numbers match—and they should—click the Yes button to complete the addition of the new slave. You can configure parameters for the VPN by double-clicking the master server's entry in the list to bring up the VPN Member dialog.

F I G U R E   8 . 1 5

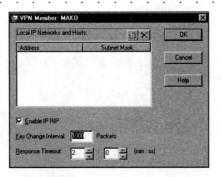

You can add other slave VPN servers from the Virtual Private Networking detail page under NWAdmin. By selecting the ⬚ button, you can set options that describe the slave to the rest of the VPN partners.

The *Local IP Networks and Hosts* section lists the static routes that have been defined for the VPN. All routes listed here are synchronized with all members of the VPN. There, they are merged with each server's routing table to permit encrypted data to be routed through the VPN tunnels to other VPN members. You should define static routes for your VPN if:

▶ You do not want VPN servers to exchange routing information. Because static routes reduce network traffic, they are typically used with on-demand connections between remote sites.

▶ You want to use your VPN for both site-to-site and site-to-Internet connections. In this case, having a static route prevents unencrypted traffic from reaching the Internet while the VPN is being established between sites.

To define static routes for your VPN, click the ⬚ button or double-click an empty row in the local IP networks and hosts list. The snap-in will display the Static Network Address dialog box shown in Figure 8.16.

Static routes (instead of
RIP-discovered routes) are
an option when adding a
new member to the VPN.

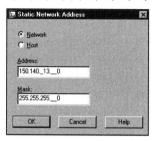

In the Static Network Address dialog box, you select whether the route is to a Network or a Host. Enter the IP address of the network or host being routed to in the Address field. For network routes, enter the network mask in the Mask field. If you haven't defined static routes, select the *Enable IP RIP* option to enable dynamic routing information to be sent across the encrypted tunnel to the other VPN members.

The *Key Change Interval* specifies how many packets can pass through the encrypted tunnel before the encryption key must be changed. The number of packets is randomly selected each time; they range from 75 percent to 100 percent of the key change interval value. If the key change interval is set too low, performance on your VPN will be noticeably degraded.

The VPN master controls the propagation of the new key information, as well as the key-change timing to the slave servers over the encrypted tunnel. The *Response Timeout* lets you determine how long the server will wait for a response from another VPN.

Control Options When you press the Control Options button on the Virtual Private Network page, the snap-in displays the Control Options dialog. From the control options dialog box, you can determine how your VPN will operate.

Select Protocols For Encryption provides options for choosing whether IP and IPX data will be encrypted and routed between the member server across the secure tunnel. *Connection Initiation* lets you choose whether only One Side or Both Sides of a VPN connection is permitted to initiate the connection.

VPN Network Topology sets your virtual private network's topology as full mesh, star, or ring topology, as follows:

▶ Full Mesh is the default topology. All servers are interconnected to form a web with only one hop to any VPN member. Direct communication is enabled between every member in the VPN, whether required or not. This topology is the most fault-tolerant.

▶ Star sets the master server as a hub, with all communications radiating outward to other servers and returning to the master server. This is the least traffic-intensive topology, but the master is the single point of failure.

▶ In a Ring configuration, each member communicates with its immediate neighbor. The ring loops from the master server to subsequent slave servers and back to the master server.

Update Interval specifies the frequency with which the master server attempts to contact the slave servers when topology, encryption, or other VPN settings need updating. The master tries to update the slave servers at the specified interval until the update succeeds.

Connect Timeout sets the amount of time the master will wait for a connection to a slave before determining that the slave server is unavailable. *Response Timeout* determines how long the master server waits for a response from a slave server before terminating the connection during a synchronization update.

Status When you press the Status button on the Virtual Private Network page, the snap-in displays the Synchronization Status dialog box. The list shows the current status of each server in your VPN. Possible states for the servers are as follows:

▶ Being Configured — The server still needs to receive the newest topology and encryption information.

▶ Up-to-Date — The last server update with the newest topology and encryption information completed successfully.

▶ Being Removed — The server is being removed from the VPN.

The synchronization status dialog box also provides access to auditing and activity information for your VPN. Press the Audit Log button to display the Audit Log dialog shown in Figure 8.17.

FIGURE 8.17

Detailed audit logs are provided as part of the VPN configuration; this details all information regarding one VPN partner and its status.

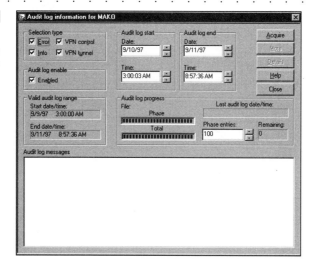

For details on how to set the options to show the auditing data just the way you like it, refer to BorderManager documentation or press the Help button. To display real-time statistics for your VPN, press the Activity button from the VPN Status Page. The Associated Connection box on the VPN activity dialog shows the current state of the protocol tunnels on the selected server (see Figure 8.18).

Activity of the VPN partner can also be obtained through NWAdmin and the Virtual Private Networking detail page.

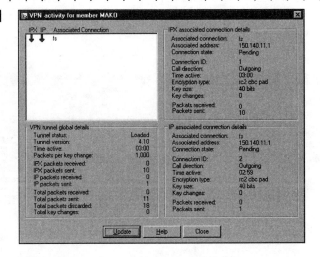

The red, green, or yellow arrows indicate data flow across the encrypted tunnel:

- Green—The encrypted tunnel is currently active between the selected VPN member and the associated connection. This arrow indicates that packets have been sent or received within the last 30 to 60 seconds.

- Yellow—The encrypted tunnel is currently pending between the selected VPN member and the associated connection. This arrow indicates that packets have been sent and received at one time, but not in the last 30 to 60 seconds.

- Red—The encrypted tunnel is currently down between the selected VPN member and the associated connection. This arrow indicates that packets have not been received across this encrypted tunnel. Check the Audit Log for both VPN members to determine why this encrypted tunnel is down.

Outgoing Rules

Outgoing Rules enable us to take advantage of the hierarchy provided by NDS and ease our jobs in managing the network services. The Outgoing Rules page on Server objects is also available on Organization and Organizational Unit objects.

The description contained here applies to the Outgoing Rules page on container objects, as well.

Enabling Outgoing Rules Before defining or editing rules, check the BorderManager Setup detail page to make sure the Enforce Rules option is enabled (see Figure 8.19). If that option is not set, none of the rules defined will be applied.

FIGURE   8.19

The Outgoing Rules page enables the administrator to decide which services are permitted outbound to users. Access is based on your NDS name and where you are in the tree.

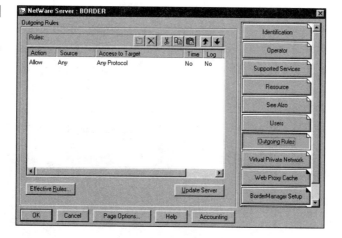

Rule Ordering and Determining Effective Rules The Rules section of the page lists all of the rules defined on the current object. It also provides tools to add, delete, cut, copy, paste, and change a rule's position in the list. The position a rule holds in the list is critical because it determines the rule's priority of application. BorderManager starts from the top of the list of effective rules and continues checking each rule against the current request until it finds a rule that matches the request. For example, you may have a rule that denies everyone access to http://www.girlymagazine.com, but if that rule is below a rule that grants Frank access to everything, Frank will have access to http://www.girlymagazine.com. You can see the list of effective rules by pressing the Effective Rules button.

Because rules are inherited through NDS containment, the effective rule set is a composite set built up from rules set on various NDS objects. The top of the list contains rules defined on the BorderManager server through which the access request is coming. From there, the order of priority starts from the BorderManager's container and works down to the root of the NDS tree.

If the requesting user is not authenticated through NDS, the rules that apply to a specific user or group will be ignored. At the bottom of every list of effective rules sits one default rule that cannot be deleted or modified. This catchall rule denies anyone access to anything. Unless the BorderManager rule manager finds a rule with higher priority than the default rule that permits the requesting user to access the destination site, it will deny the request.

You can edit an existing rule or create a new rule by double-clicking a rule, or empty row, in the rules list. Although the Rule Definition dialog box may appear a bit intimidating at first (see Figure 8.20), it is actually quite simple to define or edit a rule. Click the left-most button (next to the X) to create a new rule.

F I G U R E   8.20

You can create new Outgoing Rules with a variety of options, such as time restrictions, source addresses, and protocol access.

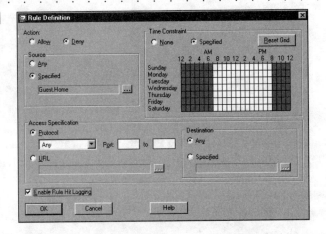

Action lets you choose whether the rule will Allow or Deny someone access to something. The *Source* section identifies which requesting clients will be affected by the rule, as follows:

► Any—This setting means that no matter who makes the request, the rule will apply if the destination matches.

► Specified—NDS User or Group enables you to select users or groups of users to whom the rule will apply.

▶ Specified—DNS Hostname enables you to provide one or more DNS names of requesting hosts to which the rule applies.

▶ Specified—Host IP Addresses specifies a single host, or range of hosts, that will be affected by this rule.

▶ Specified—Subnet Addresses applies the rule to a list of IP network/subnet mask addresses.

When you choose specified sources, any number of sources of any specified type may be added into the source list. The rule will be applied to all sources in the specified list.

The *Time Constraint* box enables you to select times when the rule will be effective. The time grid is based on the time zone of the administrator's workstation—it is assumed that the requesting client is in the same time zone as the BorderManager server. Therefore, you must adjust the hours if the server is in another time zone.

Access Specification controls which protocols, ports, or destinations are affected by this rule. The Protocol selection enables you to specify one of the standard Internet protocols to be managed. The Port fields enables you to specify a port, or range of ports, to which the rule will apply.

The URL entry enables you to manage a specific page on a particular Web site. From the URL selection dialog box (shown in Figure 8.21), you can also select Cyber Patrol categories to which the rule will apply.

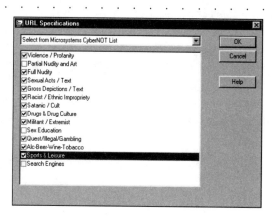

F I G U R E   8.21

You can deny access to rated sites using the Cyber Patrol add-on—these are a few sample restrictions you might use in a business environment.

The *Cyber Patrol* category selection is available only if Cyber Patrol has been installed at the server, as described in Chapter 5. When you select a category, all sites listed in the selected CyberNOT or CyberYES category are affected by the rule.

A specific Destination or Any destination must be selected for protocol- or port-based access controls. Specified destinations can include any combination of DNS hostnames, IP addresses, and Subnet addresses.

Enable Rule Hit Logging lets you choose whether or not access requests matching this rule are logged. This setting works only if logging is enabled on the circuit gateway, or the proxy through which the matching request was received.

To apply your newly defined set of rules immediately, press the Update Server button. If you don't press the button, the changed set of rules won't be applied until you close the detail pages. When the server reads the new rules, it may take a few minutes for all the changes to synchronize throughout the tree.

Managing Containers (Organizational Units and Organization Objects)

Organizational Unit and Organization objects have two new pages from which you can set parameters that apply to all objects within those containers. Attributes set in these pages use NDS inheritance to trickle down the tree to user objects. In other words, the changes here apply to all objects (such as users) in the selected container, and all containers below the selected container.

This is a tremendous asset for two reasons: first, with one rule set at the top of the tree, it will apply to all levels below (unless blocked). Second, if a user is dragged and dropped into a different container (where a different rule exists), the previous rule will no longer apply to that user while the rule of the new container will.

Outgoing Rules

The Outgoing Rules page is identical to the Outgoing Rules page for the server objects (see Figure 8.22). Refer to the preceding section for a complete description of options available in this page.

FIGURE 8.22

The Outgoing Rules detail page on an organizational unit (OU) is the same as that under the BorderManager setup detail page. Using it, you define rules for outbound access; once applied, the rule filters down into lower levels of the tree (unless blocked).

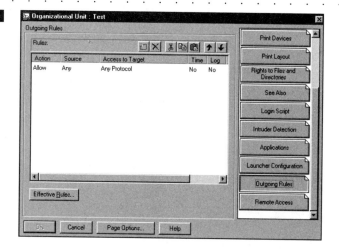

Remote Access

The Remote Access page provides settings specific to PPPRNS connections (see Figure 8.23). For details on setting up your remote-access services for PPPRNS, refer to Chapter 5 and the NetWare Connect documentation supplied with BorderManager.

FIGURE 8.23

The Idle Timeout section enables you to configure whether or not the users in this container (when connected by remote access), will be disconnected when a specified number of minutes pass without any data flowing across the connection.

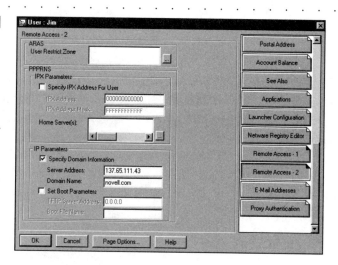

The *PPPRNS* section provides settings that control the IPX and IP addressing assigned to the user when the user connects through PPPRNS. The settings are as follows:

▸ The Specify IPX Address For User option enables you to force a specific IPX address to be assigned to a user each time he/she makes a PPPRNS connection that routes IPX data.

▸ If you select the Specify IPX Address option, you must specify the IPX Address and IPX Address Mask that will be assigned to the user.

▸ The Home Servers list lets you choose which server, or servers, the user will attach through when making dial-in connections. Press the ▨ button to modify this list.

▸ If you select the Specify Domain Information option, you can set the DNS Server Address that the user will use to resolve DNS names to IP addresses, and the Domain Name that will be appended to all local host names when resolving those names.

▸ The Set Boot Parameters lets you specify the TFTP Server Address that will be used for BOOTP requests, and the optional Boot File Name where the BOOTP information will be found.

Managing Users

When you install the BorderManager snap-ins for NWAdmin, three new pages appear on User objects. These new pages enable you to administer proxy-authentication and remote-access options for each user. If these options are already set in a container where the object (such as a user) exists, setting them may not be necessary. One reason to set them, however, is to override the default policy of the container. In this case, setting explicit policies on a user will affect only that user. Next, we will explore the options available in those three pages.

Proxy Authentication

The Proxy Authentication page lets you set up users to log in to the proxy server through Web browsers (see Figure 8.24). Those who are not using Novell's latest Client 32 with the IP gateway client can only identify themselves to the proxy through proxy authentication. If the proxy can't identify the NDS object making a request, it can't enforce user- and group-based rules.

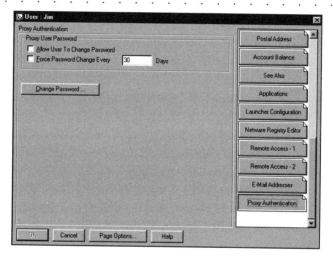

You can require a proxy authentication when a user attempts to use the BorderManager services; this can be configured on a user-by-user basis.

To avoid compromising the security of NDS passwords, proxy authentication uses a separate password. Because the proxy-authentication password will be passed over the wire to the proxy server in cleartext, it's not a good idea to enable the proxy authentication password to be set to the same password someone uses for NDS.

Allow User To Change Password lets users change their proxy login passwords from NWAdmin. If you leave this option cleared, only system administrators will be able to set proxy passwords for users. Permitting users to set their own passwords may be more convenient, but it's risky—some users will change their proxy-authentication passwords to match their NDS passwords.

Force Password Change Every x Days sets up the proxy server to make sure passwords are routinely changed. The Change Password button pulls up the Change Proxy User Password dialog box. The Change Proxy User dialog box has two fields to enter and re-enter the new password. If the two entries match, the password will be changed immediately.

Remote Access - 1 The first remote access page, aptly named *Remote Access - 1*, is shown in Figure 8.25. It enables you to configure password, connect time, timeout, and dial-back information for a single user.

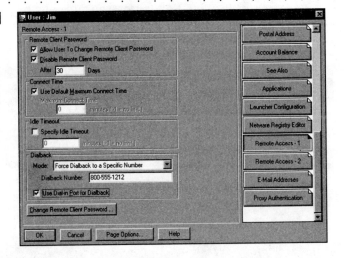

F I G U R E   8.25

You can configure remote options for users via NWAdmin. The first detail page, Remote - 1, enables you to configure dial-in and callback options.

The *Allow User To Change Remote Client Password* setting does just what it says. If this option is set, the user can run NWAdmin and change his or her own passwords. As with proxy authentication, remote access uses a separate password from NDS to avoid exposing the NDS password over unencrypted lines.

Disable Remote Client Password After x Days lets you expire remote-access passwords periodically, forcing changes at the specified interval.

Use Default Maximum Connect Time sets the amount of time the user is permitted to connect per day. If this is not set, an override value can be set.

Maximum Connect Time specifies a number of minutes per day that the user can access remote services. This value overrides the system default maximum connect time.

Set the Specify Idle Timeout option if you want the user's connections to remote access to be dropped if no activity occurs for the specified period of time. The number of minutes of inactivity can be entered when the set idle timeout option is checked.

Dialback controls whether the system must call the user back before connecting him or her to system resources. Dialback provides additional security to your dial-in service. Select the option that fits the remote-access needs of the user and still meets the security requirements of your company.

If dialback mode is set to Force Dialback to a Specific Number, enter that number in the Dialback Number field. Doing so restricts the user from accessing dial-in remote services from anywhere but the specified phone number.

If a dialback option is selected, you can choose Use Dial-in Port for Dialback to force remote-access services to use the same modem port from which the user called. The *Change Remote Client Password* button pulls up a change password dialog, prompting you to type and retype the new password for this user.

Remote Access - 2 The second remote access page added to user objects, *Remote Access - 2*, provides settings specific to ARAS and PPPRNS connections for the user (see Figure 8.26). There are two Remote Access pages available under a User object. They permit the configuration of AppleTalk Zone restrictions, dial-in network address assignments, and IP dial-in parameter configurations. The *PPPRNS* section is identical to the PPPRNS section of the Remote Access page on container objects—OUs and Os.

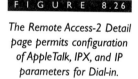

FIGURE 8.26

The Remote Access-2 Detail page permits configuration of AppleTalk, IPX, and IP parameters for Dial-in.

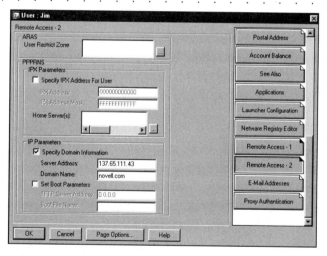

ARAS User Restrict Zone lets you specify AppleTalk zones to which the user will be restricted during ARAS connections. Click the browse button next to the User Restrict Zone field to display the Edit User Restrict Zone List dialog and modify the list of restricted zones.

BorderManager Monitor View

Included among the BorderManager snap-ins to NWAdmin is the BorderManager Monitor snap-in, shown in Figure 8.27. This snap-in provides real-time monitoring of the status and activity on the primary BorderManager services: Virtual Private Network, Proxy Cache, and IP Gateway. To access the BorderManager Monitor from the NWAdmin browser window, select a server object that has BorderManager installed, and then select Novell BorderManager from the Tools menu.

NOTE

The BorderManager Monitor snap-in that shipped with the initial release of BorderManager, BSMON.DLL dated 7/2/97, had a memory leak that would deplete your system memory if NWAdmin was left running for an extended time. Be sure to download the latest BorderManager patches from Novell to correct this problem.

F I G U R E   8.27

The options off of the NWAdmin Toolbar enable you to monitor different BorderManager services.

Service	Status	Up Time	Version
Virtual Private Network	Down		
Proxy Cache	Down		
IP Gateway	Up	1 day 14:00:52	4.2.19

You can display detailed information for each service by double-clicking the service from the main monitor list.

Monitoring VPN

Double-clicking the Virtual Private Network entry brings up the VPN monitor shown in Figure 8.28. From the VPN monitor you can examine the up-to-date statistics of VPN activity.

F I G U R E   8.28

The VPN monitor enables you to monitor active connections and traffic throughput under NWAdmin.

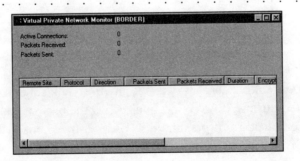

If you click the right mouse button, a context menu appears from which you can choose to View Member Activity/Log for more detail on a particular member of the VPN.

Monitoring Proxy/Cache

When you double-click the Proxy Cache entry in the monitor list, the snap-in will display the Proxy Cache Monitor screen (see Figure 8.29).

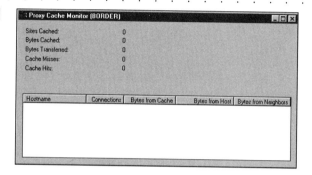

FIGURE 8.29

The Proxy Cache Monitor under NWAdmin enables you to monitor cached sites and host information.

Options on the context menu in the Proxy Cache monitor enable you to view the proxy log files in common, extended, or audit format, as well as showing cache statistics. The available log files and the level of detail entered into those logs is controlled from the BorderManager Setup page on the proxy server object. The Statistics dialog box provides pages to show you the statistics for connections, DNS, HTTP, FTP and Gopher activity (see Figure 8.30).

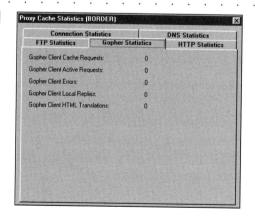

FIGURE 8.30

There are five different statistic types you can monitor for Proxy services under NWAdmin with the BorderManager snap-ins.

Monitoring Circuit Gateways

Double-click the IP Gateway service in the BorderManager monitor to display the IP Gateway Monitor screen shown in Figure 8.31.

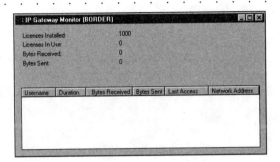

F I G U R E   8.31

You can monitor information about the IP/IP gateway under NWAdmin, including active users.

This screen shows the current data for all active gateway users. If you want to view historical activity through the gateway, select View Audit Log from the context menu. The IP Gateway Access Statistics screen displays the audit log sorted by user (see Figure 8.32). This way, you can see just how many times Frank has accessed http://www.girlymagazine.com, and how many bytes have been transferred from the site.

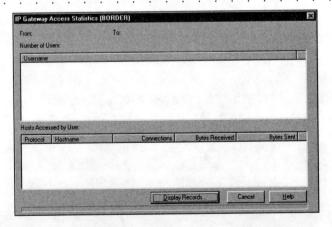

F I G U R E   8.32

Other options you can monitor for the IP/IP gateway include which hosts have been accessed, and which users are active.

Viewing Logs

From any of the monitor context menus, you can select the Novell BorderManager submenu. This submenu enables you to access various log viewers.

Access Control Log The Access Control Log viewer is shown in Figure 8.33. This lists every access request (that met the parameters of a rule defined through the Outgoing Rules pages) if the rule definition set the log access flag.

FIGURE 8.33

The BorderManager snap-ins also enable you to monitor access controls by rule.

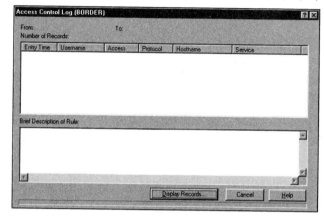

Packet Filtering Log The Packet Filtering Log viewer displays information about the activity of filters. These are specified in the filter, or exception, lists defined through FILTCFG, that had logging enabled (see Figure 8.34).

FIGURE 8.34

If logging is enabled, you can trace which packets meet the filter criteria by viewing the packet filter log under NWAdmin.

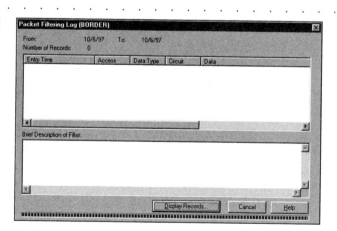

Information Logs The Information and System Logs viewer displays the BorderManager information log and the SYS$LOG.ERR log. This enables viewing of both the server-specific error logs and BorderManager logging information.

Administering BorderManager Server-Side Configurations

There are times when it is necessary to manage components that can only be accessed from the server console. When this happens, there are several ways to load the required utilities and manage the system, including the following:

▶ Run the RCONSOLE utility, provided that the REMOTE.NLM and RSPX.NLM modules have been loaded at the server in question (and you know the password!).

▶ Dial-in via the asynchronous dialup support built into RCONSOLE and REMOTE.NLM. This is extremely useful for field-based support.

▶ Go directly to the server console, load the utility, and run it.

The components that must be managed at the server console aren't items that will change everyday (such as handling packet filters, NAT tables, and clearing the proxy cache). You might be assigning new Outgoing Rules on a daily basis—if you have a growing network. Fortunately, Outgoing Rules are configured using NWAdmin.

NOTE Novell plans to provide the option to configure the rest of the server options (such as packet filters) using **NWAdmin** and **NDS.** This would obviate the need to **RCONSOLE** the server, or manually run the utilities, from the server console.

Configurations Performed at the Server

There are several proxy-server management options that can be done only at the server, and require you to either run RCONSOLE or access the server. They include:

▸ configuring packet filters

▸ configuring the NAT (Network Address Translation)

▸ installing remote services

▸ generating keys used by VPN (Virtual Private Networking)

▸ installing new network boards, WAN cards, and binding protocols

Several of these options have already been covered in Chapter 5, so we won't be covering them here. Some (like Packet Filter setups) aren't necessarily done everyday, but they may need to be configured more often than installing a new WAN or LAN board. Descriptions of screening routers and bastion hosts, as well as the need for both, are covered in Chapters 1 and 2.

In Table 8.1 is a summary of functions and the server-side utilities that manage them.

TABLE 8.1	SERVER-SIDE PROXY SERVER MANAGEMENT UTILITIES	
In some cases, you'll need to use server-side utilities to manage aspects of BorderManager. These are usually one-time setup options, or components that are seldom configured. Most day-to-day administration is done using NWAdmin. This table summarizes the functions that may require the use of a server-side utility.	**FUNCTION**	**SERVER-SIDE UTILITY**
	Create and maintain server-centric packet filters: this is used to strengthen the firewall at the server.	FILTCFG
	Enable IP/IPX protocol options, enable packet filtering, and add new LAN/WAN boards.	INETCFG
	Create new keys for Virtual Private Networking (VPN) master and slaves.	VPNCFG
	Configure remote ports for dial in/out. Configure support for AppleTalk, IP, and IPX dial in.	NIASCFG

Configuring BorderManager as a Screening Router

Packet filters are implemented on routers. Routers with filtering capabilities are commonly called *screening routers*, and sometimes, *chokes*. Because the screening router is actually a router, packet filtering can take place in a number of ways, depending on where you place the filtering router (or routers).

As an administrator, you may be called upon to modify or install packet filtering on your BorderManager server. As we stated earlier, you may not have to do this everyday, but you'll likely do it more than once.

Types of Filters

How do we configure BorderManager to be a screening router for a Web server host? This depends on what type of screening router we want. BorderManager can filter packets based on one, or several, criteria as follows:

▸ restricting IP traffic by routing (inbound/outbound RIP and EGP, as well as OSPF external routes), and packet forwarding (one of the most common)

▸ restricting IPX packets inbound (RIP/SAP), outbound (RIP/SAP), and NetBIOS packets

▸ restricting Source Routing by Protocol ID or Ring Number

▸ packet filtering AppleTalk packets—incoming, outgoing, and restricting visibility to certain devices

Now you may be configuring your routers (borders) to allow/deny propagating routing information or service broadcasts across the Internet. At the very least, you'll be configuring the services that are accessible from the Internet. The best way to configure them is by creating a packet-forwarding filter.

Configuring a Sample IP Packet-Forwarding Filter
A screening router is commonly used with IP packet-forwarding filters. The filters permit service requests to go to the Web server—but very little else. To configure the BorderManager as a screening router, we must tell the router that we need to create some filters.

We should have a filter that denies all incoming requests of any protocol, except HTTP (which will be permitted to our bastion host, only). In this case, the bastion host is hosting a Web server. We also need to permit our network's HTTP users to browse the Internet.

. At this point, we've already installed BorderManager. The utility used to configure all packet filters is called FILTCFG.NLM. It must be run on the BorderManager console. We'll assume that your WAN link is already configured. In our example, the WAN link is a dialup modem to our ISP.

We must enable TCP/IP filtering in two places. First, it should be enabled for the NetWare TCP/IP protocol stack, and second, we must enable and configure a TCP/IP filter (see Figure 8.35). Several steps must be taken to do this, including the following:

1 • Enable IP Filtering Support using the NetWare INETCFG.NLM utility.

2 • At the Border Manager console, run INETCFG. You may use the NetWare RCONSOLE utility if you like.

3 • Choose the Protocols option from the Internetworking Configuration menu of INETCFG.

4 • Select "TCP/IP" from the Protocol Configuration menu.

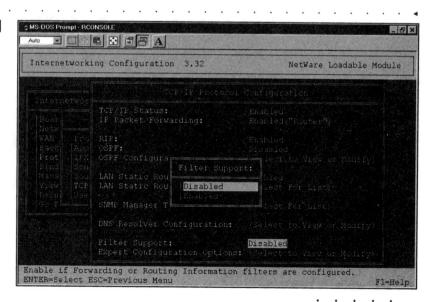

FIGURE 8.35

You must first enable packet filters in INETCFG before any configured ones can take effect.

5 • Select Filter Support from the TCP/IP Protocol Configuration menu and choose the Enable option. Press Enter to save.

6 • Exit TCP/IP configuration by pressing Esc and choosing Yes to the question "UpdateTCP/IP Configuration?"

7 • For this to take effect, you need to choose the Reinitialize System option from the main Internetworking Configuration menu.

Configuring TCP/IP Filters Using FILTCFG To configure TCP/IP filters with FILTCFG, run FILTCFG.NLM on the BorderManager console. (You may use the NetWare Remote Console facility if you like.) Then choose Configure TCP/IP Filters from the main Filter Configuration Available Options menu.

To enable TCP/IP filtering, choose Packet-forwarding filters from the TCP/IP menu. Then, enable Packet-forwarding filters by changing the status to Enabled. Upon enabling packet-forwarding filters, you will see the message shown in Figure 8.36.

F I G U R E   8 . 3 6

When packet filtering has been enabled, the default will prevent any packets from being forwarded. The next step is to define the filters desired.

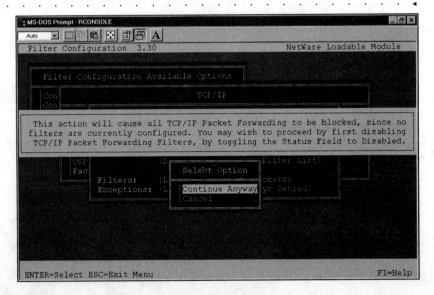

Not to worry. You don't have any filters defined to pass any TCP/IP packets across the router. As a result, no packets will be forwarded at all; however, we are about to correct this so choose Continue Anyway.

Finally! Now this is where the fun starts. There are two ways to configure packet filters. We can open the floodgates and say that everything is permitted, except those items we explicitly deny, or we can shut down everything except that which we explicitly permit. If you open the floodgates and try to lock down everything by hand you will miss some things and, of course, that will be the window through which the hacker will slip. We want to lock everything down. Choose Permit Packets in Filter List, to permit only those types of packets that we choose.

Now we need to tell BorderManager what types of packets we care about. We want to create five filters. One will permit HTTP to and from the Internet over UDP or TCP, another two will permit DNS (over TCP and UDP) and ICMP from the Internet to our network. Select List of Permitted Packets and press Enter to look at the list.

At the moment, the list is empty so press Insert to create a new filter.

The first thing you can configure is the source and destination interfaces. This may be necessary if you have more than one WAN connection and more than one LAN interface in your server. For our example, leave it at the default (Interface and All Interfaces) setting.

Highlight Packet Type and press <enter>. At this point, you'll see many different packet types you can filter on. Select www-http. This will filter Web requests coming over TCP.

Under Source and Destination, you can select a particular host, a range of hosts (network), or ALL addresses. This way, we can restrict at a very granular level who can come in via our border, and to which (destination) Web server they can connect. Remember that we are defining this as an ALLOW filter. Therefore, any packet that matches these criteria will be permitted.

You can also choose to select Logging, which enables you to see which packets met the criteria and were permitted in.

To complete our sample, we need to create several more rules to permit the following packet types: www-http/udp, domain, domain/tcp, icmp (see Figure 8.37). This way, consumers of our Web servers can come in either with UDP or TCP (HTTP) and resolve DNS names either over TCP or UDP, and ping our servers to see if they're alive (ICMP).

With that, we have completed a basic rule set to accomplish our security goals. We will provide Web access to all of our Web servers while denying all other services (such as FTP, TFTP, and Telnet).

F I G U R E   8.37

Once packet filtering has been enabled, FILTCFG enables you to create one or more filters on the router.

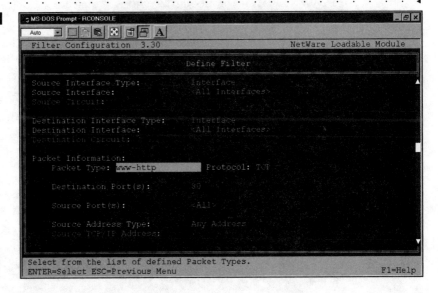

Configuring a Sample NCP Packet Forwarding Filter   The threat of an attack (from the Internet into an intranet) is greatly reduced with NetWare NCP (NetWare Core Protocol) services. However, you may need to deny services to certain outside hosts in some instances (this might be the case if you are using IP throughout your entire intranet). If you are, a NetWare IP client could attempt to gain access to NetWare NCP server over the Internet via BorderManager (provided the hacker has either a password for an established user, or has figured out how to crack RSA public/private key pairs—highly unlikely!).

If NetWare services are provided over IPX, the threat is even further reduced. Internet hosts can't even talk to the NetWare services if they are not being provided over IP.

NOTE

Enabling NCP packet-forwarding filters is similar to setting them for IP. The following steps must be completed to effectively create an NCP Filter:

1 • In INETCFG, select Protocols, and then select IPX.

2 • Select Filtering Support and set it to Enabled. This merely tells the server to look at any packet filters that have been set up in INETCFG (as with TCPIP filters).

3 • To create filters, you must run FILTCFG and create the necessary filters.

4 • Load FILTCFG at the server or via RCONSOLE.

5 • Choose Configure IPX Filters.

6 • Choose NetBIOS and Packet Forwarding Filters.

7 • Under Status, choose Enabled.

8 • Under Packet Forwarding Filters, choose Deny Packets in Filter List.

9 • Choose Filters.

10 • The filters may be empty if this is a new system. To create a filter, press the Insert key.

At this point, you have a screen similar to the IP Packet Forwarding Filters screen. You can screen based on Source and Destination addresses if you have more than one WAN board and one LAN board.

11 • Select Packet Description. At this point, you have a variety of NCP services that you can deny (because that's how we set the rule). To prevent requests from getting server info, choose NCPGetServerInf (see Figure 8.38). We can now restrict to an IPX network address, or a fully distinguished IPX address (network and node address).

12 • If you wish to enable logging for packets matching this rule, select Enabled under Logging. At this point, you have an NCP filter that will prevent nodes from gaining information about your server. Note that anyone inside the firewall won't have problems accessing information because they won't be going through BorderManager. Any potential intruders, however, will be stopped at the border!

F I G U R E   8.38

NCP packet filters can be created providing an extra layer of protection against unwanted intruders.

Route Filtering

As discussed, another way to filter packets is by route. This delves into the way routers exchange information about other routers in the infrastructure. Why is this important? There are two reasons:

▶ Inbound filters keep the intranet routers from displaying other networks on the Internet.

▶ Outbound filters will keep other Internet hosts from knowing what network addresses you publish internally.

Ideally, you should prevent this by fully disabling any route propagation (IP or IPX) externally. Then use static routing (described in Chapter 5) to give enough information to the routers on the other end for communications purposes.

A Sample Outbound-IP Route Filter Because the filters are so similar, we will show just an IP-outbound route filter. To create and activate such a filter, follow these steps:

1 • Under INETCFG, enable filters under the Protocol option just like a Packet Forwarding Filter. If you haven't enabled this already, you must issue a Reinitialize System request for the setting to be active.

2 • Load FILTCFG.

3 • Choose Configure TCP/IP Filters.

4 • Choose Outgoing RIP Filters.

5 • Choose Enabled for the status.

6 • Choose the allow/deny option. The default is Deny Routes in Filter List. This means all other routes will be permitted. Conversely, you can enable only routes in the list. To make the border as secure as possible, choose Permit Routes in Filter List.

7 • Choose Filters.

8 • To insert a new filter, choose Insert (from the keyboard).

9 • To do this, first choose the target filtered route; All Routes is the default setting. You can choose a specific host address, network address, or all. Typically, you will deny/allow based on a network address.

10 • Next, you can choose where the chosen network/host addresses will be advertised to by LAN/WAN interface. This means you can allow/deny to the intranet as well as to the Internet.

11 • Advertised Hop Count (shown in Figure 8.39) enables you to increase the cost of the address. Using this option, you can prevent this address from being chosen by a router by choosing a high cost.

12 • Last, of course, you can choose to enable logging of packets that match the criteria of the filter.

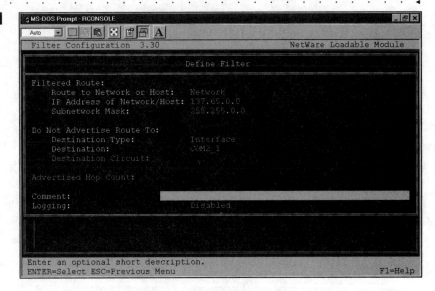

FIGURE 8.39

Route Filters (such as this outbound-IP filter) prevent unauthorized users from seeing internally advertised routes in the intranet.

One thing to be aware of when creating route filters (particularly with Novell Directory Services) is that you may prevent one node from communicating with another—even though you want them to communicate. Following is an example:

You have a NetWare service advertised (such as an NDS tree) on a server. You have denied advertisement of a RIP (IPX) route that one NDS server requires to talk to the advertising server in the tree. You will get service advertisements from the NetWare/NDS server, yet not be able to reach it because you cannot determine the route to that server.

Filtering IP RIP/EGP traffic is usually less of a consideration. Static routes are typically used and no service, such as NDS on the Internet, needs such full connectivity. With the intranet, however, beware!

Service Filtering (NetWare NCP)

If you have an Internet focus, skip this section. This pertains to internal users of NetWare and BorderManager.

SAP (Service Advertising Protocol) is a service that is used to enable a client to find services (such as NetWare servers, Print Servers, and so on) on the LAN. Since NDS became available, Novell has significantly reduced its dependency on SAP (but a number of services still use it). The problem with SAP is that it advertises every 60 seconds (configurable, in INETCFG) to all other routers on each LAN segment to which the router is attached. In some cases, therefore, SAP filtering is used to reduce network traffic. Of course when you do that, some clients (on the other side of the BorderManager server) won't see the services that have been filtered.

The following scenario offers a good example of when SAP filtering could be used:

At a law office, each group of lawyers on a project is on its own network segment. Each group also has its own set of printers, which use SAP to announce their presence. For confidentiality reasons, none of the groups share printers.

In this case, the BorderManager (or NetWare router) between each lawyer group could filter printer advertisements. This is a very simplistic example, but you get the general idea.

A Sample SAP Filter

Let's set up this particular scenario. In the following steps, we create a SAP filter to prevent a SAP advertisement from being propagated (see Figure 8.40).

1 • Once again, using INETCFG, choose Protocols and select Enable under Filtering Support. Then choose Reinitialize System for the change to take affect.

2 • Load FILTCFG.

3 • Choose Configure IPX Filters.

4 • Choose Incoming SAP Filters.

5 • Choose Enable under Status.

6 • Under Action, be sure that Deny Services in Filter List has been set (this denies the service we specify from being advertised).

7 • Choose Filters and press the Insert key to create a new filter.

8 • Under Service Type, enter the advertising number that identifies the service. To simplify this, highlight the field for Service Type and press the Insert key. A noncomprehensive list of defined types will appear. Choose Advertising Print Server.

If you want to block advertisements from a specific LAN/WAN card, you can select a particular interface from the Destination option. For our purposes, we'll leave it at the default.

Note that we could create an Exception filter. We may do this to advertise the print servers to a segment the administrator's workstation resides on. This would enable you to manage from a workstation not attached to the same segment as the print servers.

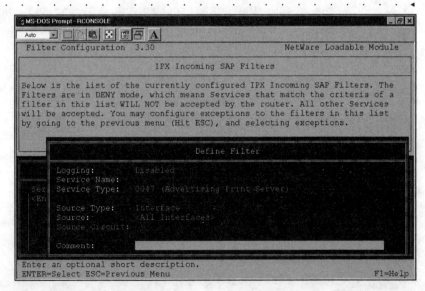

An important thing to note is that we blocked all incoming Print Server Advertisements. If we had merely kept our print servers from advertising, we would have to trust that the other lawyer groups had properly filtered their print servers (unless we set up more filters, of course). By blocking the advertisement inbound, we are guaranteed to have external advertisements filtered.

Summary of Server-Only Administration Tools

As previously discussed, your day-to-day administration of BorderManager can be done via NWAdmin. For those times when seldom-configured components need to be tweaked, you know where to go and what to do. A significant amount of documentation is included with BorderManager and can guide you on further filtering options. Now that we've covered the administration of the BorderManager server, we'll discuss the measures you must take to ensure the browser can take advantage of it.

Configuring Web Browsers to Use the Proxy

Before your users can access Internet Web sites through Proxy Cache Services, you need to configure their Web browsers to use the Novell BorderManager proxy server. This section describes the required configuration for the most popular browsers on Windows platforms. If your users have other browsers, refer to the browser's documentation to specify where Proxy servers are configured.

Netscape Navigator

BorderManager ships with the Netscape Navigator browser. To configure it for use with the proxy server, select Network Preferences from the Options menu. This displays the Preferences dialog box, from which you choose the Proxies tab. On the Proxies tab, select Manual Proxy Configuration and press the View button to display the Manual Proxy Configuration dialog box (see Figure 8.41).

To use the BorderManager Proxy, you need to configure the browser to contact the proxy server by DNS name or IP address.

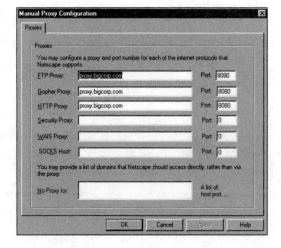

In the FTP Proxy, Gopher Proxy, and HTTP Proxy fields, enter the host name and proxy listening port of your proxy server. After you click OK to dismiss both dialog boxes, your browser is configured for proxy access to your proxy server.

Netscape Communicator

Netscape Communicator is configured almost the same as Navigator; the difference is that the options have been moved. From the Edit menu, select Preferences to display the preferences dialog box shown in Figure 8.42. In the Category list, expand Advanced and select the Proxies option.

F I G U R E   8.42

To use the BorderManager Proxy server, you need to configure the Communicator browser to point at the Proxy server by DNS Name or IP address.

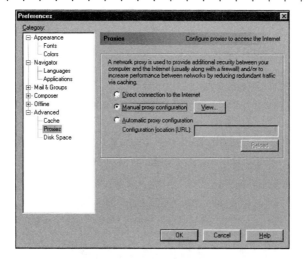

From here, the process is the same as it is for Navigator. Select Manual Proxy Configuration and press the View button to display the Manual Proxy Configuration dialog. In the FTP Proxy, Gopher Proxy, and HTTP Proxy fields, enter the host name and proxy listening port of your proxy server.

Netscape Automatic Proxy Configuration

You can also configure Netscape Navigator and Communicator for Automatic Proxy Configuration. This enables you to write a JavaScript routine that will provide the browser with the proxy information for each URL request. For information on writing the auto-configuration script, refer to:

```
http://home.netscape.com/eng/mozilla/2.0/relnotes/demo/proxy-
live.html.
```

After writing your script and saving it on a Web server that has the application/x-ns-proxy-autoconfig mime type configured, follow the previous steps to get to the proxy dialog. Instead of choosing Manual Proxy Configuration, choose Automatic Proxy Configuration and enter the URL to your script file. Now, each time the browser starts, it will load the script from your Web server. Then, the URL for each request will be passed to the script's FindProxyForURL routine.

This can be a tremendous time-saver, however, you must have configured the browser at least once to use a proxy server (manual or automatic). The difference is that once you have configured a browser (or browsers) to use automatic proxy, you need only update the proxy script to reconfigure one, ten, or a thousand browsers!

Microsoft Internet Explorer

To configure proxy access in Microsoft's browser (Internet Explorer 4.0, or IE4), select Internet Options from the View menu to display the Internet Options dialog box. In the Internet options dialog box, click the Connection tab (shown in Figure 8.43) and select Access the Internet using a proxy server.

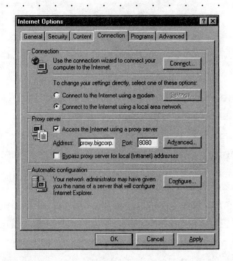

F I G U R E   8.43

Point to the proxy server by DNS Name, or IP address, under Connection/Internet Options to make Internet Explorer point to a BorderManager Proxy server.

Enter your proxy server's Address and Port into the appropriate fields, and you are set. You can also configure Internet Explorer 4 to use the same automatic-proxy configuration scripts that you use for Netscape Communicator. To do so, press the Configure button in the Automatic Configuration section at the bottom of the connection tab. This brings up the Automatic Configuration dialog box which enables you to enter a URL to the proxy configuration script.

Summary

What a lot of territory! If you have read this book sequentially, our hats are off to you! We've covered a significant amount of management tasks that deal with day-to-day administration in this chapter.

From here, the best thing to do is delve into BorderManager documentation. Take advantage of the many books that address border management, proxy servers, firewalls, and so on. One suggestion: the best approach is to install BorderManager in your nonproduction laboratory and get to know all the features we have discussed in these chapters.

The IP Network Address Translator (NAT)

Network Working Group
Category: Informational
By K. Egevang, P. Francis, Cray Communications
May 1994

Status of this Memo

This memo provides information for the Internet community. This memo does not specify an Internet standard of any kind. Distribution of this memo is unlimited.

Abstract

The two most compelling problems facing the IP Internet are IP address depletion and scaling in routing. Long- and short-term solutions to these problems are being developed. The short-term solution is CIDR (Classless InterDomain Routing). The long-term solutions consist of various proposals for new internet protocols with larger addresses.

It is possible that CIDR will not be adequate to maintain the IP Internet until the long-term solutions are in place. This memo proposes another short-term solution, address reuse, that complements CIDR or even makes it unnecessary. The address reuse solution is to place Network Address Translators (NAT) at the borders of stub domains. Each NAT box has a table consisting of pairs of local IP addresses and globally unique addresses. The IP addresses inside the stub domain are not globally unique. They are reused in other domains, thus solving the address depletion problem. The globally unique IP addresses are assigned according to current CIDR address allocation schemes. CIDR solves the scaling problem. The main advantage of NAT is that it can be installed without changes to routers or hosts. This memo presents a preliminary design for NAT and discusses its pros and cons.

Acknowledgments

This memo is based on a paper by Paul Francis (formerly Tsuchiya) and Tony Eng, published in Computer Communication Review, January 1993. Paul got the concept of address reuse from Van Jacobson.

Kjeld Borch Egevang edited the paper to produce this memo and introduced adjustment of sequence-numbers for FTP. Thanks to Jacob Michael Christensen for his comments on the idea and text (we thought for a long time that we were the only ones who had the idea).

1. Introduction

Until the long-term solutions are ready, an easy way to hold down the demand for IP addresses is through address reuse. This solution takes advantage of the fact that a very small percentage of hosts in a stub domain are communicating outside of the domain at any given time. (A stub domain is a domain, such as a corporate network, that handles only traffic originated or destined to hosts in the domain). Indeed, many (if not most) hosts never communicate outside of their stub domain. Because of this, only a subset of the IP addresses inside a stub domain need be translated into IP addresses that are globally unique when outside communications are required.

This solution has the disadvantage of taking away the end-to-end significance of an IP address and making up for it with increased state in the network. There are various work-arounds that minimize the potential pitfalls of this. Indeed, connection-oriented protocols are essentially doing address reuse at every hop.

The huge advantage of this approach is that it can be installed incrementally, without changes to either hosts or routers. (A few unusual applications may require changes.) As such, this solution can be implemented and experimented with quickly. If nothing else, this solution can provide temporary relief while other, more complex and far-reaching solutions are worked out.

2. Overview of NAT

The design presented in this memo is called NAT, for Network Address Translator. NAT is a router function that can be configured as shown in Figure A.1. Only the stub border router requires modifications.

NAT's basic operation is as follows: the addresses inside a stub domain can be reused by any other stub domain. For instance, a single Class A address could be used by many stub domains. At each exit point between a stub domain and backbone, NAT is installed. If there is more than one exit point, it is of great importance that each NAT has the same translation table.

FIGURE A.1

NAT Configuration

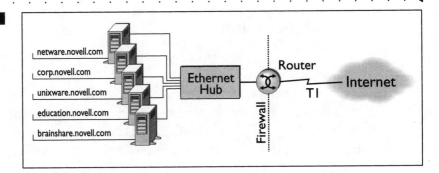

In the example of Figure A.2, both stubs A and B internally use class A address 10.0.0.0. Stub A's NAT is assigned the class C address 198.76.29.0, and Stub B's NAT is assigned the class C address 198.76.28.0. The class C addresses are globally unique — no other NAT boxes can use them.

Basic NAT Operation

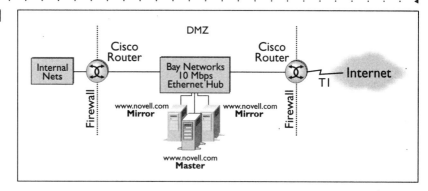

When stub A host 10.33.96.5 wishes to send a packet to stub B host 10.81.13.22, it uses the globally unique address 198.76.28.4 as destination, and sends the packet to its primary router. The stub router has a static route for net 198.76.0.0 so the packet is forwarded to the WAN-link. However, NAT translates the source address 10.33.96.5 of the IP header with the globally unique 198.76.29.7 before the package is forwarded. Likewise, IP packets on the return path go through similar address translations.

Notice that this requires no changes to hosts or routers. For instance, as far as the stub A host is concerned, 198.76.28.4 is the address used by the host in stub B. The address translations are completely transparent. Of course, this is just a simple example. There are numerous issues to be explored.

3. Various Aspects of NAT

3.1 Address Spaces

Partitioning of Reusable and Non-reusable Addresses

For NAT to operate properly, it is necessary to partition the IP address space into two parts—the reusable addresses used internally to stub domains, and the globally unique addresses. We call the reusable addresses *local addresses*, and the globally unique addresses *global addresses*. Any given address must either be a local address or a global address. There is no overlap.

The problem with overlap is the following: say a host in stub A wished to send packets to a host in stub B, but the local addresses of stub B overlapped the local addressees of stub A. In this case, the routers in stub A would not be capable of distinguishing the global address of stub B from its own local addresses.

Initial Assignment of Local and Global Addresses

A single class A address should be allocated for local networks. (See RFC 1597 [3].) This address could then be used for intranets with no connection to the Internet. NAT then provides an easy way to change an experimental network to a "real" network by translating the experimental addresses to globally unique Internet addresses.

Existing stubs that have unique addresses assigned internally, but are running out of them, can change addresses subnet by subnet to local addresses. The freed addresses can then be used by NAT for external communications.

3.2 Routing Across NAT

The router running NAT should never advertise the local networks to the backbone. Only the networks with global addresses may be known outside the stub. However, global information that NAT receives from the stub border router can be advertised in the stub the usual way.

Private Networks that Span Backbones

In many cases, a private network (such as a corporate network) will be spread over different locations and will use a public backbone for communications between those locations. In this case, it is not desirable to do address translation because large numbers of hosts may want to communicate across the backbone (thus requiring large address tables), and also because there will be more applications that depend on configured addresses—as opposed to going to a name server. We call such a private network a backbone-partitioned stub.

Backbone-partitioned stubs should behave as though they were a nonpartitioned stub. That is, the routers in all partitions should maintain routes to the local address spaces of all partitions. Of course, the (public) backbones do not maintain routes to any local addresses. Therefore, the border routers must tunnel through the backbones using encapsulation. To do this, each NAT box will set aside one global address for tunneling. When a NAT box x in stub partition X

wishes to deliver a packet to stub partition *Y*, it will encapsulate the packet in an IP header with destination address set to the global address of NAT box *y* that has been reserved for encapsulation. When NAT box *y* receives a packet with that destination address, it decapsulates the IP header and routes the packet internally.

3.3 Header Manipulations

In addition to modifying the IP address, NAT must modify the IP checksum and the TCP checksum. Remember, TCP's checksum also covers a pseudoheader which contains the source and destination address. NAT must also look out for ICMP and FTP and modify the places where the IP address appears. Undoubtedly, there are other places where modifications must be done. Hopefully, most such applications will be discovered during experimentation with NAT.

The checksum modifications to IP and TCP are simple and efficient. Because both use a 1's complement sum, it is sufficient to calculate the arithmetic difference between the before-translation and after-translation addresses and add this to the checksum. The only tricky part is determining whether the addition resulted in a wrap-around (in either the positive or negative direction) of the checksum. If so, 1 must be added or subtracted to satisfy the 1's complement arithmetic. Sample code (in C) for this is as follows:

```
...void checksumadjust(unsigned char *chksum, unsigned char *optr,
...int olen, unsigned char *nptr, int nlen)
.../* assuming: unsigned char is 8 bits, long is 32 bits
...- chksum points to the chksum in the packet
...- optr points to the old data in the packet
...- nptr points to the new data in the packet
*/
{
  long x, old, new;
  x=chksum[0]*256+chksum[1];
  x=~x;
  while (olen) {
   if (olen==1) {
    old=optr[0]*256+optr[1];
    x-=old & 0xff00;
```

```
            if (x<=0) { x-; x&=0xffff; }
            break;
        }   else {
            old=optr[0]*256+optr[1]; optr+=2;
            x-=old & 0xffff;
            if (x<=0) { x-; x&=0xffff; }
            olen-=2;
        }
    }
    while (nlen) {
     if (nlen==1) {
        new=nptr[0]*256+nptr[1];
        x+=new & 0xff00;
        if (x & 0x10000) { x++; x&=0xffff; }
        break;
     }
     else {
        new=nptr[0]*256+nptr[1]; nptr+=2;
        x+=new & 0xffff;
        if (x & 0x10000) { x++; x&=0xffff; }
        nlen-=2;
     }
    }
    x=~x;  chksum[0]=x/256; chksum[1]=x & 0xff;
}
```

The arguments to the File Transfer Protocol (FTP) PORT command include an IP address (in ASCII!). If the IP address in the PORT command is local to the stub domain, then NAT must substitute this. Because the address is encoded in ASCII, this may result in a change in the size of the packet (for instance, 10.18.177.42 is 12 ASCII characters, while 193.45.228.137 is 14 ASCII characters). If the new size is the same as the previous, only the TCP checksum needs adjustment (again). If the new size is less than the previous, ASCII 0's may be inserted, but this is not guaranteed to work. If the new size is larger than the previous, TCP sequence numbers must be changed, too.

A special table is used to correct the TCP sequence and acknowledge numbers with source port FTP, or destination port FTP. The table entries should have source, destination, source port, destination port, initial sequence number, delta for sequence numbers, and a timestamp. New entries are created only when FTP PORT commands are seen. The initial sequence numbers are used to find out if the sequence number of a packet is before, or after, the last FTP PORT command (delta may be increased for every FTP PORT command). Sequence numbers are incremented and acknowledge numbers are decremented. If the FIN bit is set in one of the packets, the associated entry may be deleted soon after (one minute should be safe). Entries that have not been used for approximately 24 hours should be safe to delete, also.

The sequence number adjustment must be coded carefully, so as not to harm performance for TCP in general. Of course, if the FTP session is encrypted, the PORT command will fail.

If an ICMP message is passed through NAT, it may require two address modifications and three checksum modifications. This is because most ICMP messages contain part of the original IP packet in the body. Therefore, for NAT to be completely transparent to the host, the IP address of the IP header (embedded in the data part of the ICMP packet) must be modified, the checksum field of the same IP header must correspondingly be modified, and the ICMP header checksum must be modified to reflect the changes to the IP header and checksum in the ICMP body. Furthermore, the normal IP header must also be modified as already described.

It is not entirely clear if the IP header information in the ICMP part of the body really needs to be modified. This depends on whether any host code actually looks at this IP header information. Indeed, it may be useful to provide the exact header seen by the router or host that issued the ICMP message to aid in debugging. In any event, no modifications are needed for the Echo and Timestamp messages, and NAT should never need to handle a Redirect message.

SNMP messages could be modified, but it is even more dubious that it will be necessary for ICMP messages.

Applications with IP-Address Content

Any application that carries (and uses) the IP address inside the application will not work through NAT unless NAT knows of such instances and does the appropriate translation. It is not possible, or even necessarily desirable, for NAT to know of all such applications. If encryption is used, it is impossible for NAT to make the translation.

It may be possible for such systems to avoid using NAT, if the hosts in which they run are assigned global addresses. Whether or not this can work depends on the capability of the intradomain routing algorithm and the internal topology. This is because the global address must be advertised in the intradomain routing algorithm. With a low-feature routing algorithm, such as RIP, the host may require its own class C address space that must be advertised internally and externally (thus hurting global scaling). With a high-feature routing algorithm, such as OSPF, the host address can be passed around individually, and can come from the NAT table.

Privacy, Security, and Debugging Considerations

Unfortunately, NAT reduces the number of options for providing security. With NAT, nothing that carries an IP address or information derived from an IP address (such as the TCP-header checksum) can be encrypted. While most application-level encryption should be OK, this prevents encryption of the TCP header.

On the other hand, NAT itself can be seen as providing a kind of privacy mechanism. This comes from the fact that machines on the backbone cannot monitor which hosts are sending and receiving traffic (assuming, of course, that the application data is encrypted).

The same characteristic that enhances privacy potentially makes debugging problems (including security violations) more difficult. If a host is abusing the Internet in some way (such as trying to attack another machine or even sending large amounts of junk mail), it is more difficult to pinpoint the source of the trouble because the IP address of the host is hidden.

4. Conclusions

NAT may be a good short-term solution to the address depletion and scaling problems. This is because it requires very few changes and can be installed incrementally. NAT has several negative characteristics that make it inappropriate as a long-term solution, and may make it inappropriate even as a short-term solution. Only implementation and experimentation will determine its appropriateness.

The negative characteristics are as follows:

- ▶ It requires a sparse end-to-end traffic matrix. Otherwise, the NAT tables will be large, thus giving lower performance. While the expectation is that end-to-end traffic matrices are indeed sparse, experience with NAT will determine whether or not they are. In any event, future applications may require a rich traffic matrix (for instance, distributed resource discovery), thus making long-term use of NAT unattractive.

- ▶ It increases the probability of misaddressing.

- ▶ It breaks certain applications (or at least makes them more difficult to run).

- ▶ It hides the identity of hosts. While this has the benefit of privacy, it is generally a negative effect.

- ▶ It has problems with SNMP, DNS . . . you name it.

Current Implementations

Paul and Tony implemented an experimental prototype of NAT on public domain KA9Q TCP/IP software [1]. This implementation manipulates addresses and IP checksums.

Kjeld implemented NAT in a Cray Communications IP-router. The implementation was tested with Telnet and FTP. This implementation manipulates addresses, IP checksums, TCP sequence/acknowledge numbers, and FTP PORT commands.

The prototypes have demonstrated that IP addresses can be translated transparently to hosts within the limitations described in this paper.

References

[1] Karn, P., "KA9Q", anonymous FTP from ucsd.edu (hamradio/packet/ka9q/docs).

[2] Fuller, V., Li, T., and J. Yu, "Classless Inter-Domain Routing (CIDR) an Address Assignment and Aggregation Strategy", RFC 1519, BARRNet, cisco, Merit, OARnet, September 1993.

[3] Rekhter, Y., Moskowitz, B., Karrenberg, D., and G. de Groot, "Address Allocation for Private Internets", RFC 1597, T.J. Watson Research Center, IBM Corp., Chrysler Corp., RIPE NCC, March 1994.

Security Considerations

Security issues are not discussed in this memo.

Request for Comments 1918 Address Allocation for Private Internets

Network Working Group
Category: Best Current Practice
Y. Rekhter, B. Moskowitz, D. Karrenberg, G. J. de Groot, E. Lear
February 1996

Status of this Memo

This document specifies an Internet Best Current Practices for the Internet community and requests discussion and suggestions for improvements. Distribution of this memo is unlimited.

1. Introduction

For the purposes of this document, an enterprise is an entity autonomously operating a network using TCP/IP and, in particular, determining the addressing plan and address assignments within that network.

This document describes address allocation for private intranets. The allocation permits full network-layer connectivity among all hosts inside an enterprise, as well as among all public hosts of different enterprises. The cost of using private Internet address space is the potentially costly effort to renumber hosts and networks between public and private.

2. Motivation

With the proliferation of TCP/IP technology worldwide, including outside the Internet, an increasing number of nonconnected enterprises use this technology and its addressing capabilities for sole intraenterprise communications, without any intention to ever directly connect to other enterprises or the Internet.

The Internet has grown beyond anyone's expectations. Sustained exponential growth continues to introduce new challenges. One challenge is a concern within the community that globally unique address space will be exhausted. A separate and far more pressing concern is that the amount of routing overhead will grow beyond the capabilities of Internet Service Providers. Efforts are in progress within the community to find long-term solutions to both of these problems. Meanwhile, it is necessary to revisit address-allocation procedures and their impact on the Internet routing system.

To contain growth of routing overhead, an Internet Provider obtains a block of address space from an address registry, and then assigns to its customers addresses from within that block based on each customer requirement. The result of this process is that routes to many customers will be aggregated together and will appear to other providers as a single route [RFC1518], [RFC1519]. In order for route aggregation to be effective, Internet providers encourage customers joining their network to use the provider's block and thus renumber their computers. Such encouragement may become a requirement in the future.

With the current size of the Internet and its growth rate, it is no longer realistic to assume that by virtue of acquiring globally unique IP addresses out of an Internet registry an organization that acquires such addresses would have Internet-wide IP connectivity once the organization gets connected to the Internet. To the contrary, it is quite likely that when the organization connects to the Internet to achieve Internet-wide IP connectivity, the organization would need to change IP addresses (renumber) all of its public hosts (hosts that require Internet-wide IP connectivity), regardless of whether the addresses used by the organization initially were globally unique.

It has been typical to assign globally unique addresses to all hosts that use TCP/IP. In order to extend the life of the IPv4 address space, address registries are requiring more justification than ever before, making it harder for organizations to acquire additional address space [RFC1466].

Hosts within enterprises that use IP can be partitioned into three categories:

▸ Category 1: hosts that do not require access to hosts in other enterprises or the Internet at large; hosts within this category may use IP addresses that are unambiguous within an enterprise, but may be ambiguous between enterprises.

▸ Category 2: hosts that need access to a limited set of outside services (e.g., e-mail, FTP, netnews, remote login) which can be handled by mediating gateways (e.g., application-layer gateways). For many hosts in this category an unrestricted external access (provided via IP connectivity) may be unnecessary and even undesirable for privacy/security reasons. Just like hosts within the first category, such hosts may use IP addresses that are unambiguous within an enterprise, but may be ambiguous between enterprises.

▶ Category 3: hosts that need network-layer access outside the enterprise (provided via IP connectivity); hosts in the last category require IP addresses that are globally unambiguous.

We will refer to the hosts in the first and second categories as *private*. We will refer to the hosts in the third category as *public*.

Many applications require connectivity only within one enterprise and do not need external (outside the enterprise) connectivity for the majority of internal hosts. In larger enterprises it is often easy to identify a substantial number of hosts using TCP/IP that do not need network-layer connectivity outside the enterprise. Some examples, where external connectivity might not be required, include:

▶ A large airport that has its arrival/departure displays individually addressable via TCP/IP. It is very unlikely that these displays need to be directly accessible from other networks.

▶ Large organizations, such as banks and retail chains, are switching to TCP/IP for their internal communication. Large numbers of local workstations, such as cash registers, money machines, and equipment at clerical positions rarely need to have such connectivity.

▶ For security reasons, many enterprises use application-layer gateways to connect their internal network to the Internet. The internal network usually does not have direct access to the Internet; thus only one or more gateways are visible from the Internet. In this case, the internal network can use nonunique IP network numbers.

▶ Interfaces of routers on an internal network usually do not need to be directly accessible from outside the enterprise.

3. Private Address Space

The Internet Assigned Numbers Authority (IANA) has reserved the following three blocks of the IP address space for private intranets:

10.0.0.0 - 10.255.255.255 (10/8 prefix)

172.16.0.0 - 172.31.255.255 (172.16/12 prefix)

192.168.0.0 - 192.168.255.255 (192.168/16 prefix)

We will refer to the first block as *24-bit block*, the second as *20-bit block*, and to the third as *16-bit block*. Note that (in pre-CIDR notation) the first block is nothing but a single class A network number, while the second block is a set of 16 contiguous class B network numbers, and third block is a set of 256 contiguous class C network numbers.

An enterprise that decides to use IP addresses out of the address space defined in this document can do so without any coordination with IANA or an Internet registry. The address space can thus be used by many enterprises. Addresses within this private address space will be unique only within the enterprise, or the set of enterprises that choose to cooperate over this space so they may communicate with each other in their own private intranet.

As before, any enterprise that needs globally unique address space is required to obtain such addresses from an Internet registry. An enterprise that requests IP addresses for its external connectivity will never be assigned addresses from the blocks previously defined.

In order to use private address space, an enterprise needs to determine which hosts do not need to have network-layer connectivity outside the enterprise in the foreseeable future and, thus, could be classified as private. Such hosts will use the private address space previously defined. Private hosts can communicate with all other hosts inside the enterprise, both public and private. However, they cannot have IP connectivity to any host outside the enterprise. While not having external (outside of the enterprise) IP connectivity, private hosts can still have access to external services via mediating gateways (e.g., application-layer gateways).

All other hosts will be public and will use globally unique address space assigned by an Internet Registry. Public hosts can communicate with other hosts inside the enterprise, both public and private, and can have IP connectivity to public hosts outside the enterprise. Public hosts do not have connectivity to private hosts of other enterprises.

Moving a host from private to public or vice versa involves a change of IP address, changes to the appropriate DNS entries, and changes to configuration files on other hosts that reference the host by IP address.

Because private addresses have no global meaning, routing information about private networks shall not be propagated on interenterprise links, and packets with private source or destination addresses should not be forwarded across such links. Routers in networks not using private address space, especially those of Internet service providers, are expected to be configured to reject (filter out) routing information about private networks. If such a router receives such information, the rejection shall not be treated as a routing protocol error.

Indirect references to such addresses should be contained within the enterprise. Prominent examples of such references are DNS Resource Records and other information referring to internal private addresses. In particular, Internet service providers should take measures to prevent such leakage.

4. Advantages and Disadvantages of Using Private Address Space

The obvious advantage of using private address space for the Internet at large is to conserve the globally unique address space by not using it where global uniqueness is not required.

Enterprises themselves also enjoy a number of benefits from their usage of private address space: they gain a lot of flexibility in network design by having more address space at their disposal than they could obtain from the globally unique pool. This enables operationally and administratively convenient addressing schemes, as well as easier growth paths.

For a variety of reasons the Internet has already encountered situations in which an enterprise that has not been connected to the Internet had used IP address space for its hosts without getting this space assigned from the IANA. In some cases, this address space had already been assigned to other enterprises. If such an enterprise later connects to the Internet, this could create very serious problems, as IP routing cannot provide correct operations in presence of ambiguous addressing. Although, in principle, Internet service providers should guard against such mistakes through the use of route filters, this does not always happen in practice. Using private address space provides a safe choice for such enterprises, avoiding clashes once outside connectivity is needed.

A major drawback to the use of private address space is that it may reduce an enterprise's flexibility to access the Internet. Once one commits to using a private address, one is committing to renumber part (or all) of an enterprise, should one decide to provide IP connectivity between that part (or all of the enterprise) and the Internet. Usually, the cost of renumbering can be measured by counting the number of hosts that have to transition from private to public. As discussed earlier, however, even if a network uses globally unique addresses, it may still have to renumber in order to acquire Internet-wide IP connectivity.

Another drawback to the use of private address space is that it may require renumbering when merging several private intranets into a single private intranet. If we review the examples listed in Section 2, we note that companies tend to merge. If such companies prior to the merge maintained their uncoordinated intranets using private address space, and if after the merge, these private intranets would be combined into a single private intranet, some addresses within the combined private intranet may not be unique. As a result, hosts with these addresses would need to be renumbered.

The cost of renumbering may well be mitigated by development and deployment of tools that facilitate renumbering (e.g. Dynamic Host Configuration Protocol—DHCP). When deciding whether to use private addresses, we recommend to inquire computer and software vendors about availability of such tools. A separate IETF effort (PIER Working Group) is pursuing full documentation of the requirements and procedures for renumbering.

5. Operational Considerations

One possible strategy is to design the private part of the network first and use private address space for all internal links. Then plan public subnets at the locations needed and design the external connectivity.

This design does not need to be fixed permanently. If a group of one or more hosts requires a status change (from private to public or vice versa) later, this can be accomplished by renumbering only the hosts involved, and changing physical connectivity, if needed. In locations where such changes can be foreseen (machine rooms, etc.), it is advisable to configure separate physical media for public and private subnets to facilitate such changes. In order to avoid major network disruptions, it is advisable to group hosts with similar connectivity needs on their own subnets.

If a suitable subnetting scheme can be designed and is supported by the equipment concerned, it is advisable to use the 24-bit block (class A network) of private address space and make an addressing plan with a good growth path. If subnetting is a problem, the 16-bit block (class C networks), or the 20-bit block (class B networks) of private address space can be used.

One might be tempted to have both public and private addresses on the same physical medium. While this is possible, there are pitfalls to such a design (note that the pitfalls have nothing to do with the use of private addresses, but are due to the presence of multiple IP subnets on a common Data Link subnetwork). We advise caution when proceeding in this area.

It is strongly recommended that routers which connect enterprises to external networks are set up with appropriate packet and routing filters at both ends of the link, in order to prevent packet and routing information leakage. An enterprise should also filter any private networks from inbound routing information to protect itself from ambiguous routing situations which can occur if routes to the private address space point outside the enterprise.

It is possible for two sites, which both coordinate their private address space, to communicate with each other over a public network. To do so, they must use some method of encapsulation at their borders to a public network, thus keeping their private addresses private.

If two (or more) organizations follow the address allocation specified in this document and then later wish to establish IP connectivity with each other, then there is a risk that address uniqueness would be violated. To minimize the risk, it is strongly recommended that an organization using private IP addresses choose randomly from the reserved pool of private addresses when allocating subblocks for its internal allocation.

If an enterprise uses the private address space, or a mix of private and public address spaces, then DNS clients outside of the enterprise should not see addresses in the private address space used by the enterprise, because these addresses would be ambiguous. One way to ensure this is to run two authority servers for each DNS zone containing both publicly and privately addressed hosts. One server would be visible from the public address space and would contain only the subset of the enterprise's addresses which were reachable using public addresses. The other server would be reachable only from the private network and would contain the full set of data, including the private addresses and whatever public addresses are reachable via the private network. In order to ensure consistency, both servers should be configured from the same data of which the publicly visible zone only contains a filtered version. There is certain degree of additional complexity associated with providing these capabilities.

6. Security Considerations

Security issues are not addressed in this memo.

7. Conclusion

With the described scheme many large enterprises will need only a relatively small block of addresses from the globally unique IP address space. The Internet at large benefits through conservation of globally unique address space which will effectively lengthen the lifetime of the IP address space. The enterprises benefit from the increased flexibility provided by a relatively large private address space. However, use of private addressing requires that an organization renumber part or all of its enterprise network, as its connectivity requirements change over time.

8. Acknowledgments

We would like to thank Tony Bates (MCI), Jordan Becker (ANS), Hans-Werner Braun (SDSC), Ross Callon (BayNetworks), John Curran (BBN Planet), Vince Fuller (BBN Planet), Tony Li (Cisco Systems), Anne Lord (RIPE NCC), Milo Medin (NSI), Marten Terpstra (BayNetworks), Geza Turchanyi (RIPE NCC), Christophe Wolfhugel (Pasteur Institute), Andy Linton (connect.com.au), Brian Carpenter (CERN), Randy Bush (PSG), Erik Fair (Apple Computer), Dave Crocker (Brandenburg Consulting), Tom Kessler (SGI), Dave Piscitello (Core Competence),

Matt Crawford (FNAL), Michael Patton (BBN), and Paul Vixie (Internet Software Consortium) for their review and constructive comments.

9. References

[RFC1466] Gerich, E., "Guidelines for Management of IP Address Space," RFC 1466, Merit Network, Inc., May 1993.

[RFC1518] Rekhter, Y., and T. Li, "An Architecture for IP Address Allocation with CIDR," RFC 1518, September 1993.

[RFC1519] Fuller, V., Li, T., Yu, J., and K. Varadhan, "Classless Inter-Domain Routing (CIDR): an Address Assignment and Aggregation Strategy," RFC 1519, September 1993.

Web Server Acceleration with Novell BorderManager: A Case Study of www.novell.com

Ron Lee, Senior Research Engineer, Advanced Development Group Information businesses around the globe are rushing to hang their shingle on the World Wide Web (WWW). Most are counting on Web presence to boost their name recognition and enhance their image as worldwide enterprises, with the hopes of forming new customer relationships and ultimately generating more sales. Many are telling phenomenal and surprising success stories. With over 1,000,000 hits per day, Novell's corporate Web site, `www.novell.com`, is one of those success stories.

Novell's corporate Web site is strategic to the company, providing visitors a view of the company and presenting up-to-the-minute information about our products, solutions, programs, and channel partners. It's also an interactive site where communication and feedback can take place between the visitor and Novell. Like many successful sites, `www.novell.com` handles a lot of traffic and is constantly growing. It is also susceptible to all of the traditional problems related to hosting a corporate Web site, including Internet security, 24-hours-a-day, 7-days-per-week reliability, and performance. In fact, there's quite an investment of time and money required to keep a large and dynamic Web site up and running.

As an early implementer, Novell quickly saw the need to simplify its Web publishing operations and infrastructure. In the process, Novell's IT management and Webmasters found a remarkably simple solution to the sometimes nightmarish problems of managing a corporate Web site (such as trying to centrally manage a distributed content set while trying to increase performance for customers worldwide).

This AppNote narrates Novell's quest for a solution and describes its eventual use of Novell BorderManager to redesign its Web configuration and increase security and reliability, while boosting performance by an order of magnitude. This case study is targeted to IT executives, corporate Webmasters, and network engineers who are interested in applying Web server acceleration to their Web infrastructures. Whether you're still waiting to enter the fray, or you're already holding the Internet tiger by the tail, this case study will give you a blueprint to implement BorderManager so you can achieve similar results.

The Evolution of www.novell.com

Novell's story begins long before the Web was widely recognized as the next great frontier of corporate marketing. By the mid-1980s, Novell had developed a very large presence on CompuServe and delivered marketing, sales channel support, and customer support through CompuServe forums and FTP download sites.

Early Outsourcing

When the World Wide Web began to emerge as a viable alternative for delivering information, Novell outsourced all of its original Web site development and hosting (with the exception of `www.support.novell.com`) to a third-party Web development agency. All of the organizations within Novell that had used CompuServe facilities for everything from marketing to support jumped into the Web publishing business. As a result, the initial `www.novell.com` was composed of a number of sites all served by separate Web servers: a `www.corp.novell.com`, a `www.netware.novell.com`, a `www.education.novell.com`, and various other servers, each with its own content set, authoring system, and the normal headaches associated with having multiple systems when one would have been sufficient.

Moving www.novell.com In-House

Novell hired a corporate Webmaster who re-evaluated the design of the Web site. The main objective of the new design was to provide Novell's company information and all the traditional content and functionality that Internet-savvy customers had come to expect from a corporate Web site. Additionally, the design required 24x7 reliability for 100 percent uptime and adequate capacity for the rapidly expanding site.

To meet these overall success factors for the site, the new Web team decided on two primary goals:

> ▶ First, they had to centralize the content set. This would enable them to manage what would otherwise be duplicate copies of the same content set distributed across many servers located all over the world.

Centralizing the Web server resources would also ease their efforts to provide redundant systems for fail-over.

▸ The second goal was to distribute access to the site internationally so that countries with poor communications infrastructures could have appreciably better access than they had with Novell's existing single point of presence.

The Web team and IT management knew they had a pretty big challenge right from the beginning. Based on their experience with too many Web servers, Novell came to believe that, for the purposes of managing a Web site, the fewer Web servers you have the better. So, the Web team formulated a plan to try to condense the contents and collate them under one server. After factoring in the need for 24x7 reliability, the design was expanded to include two additional servers.

The additional servers would be identical mirrors of the first and include a fail-over process in the event one of the servers crashed.

Shortly thereafter, IS installed the three Web servers, mirrored the contents, and placed them on the Web. By registering all of the systems' IP numbers as www.novell.com, the DNS resolution of www.novell.com randomly provides one of the three addresses to clients all over the world, thereby enabling the three servers to handle requests on a pseudoround-robin basis—each handling approximately one-third of the load.

At first, the only page that went up on the new servers was a home page. The remainder of Novell's corporate content was still located on the Web servers operated by the third-party agency. Because Novell didn't know what kind of traffic to expect on the new consolidated Web site, the new site ran with just this single home page for several months. This was obviously an extreme case of overkill to have a single HTML document being served by a set of three Compaq 4500 systems, each with four 100MHz Pentiums, 256MB of RAM, and 16GB RAID subsystems. However, with all of the content on the outsourced Web servers, this was the perfect opportunity to see what kind of traffic a single Novell Web server would attract.

The communications infrastructure for www.novell.com started out with a single T1 line. Within several months Novell needed two T1 lines, and several months later needed four, and soon after six. It was clear that demand would stay ahead of any new infrastructure Novell could put in place.

At the same time, the Novell Web team was dealing with the time-consuming effort of consolidating the content from multiple outsourced servers. Sadly, the existing content couldn't simply be copied en masse onto the new server because of considerable name space overlap in the top-level directories. There was no way to resolve the mismatches without completely reorganizing the content, a tremendously painful, time-consuming, and error-prone process.

Performance Problems and a Short-Term Solution

During the Web server consolidation, Novell's content became evenly split between the new in-house master server and the outsourced servers. The popularity of the site was also growing and overrunning the communication lines. At this point, Novell began to see system utilization on www.corp.novell.com that was unacceptable. There were two possible solutions:

- ▸ buy a larger server

- ▸ balance the load by breaking up the consolidated content set and moving the content onto multiple servers

In an attempt to overcome burgeoning Web server workloads and bandwidth problems in Provo, Novell's www.support.novell.com Web team (separate from the corporate Web team) began to distribute mirrors of the support Web servers to other parts of the world. Web servers were introduced in Germany and the United Kingdom that initially were independent of the Provo server system. Their contents were manually generated replicas of the most popular portions of the corporate server.

Although these systems improved access for customers in those regions, the mirrors quickly became labor intensive because the content wasn't automatically synchronized. A better long-term solution had to be found.

Diverging Paths

At this point in the redesign process, the solutions to Novell's two original goals began to take diverging paths. By consolidating the content set onto one mirrored set of central Web servers, Novell had simplified the process of making the whole site redundant. They had also improved the ability to manage the site because the content sets were now all adjacent rather than distributed throughout the network. However, the performance of both the Web servers and the Internet connection was unable to keep up with demand. Now, the short-term solution used by the `www.support.novell.com` team—placing additional mirrored sites around the globe—was adding enormous complexity and resource burdens to an already overloaded Web team.

Content Caching: The Web's Equivalent to a Free Lunch

While searching for ways to speed up these systems, Novell's corporate Webmaster came across a Web site that described a new type of WWW content caching software called *Harvest* and another called *Squid*. The Harvest cache was designed by the Computer Science Departments at the University of Southern California and the University of Colorado, Boulder (`<http://excalibur.-usc.edu/cache-html/cache.html>http://excalibur.usc.edu/cache-html/cache.html`), and the Squid cache was developed at the National Laboratory for Applied Network Research (NLANR - `<http://squid.nlanr.-net>http://squid.nlanr.net`). Both provided something called *Web server acceleration* to reduce the Web's burden on popular Web servers. Several organizations with large Internet sites were successfully using this technology to reduce costs and keep pace with the popularity of their sites. Beyond easing the load on Web servers, caching could also save bandwidth, increase the speed of service requests, and protect the Web servers from clients that generate repeated requests.

By placing a Harvest or Squid cache in front of a Web server, the cache pretends to be the Web server and forwards requests that aren't cached to the real Web server. Requests for cacheable objects, such as HTML pages and graphics, are served by the cache, providing Web server acceleration, while requests for noncacheable objects, such as CGI-BIN programs, are served by the true Web server. Because the majority of Web sites are made up of over 95 percent cacheable objects, Web server acceleration can dramatically reduce a Web server's workload and increase the performance of a Web server by an order of magnitude—all without degrading the site's performance.

To Novell's Webmaster, this ability to accelerate a Web site sounded like a free lunch. He downloaded the source code for the Squid cache (which was available under the GNU Public License), compiled it, and placed the cache software in front of the Web server process on one of the outsourced Web servers. The result — the load on the Web server process dropped dramatically.

Achieving Webmaster Nirvana

Novell's Webmaster wondered if he would gain the same benefit by running the Squid cache on a different system at some other location. So, the Webmaster installed a Squid cache in his office in San Jose, CA and configured it to cache the www.novell.com server located in Provo, UT. He hoped to gain cached access to the corporate Web site which resided on a loaded server, behind a loaded T1 connection and a loaded firewall. The result was instantaneous cached access to the Provo content and an end to his long response times.

Novell's Webmaster couldn't believe what he was seeing. He had cached his working set of www.novell.com—Novell's entire corporate content, with the exception of the one home page—on a 486/66 PC with 16MB of RAM allocated to the cache and 100MB of disk space. This small system made an impressive difference in the load on a very expensive Web server. If that was all it cost to cut the load on his server in half, than he had found Webmaster nirvana.

It was at that point, about a year into the lifetime of the site, that the Web team realized the two goals of central management and distributed performance weren't really at odds with each other. They could cache their centralized content set and distribute those caches in areas of high traffic and achieve the second goal of globally distributing the content set without pushing high cost, high maintenance Web server mirrors to the four corners of the globe.

Novell had achieved its first goal of central management by condensing the contents into the set of the three mirrored servers. Now, it achieved the second goal by distributing caches of the central site around the world. These successful experiences helped Novell's Web team realize that caching was the best way to achieve these goals.

A Better Cache

About the same time that Novell's corporate Webmaster was discovering the power of Web caches, Novell's Advanced Development Group began to develop an Internet object cache of its own. Based on years of caching research and development from the development of NetWare and IntranetWare, Novell designed an Internet object cache that provides both proxy caching and Web server acceleration with performance and scalability unmatched by the Harvest and Squid solutions. In fact, the Novell cache can service close to 4,000 connections per second and deliver up to 32MB of payload per second, which is up to 10 times the capacity of existing UNIX and NT solutions. These results were produced on a uniprocessor Pentium Pro system. Therefore, the Squid caches originally used by Novell's corporate Web team have now been replaced by Novell's Internet object cache which is included in Novell's BorderManager suite of Internet technologies.

That is what led Novell's Web team to the point they are at now. Novell has substantial content along with an authoring system that enables any authorized Novell employee (anywhere in the world) to submit his/her content to the centralized server. Their centralized Web servers are now the target of BorderManager caches placed around the world to speed worldwide access.

Novell's Current Web Site Solution

The results of Novell's early experimentation with caching and eventual installation of Novell's own BorderManager technologies are still hard to believe. It isn't often that elegant solutions are as simple and inexpensive as BorderManager's Web server acceleration capabilities.

The addition of BorderManager has enabled Novell to make a dramatic change to their Internet infrastructure. Internet Web servers have traditionally been placed between an organization's inner and outer firewalls which leave the servers exposed to the world, distrusted by the organization, and difficult for Web publishers to manage through the firewall. Using BorderManager, this traditional configuration can be redrawn to your advantage.

Today, the only www.novell.com systems located within the DMZ—the "no man's land" in front of Novell's inner firewall—are two BorderManager servers which are configured as Web server accelerators. These two servers handle all requests for cacheable objects, including all HTML pages and graphics files. The result is that 90 percent of the total Web traffic aimed at www.novell.com has been offloaded from the Web servers.

High Availability

From a performance perspective, one BorderManager Web server accelerator is sufficient to handle the equivalent of five T3 lines (32MB of payload per second), but Novell's high-availability Web site justifies additional equipment to provide sufficient fail-over mechanisms in the case of failure. Novell's Web server accelerators operate on two servers whose IP numbers are registered as www.novell.com. Both actively service requests and are available if one of the servers fails. A third BorderManager server is configured and ready to run as a hot standby system. These precautions eliminate the single point of failure in the system and also protect against conditions that might lead to a single point of failure.

Improved Firewall Security and Web Server Access

The Web servers, which were originally located in the DMZ, have been moved inside Novell's firewall with significant benefits. Such improvements tighten the security of the firewall, and improve the Web authors' access to the Web servers.

The Web servers are also configured with two servers actively servicing requests from the Web server accelerators, and one hot standby system. One of BorderManager's features enables it to access multiple Web servers using a form of load balancing—a round-robin process based on the number of outstanding requests on each Web server connection. Therefore, the two Web servers are actively servicing requests, making each a perfect fail-over system.

Because the Web servers are inside the firewall, Novell's Web authors now have no reason to make connections through the firewall to get to the Web servers. This greatly simplifies Novell's firewall construction because the firewall need only permit the two Web server accelerators through to the Web servers on private connections. Content development and management processes are also simplified because the Web servers are located inside the corporate firewall. For instance, CGI applications were forced to go through a CGI-proxy to service requests on a corporate database behind the firewall. Now, with the Web servers behind the firewall, the need for that CGI-proxy goes away because the Web servers have a direct connection to the database server.

Hardware and Software Configurations

Novell's two BorderManager Web server accelerators live inside Novell's DMZ on a Bay Networks 28000-series 10/100Mbps Ethernet switch. Two Cisco 7000-series routers confine the DMZ. The BorderManager hardware platform is an Intel 200MHz Pentium Pro with 256MB of RAM, a 16GB disk subsystem, and an Intel EtherExpress PRO/100 Server Adapter. Software includes IntranetWare and the public release of BorderManager 1.0.

The Web servers are rack mounted Compaq Proliant 4500R systems. Each includes four 100MHz Pentium processors, 256MB RAM, and 16GB of disk storage. All three systems are running UNIXWare v2.1.2 and Apache v1.2*x* Web server software. Novell has been experimenting with several commercial Web server products, but plans to switch over to Novonyx's port of Netscape Enterprise Server as soon as that product is ready for release.

New System Benefits

This technology has given Novell considerable flexibility in terms of bandwidth, delivery, maintenance, and cost. Following are some of the benefits Novell can demonstrate as a direct result of using BorderManager and Web server acceleration:

▶ Enhanced company image — It's one thing to say you're a global company but it's another to be a global company. Although every Web site on the Internet is accessible around the globe, the reality is that international bandwidth and performance can prevent your target market from making use of your site without significant pain. Using the proxy cache component of BorderManager, Novell is able to distribute caches of its site into areas where bandwidth is a problem. Because this is done with low-cost PC systems and very little administrative burden, Novell's new "globally friendly" appearance is a real win.

▶ Simplified management and control — Novell is happy with the Web server accelerators because they're simple. All of the accelerator caches are essentially 100 percent hands-off autonomous systems. Nobody ever looks at them for any reason . . . they just run. It's an ideal system from an administrative point of view because Novell can distribute the BorderManager servers without the additional requirement of technical expertise at every location. It's set up and configured one time, and from then on it simply delivers. Contrast this with Novell's main servers that require constant attention.

With these simple and low-cost accelerators in place, Novell is free to maintain its strategy of centralizing the content set even while experiencing overwhelming growth and pressure from international offices to host their own Web sites. In fact, the effectiveness of centralizing the content management and distributing that content via BorderManager servers has led early detractors of the plan to change their minds. With these object caches in place, the international offices couldn't tell they were browsing content in the United States.

This newfound success in reigning international content developers led the Web team to create an authoring system that directed the entire flow of new content from around the world through a single processing system in Provo. Thus, the BorderManager caches enabled Novell to manage the content creation centrally while distributing access in a way that complimented their worldwide organization. This also made Novell more competitive because it is not stuck with a single, high-cost solution for increasing access to its site. They have a more flexible, lower-cost solution.

In Novell's experience, cache configuration and administration was an order of magnitude less burdensome than what they would have put in place if they were to replicate the Web servers with mirrored Web servers. Novell also believes they could not replace any of the BorderManager caches with standalone mirrored systems, at this point. This is true because the maintenance component would be excessive compared to what the caches require. Several reasons to provide BorderManager services follow:

> ▶ Stellar performance and scalability — BorderManager's performance characteristics are providing Novell the flexibility they need to keep their main Web site centralized, and still meet the needs of content authors around the world. In their internal marketing pitch to authors, they can guarantee them the benefit of globally cached distribution of their content without requiring a significant change in the way they construct their content. The content providers are ecstatic.

Novell is also taking advantage of BorderManager's scalability. With the addition of up to four Intel EtherExpress PRO/100 Server adapters running in polled mode, Novell's existing BorderManager hardware and software combination is capable of handling close to 4,000 connections per second with a sustained throughput of up to 32MB per second. That's not bad, especially when you consider that the three www.novell.com Web servers were handling much less than 100 connections per second to make the 1,000,000 hits-per-day mark. This leads us to another BorderManager benefit:

> ▶ Lower costs—By placing a BorderManager Web server accelerator in front of Novell's Web servers, Novell is relieving their expensive Web server systems of more than 90 percent of their workload. Novell has saved a small fortune by avoiding an otherwise natural upgrade process on those systems. In fact, all three were soon to be replaced by three Sun Enterprise 3,000 servers. Now the three Web servers will remain on Compaq equipment.

Novell has also reduced costs by placing BorderManager at sites around the world. These caches are accelerating 90 percent of the requests for www.novell.com customers in those areas. This means those requests aren't traveling to the central Web site in Provo and don't require bandwidth on Novell's Web servers or their connection to the Internet. As a result of the reduced costs, the following opportunity has emerged:

> ▶ New business opportunities—In terms of creating new business opportunities, Novell's new Web architecture enables its strategic partners to cache Novell's entire Web site for their internal benefit and the benefit of their customers. For example, a Novell reseller might cache Novell's Web site at their location using BorderManager Web server accelerators. After downloading sales materials and software once, they would be able to distribute those cached products in a rapid fashion to their customers. Another example is the ability of an organization that relies heavily on Novell products and support to cache Novell's Web site at their location. They would have much faster access to the kind of information they need to effectively run their organization.

The tremendous benefit in these situations is that BorderManager caches at the end-points are inexpensive and easy to set up and maintain. Novell's infrastructure doesn't require any special configuration and complements existing UNIX and Windows NT systems.

Perhaps best of all, Novell's authoring system is capable of expiring BorderManager cache content. If these caches located at Novell's strategic partners' sites are known to Novell, Novell can include their caches in the authoring system and guarantee the cache owners that their contents are always up-to-date. The authoring system takes on the burden of expiring the contents that are being modified on the main Web servers.

Summary

As Novell's Web site was being distributed via BorderManager caches around the world, the Web team began referring to the process as "virtualizing" the Web site. By virtualizing the entire Web site, Novell makes access to the site more convenient for a wider range of people and believes this will result in increased sales and an enhanced perception of the Novell name. Through these experiences, Novell's Web team now believes it is beginning to realize the true potential of the World Wide Web.

*I*ndex

encryption (*continued*)
protocols, 20-22
RC2 encryption, 93-94
RSA digital signatures, 95
RSA encryption, 90-92, 93, 94
SHTTP, 20, 21-22
slave VPN server configuration, 191-193
SSL, 20-21, 78
VPN encryption, 57, 90-92, 93-96, 259-260
Eng, Tony, 295, 303
errors
during ICP hierarchical caching, 87
HTTP errors and caching, 80-81
viewing logs, 272-274
See also troubleshooting
Establish Connection Timeout parameter, 253
Ethernet networks
data delivery method, 8
maximum physical receive packet size, 158
executive search firm. *See* home office example
expenses. *See* costs
Extended Format for proxy cache log, 210

F

fault tolerance and single access point, 36
FDDI networks maximum packet size, 158
file servers as bastion hosts, 42-43
File Transfer Protocol (FTP)
anonymous FTP, 13
built-in security, 40
NAT and, 181
overview, 13
packet filtering, 48
TCP and, 12
FILTCFG utility
disabling packet filtering, 160
IP packet-forwarding filter configuration, 276-278
NCP packet-forwarding filter configuration, 280-282

overview, 275
route filtering, 282-284
TCP/IP filter configuration, 278-280
See also packet filtering
firewall technologies, 38-57
access control, 70-72, 166, 273
application proxies, 54-55, 155
bastion hosts, 42-43, 63-64
BorderManager firewall services, 63-72
built-in security services and, 39-41
circuit-level gateways, 53-54, 67-70, 155
corporate office example, 109, 110
law firm example, 116
NAT (Network Address Translation), 50-51, 64-66, 182-185, 293-304
OSI model and, 38-39
packet filtering, 45-51, 63-64, 159-160, 276-284
prohibiting inbound access, 52
protocol proxies, 64-66
proxy gateways and services, 52-53
school district example, 231-236
screened-host gateways, 43-44, 63-64
screening routers, 41-42, 63-64, 276-284
tri-homed hosts, 45, 63-64
virtual private networks (VPNs), 56-57, 90-96, 186, 187-196, 254-260, 270-271
See also specific technologies
forbidden request error (403), 80-81
Force Password Change Every x Days parameter, 267
frame relay with MPR, 98
Francis and Goodfellow. *See* law firm example
Francis, Paul, 295, 303
freshness
determining for Web documents, 79-80
proxy cache parameters, 247, 249-250
time-to-live information, 79, 249-250
FTP (File Transfer Protocol)
anonymous FTP, 13

my2cents.idgbooks.com